Dear Mary

Papa and Mama, c. 1939, East River, Connecticut

Dear Mary
*Letters Home from the
10th Mountain Division*
1944–1945

Sydney M. Williams

BAUHAN PUBLISHING
PETERBOROUGH . NEW HAMPSHIRE
2019

© 2019 Sydney M. Williams III
All Rights Reserved
ISBN: 978-087233-291-1

Library of Congress Cataloging-in-Publication Data
Names: Williams, Sydney M. (Sydney Messer), 1910-1968, author. | Williams, Sydney M. (Sydney Messer), 1941- author.
Title: Dear Mary : letters home from the 10th Mountain Division (1944-1945) / Sydney M. Williams.
Other titles: Correspondence. | Letters home from the 10th Mountain Division (1944-1945)
Description: Peterborough, NH : Bauhan Publishing, [2019]
Identifiers: LCCN 2019015064 | ISBN 9780872332911 (softcover : alk. paper)
Subjects: LCSH: Williams, Sydney M. (Sydney Messer), 1910-1968—Correspondence. | Williams, Mary B. W. Hotchkiss—Correspondence. | United States. Army. Mountain Division, 10th. | World War, 1939-1945—Personal narratives, American. | World War, 1939-1945--Mountain warfare. | World War, 1939-1945—Campaigns—Italy. | United States. Army—Ski troops.
Classification: LCC D769.3 10th .W55 2019 | DDC 940.54/1273092 [B] — dc23
LC record available at https://lccn.loc.gov/2019015064

Book design by Sarah Bauhan
Text set in Bembo Book Pro
Cover design by Henry James
Printed by Versa Press

PO BOX 117 PETERBOROUGH NEW HAMPSHIRE 03458
WWW.BAUHANPUBLISHING.COM   603-567-4430

Cover: Foreground – Walt Prager, (Hq. Co. 3rd Bn.) writing a letter home. Background – A machine gunner and two riflemen of Co K, 87th Mountain Infantry, 10th Mountain Division, cover an assault squad routing Germans out of a building in the background. Sassomolare Area, Italy. Porretta Moderna Highway. 4 March 1945.

Manufactured in the United States of America

DEDICATION

To politicians, and to generals far behind the front lines, the distant actions of war might seem like no more than the movement of pins on a map—necessary but impersonal. The reality for those who fight is much more grim. Yet war is sometimes necessary, I believe, especially when freedom is at stake. For there is nothing—not the works of Shakespeare, not the music of Beethoven, not Michelangelo's art—that has been a greater gift *from* mankind *to* mankind than liberty.

That gift has come at an enormous cost in the form of the ultimate sacrifice made by hundreds of thousands of men and women over the years. That the 10th Mountain Division, in its reactivated form as a light infantry unit for mountain warfare, still produces heroic troops is evident in the story of thirty-one-year-old Staff Sergeant Travis Atkins. In Iraq in 2007, Sergeant Atkins, to protect the lives of three of his troops, hugged a suicide bomber just before the latter blew up his vest. On March 27, 2019, the Medal of Honor was awarded posthumously to his now twenty-two-year-old son, Trevor.

In compiling this book, I read the regimental history of the 87th Regiment, and perused the family letters contained herein to learn the human stories of the time. I thought of the men my father knew who had been killed in action—men like PFC Juan Barrientos, PFC Glenn Bailey, PFC Chester West, and 1st Sgt. Lester Ersland. Some of those who died in combat seventy-four years ago might otherwise still be living today. I thought of what they had missed: the love of a wife or fiancée and children. I thought of how the world had changed since their deaths: McDonald's; civil rights; the assassination of their comrade in arms, President John F. Kennedy; Neil Armstrong's walk on the moon; the growth of Walmart and Amazon; the collapse of the Soviet Union; the invention of the iPhone, personal computers, and video games; the democratization and economic revival of their former enemies—Germany and Japan.

We and the world are freer, richer, and safer because of the sacrifice such men made. They deserve our remembrance and prayers. And that is why this book is dedicated to those who served in the 10th Mountain Division during the Second World War.

CONTENTS

Preface	9
Introduction	13
The Letters	
December 11, 1944–February 13, 1945	21
February 15, 1945–March 2, 1945	50
March 10, 1945–April 13, 1945	67
April 14, 1945–May 2, 1945	141
May 3, 1945–July 27, 194	155
Epilogue	251
Acknowledgments	254

Frank, Mary, Mama holding Betsy, Papa, Sydney – August, 1944, East River, Connecticut

PREFACE

There is one front and one battle where everyone in the United States—every man, woman, and child—is in action and will be privileged to remain in action throughout this war. That front is right here at home, in our daily lives, and in our daily tasks.
Franklin D. Roosevelt (1882–1945) Radio address, April 28, 1942

Those of us born a few years before World War II have lived during a near-perfect time. We were too young for that conflict or Korea, and were either drafted or entered the army voluntarily before Vietnam. Our children have largely been fortunate as well. The First Iraq War came and went quickly. The attack on 9/11 and subsequent Second Iraq War and the ongoing wars against terrorism have been handled by volunteers, not draftees.

One cannot say the same for many other generations. Men were sometimes conscripted, as in our Civil War, or pressed into service, as happened throughout the centuries in myriad conflicts. Women were left behind to fend for themselves and their children, with loneliness, starvation, and despair constant companions. By contrast, my mother and the millions like her who remained at home during the Second World War had it easier. Even after the Depresssion, the country was richer and life was easier than it had been during earlier wars.

All five sons from my two sets of grandparents served in the global conflagration that comprised World War II. That generation became known, rightly, as the "Greatest Generation," although none ever considered themselves exceptional. Coming from every class, culture, race, and religion, they simply did what was expected of them—their duty. In 1942, the population of the United States was 135 million. Approximately 19 million Americans (14 percent of the population), including 350,000 women, served in the armed forces. Approximately 5 percent became casualties, including 416,800 who were killed. Men from the age of eighteen through their mid-thirties were drafted. Virtually every American had a son, daughter, brother, sister, father, mother, cousin, boyfriend, or girlfriend in uniform.

The war, as President Roosevelt stated, was total. It was a war unlike any before or since in that it affected almost everyone and impacted all aspects of life. Gas was rationed, as were food products. Even products not

Papa with the 1938 Chevy, complete with a goat in the back seat, suitcase on the wheel well, and "George" the dog – East River, Connecticut

rationed were in short supply. No new passenger cars, commercial trucks, or auto parts were produced between February 1942 and October 1945 (my parents drove a 1938 Chevrolet station wagon). Approximately 40 percent of US gross domestic product was devoted to defense during the war years. Labor became scarce. Women like my mother did their part, displaying a stoic willingness to suffer economic and emotional deprivation with the common goal of bringing their soldier, marine, and sailor sons, husbands, and brothers home safely, and in victory. They assumed jobs in factories and on farms that would ordinarily have been performed by men, as well as tended their homes and children. The ability to mend or fix torn or broken items, from clothes to fences, was an invaluable asset.

Books like Norman Mailer's *The Naked and the Dead* and Elie Wiesel's *The Night Trilogy* provide a sense of war's noise, horror, fear, and dread, as do movies like *The Longest Day, Saving Private Ryan, Stalingrad,* and *Fire on the Mountain.* (The latter work captures the fighting in which the 10th Mountain Division, my father's unit, was involved.) But less attention has been paid to describing the experiences of those left at home: the anguish of not knowing a loved one's whereabouts or fate; the struggle to provide young children with as normal a life as possible; the fear of being left alone. For mothers of those in combat, like both my grandmothers, the worry of losing a child must have been mind-numbing. Women on the home front called on God and did their best to harness inner strengths. Keeping one's self busy during the day was paramount, so as to fall into bed exhausted—even then, sleep often came late. Unfortunately, but understandably, many of those who stayed home took to drink, or other anesthetizing habits, to block out the fear and loneliness.

The letters in this book tell one family's story—my family's. Nevertheless, Americans who stayed home during the war years shared a common experience. It is often said there are no atheists in foxholes. These letters suggest that, at least in my family, there were no atheists on the home front either. In reading my mother's letters, I was struck by the frequency with which she invoked God. I never knew her as particularly religious, yet in 1957—twelve years after the war—she wrote a letter for the minister's monthly report of the Unitarian church in Peterborough, New Hampshire, ending with what she wanted for her children: "That hope is there for peace in the world."

It is my hope that these letters will help us better understand what those on the home front endured and to see the human side of war.

Sydney, Papa, Frank, Mary. The children he was leaving behind...

"Wyndham"

INTRODUCTION

"Please Mr. Postman, look and see. Is there a letter, a letter for me?"
                                    The Marvelettes, "Please, Mr. Postman," 1961

My father was drafted in March 1944, at age thirty-three. After basic training at Fort McClellan in Alabama, he was ordered to Camp Swift in Texas to join the 10th Mountain Division. In December he was sent to Fort Patrick Henry in Virginia, and on January 4, 1945, he boarded the USS *West Point* (built in 1940 as the SS *America*) for the trip to Naples, Italy. He was a thirty-four-year-old Private First Class in the 87th Regiment, 1st Battalion, C Company, 2nd Platoon, 2nd Squad. My mother moved from our farmhouse in New Hampshire back to her parents' home, "Wyndham," in the East River section of Madison, Connecticut in early 1944, with three small children in tow (my sister Mary, age four; me at three; my brother Frank, one) and pregnant with a fourth (my sister Betsy, due in August). In six years of marriage, my parents had never been separated.

During the war, people lived in a sort of cocoon, absent of information until the next letter arrived—a letter censored to remove any information as to exactly where the writer might be, or what casualties his unit might have suffered. Battles were reported by the press, but families did not know where their loved ones were, how they were faring, even whether they had been wounded or killed. There were no cellphones, e-mail, or instant-messaging. The World War II generation was the last of the letter writers. The letters presented in this book cover my parents' correspondence during the seven months my father was in Italy. One could argue that letters between one man and one woman reflect only their thoughts and experiences, and, thus, have little general relevance. That may be true, but their significance, in my opinion, is more universal, because of the large number of Americans who served in uniform during the war and the even larger number who stayed home. Still, these letters provide but a microscopic view. And, as they show, my parents were more fortunate than many.

For those at home, life was disrupted in many ways. There was a breakdown in social values: divorce rates increased, as did rates of truancy, juvenile delinquency, and venereal disease. Alcoholism was a problem. With women needed in the workforce, there was a growth in unsupervised, "latchkey"

Mary, Frank, Sydney – 1944, East River, Connecticut

Frank, Sydney, Betsy, Mary, 1944, East River, Connecticut

children. While unemployment declined due to conscription and expansion of war industries, so did safety nets; as spending on defense needs preempted funds for support programs, so poverty increased and income gaps widened. Gasoline rationing meant restricted travel, and food rationing meant the need for substitutions like powdered eggs and milk, and liquid paraffin for cooking oil. At one point during the war, 50 percent of the nation's vegetables were being grown at home in Victory Gardens.

In the meantime, my brother and sisters and I lived in idyllic conditions—a large house on Long Island Sound, a barn with animals, and a mother and grandparents who were attentive and loving. We were too young to understand what was happening overseas, and we were never deprived of food or a comfortable place to sleep. We were protected from the worries that consumed our elders. For me, those months were filled with the joy and wonder of childhood, a place where the guns and bombs that devastated Europe, the Middle East, and Asia could not be heard and had no meaning.

My family was fortunate in other ways. All immediate family members survived. My mother's three brothers served as naval officers; all experienced combat and all returned uninjured. Of my father's two brothers, one was a medical doctor who remained stateside, the other an army lieutenant who was wounded on Okinawa but made it home with no visible scars. Both my father's brothers-in-law served as naval officers; neither was wounded.

۞

A few years after my mother died, I read through the letters my parents had written one another. My mother's letters provided a sense of the sacrifice she made, the gaiety she showed us children, the normalcy she expressed to my father, and the torment that rended her heart, which she was unable to disguise. It was not politics or the war as a whole that consumed her; it was the personal. In an appendix to *War and Peace*, Leo Tolstoy wrote, in contrasting the differences between the way a historian views war and an artist, ". . . for the artist there cannot and should not be any heroes, but there should be people." These letters show people. They carry the all-too-human voices of those who wrote them seventy-four years ago. While not all letters survived, a surprising number did—especially given that those from home were carried by my father in his backpack across fields of battle, over the Apennines, and through the Po Valley. They crossed the Po River, to the shores of Lake Garda, and close to the Yugoslav border.

Sydney holding "Sydney kid," Mama with "Gay," Mary with "Mary kid," – 1945, East River, Connecticut

 In his biography, *Churchill: Walking with Destiny*, Andrew Roberts tells of the future prime minister writing to his wife when he went to France in November 1915, "[His letters] . . . allow us to peer into his mind better than at any other period in his life." All letters do that, especially those between spouses. Unlike Churchill's, however, the letters in this book were never written with the idea they might someday be published. That was something I had to consider when weighing the appropriateness of having the letters that make up this book transcribed and made available for all to read. In the end, I decided their value as a window on a special time in our history seemed worth whatever embarrassment might accrue to those no longer alive.

 None of these letters say anything about the geopolitics of the time, but they do show people as individuals—not made up and not idealized. This book is an attempt to derive a better understanding of that time and what life was like, for those in combat and for those left at home.

⁂

Because of the personal nature of this correspondence, not every reference will be immediately understood, especially those to people and places. I have added explanatory footnotes where appropriate. Besides letters between my parents, I have included a few letters from my father's parents, his two sisters, and one of his two brothers, as well as commentary about the war to allow readers to follow the course of the 87th Regiment in combat. Since there was every expectation that his division would be sent to Japan for the planned invasion of Japan (Operation Downfall), I have also included letters written during during the two and a half months following the surrender of Germany on May 7, before he was shipped back to the United States.

My mother makes reference to several animals in her letters—dogs, horses, goats, and even a duck, "Robert." My father, to whom these letters are addressed, obviously knew to whom or to what my mother referred, but to aid the reader, the names of animals appear in quotation marks. Minor editorial changes have also been made to the letters, such as the creation of paragraphs where none existed, and the insertion of punctuation marks and bracketed information to clarify what was written. Some letters are referenced but not shown.

In addition to these letters, I had access to the military history of the 10th Mountain Division. There is a surfeit of literature that proved helpful, in particular Hal Burton's *The Ski Troops* and Charles Hauptman's *Combat History of the 10th Mountain Division*. Especially informative was *History of the 87th Regiment* by Captain George F. Early, written in 1945, which includes a day-by-day history of the regiment's time in combat. It also includes a list of all the men who served in the regiment. And I am indebted to the Denver Public Library which houses the archives for the 10th Mountain Division, and in particular I am grateful to be able to use photos from the limited edition book, *This Was Italy,* put together in 1946 by Richard A. Rocker.

THE LETTERS

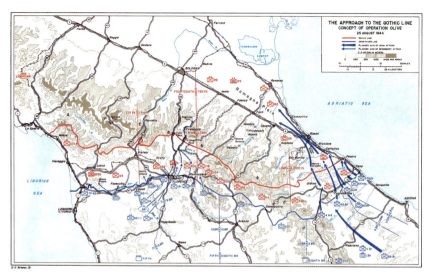

The Gothic Line, August 1944 and the concept of Operation Olive. The dark blue arrows represent major Allied attacks.

USS West Point (AP-23), on 22 April 1944

DECEMBER 11, 1944–FEBRUARY 13, 1945

On December 20, the 10th Mountain Division entrained for Fort Patrick Henry in Virginia, and on January 3, the 87th Regiment boarded the USS *West Point*—destination: Naples, Italy. On June 4, 1944, Rome had been liberated. The German armies, under Field Marshall Albert Kesselring, fell back, first to Florence and defensive positions along the Arno River, and then, on August 17, to the so-called Gothic Line. The Gothic Line ran along the southern edge of the Apennines from Marina di Carrara (source of the famous marble) on the Ligurian Sea to Pesaro on the Adriatic. The 8th Army (British, under General Sir Richard McCreery) had moved up the eastern edge of the Italian peninsula, while the 5th Army (American, under Lieutenant General Lucian K. Truscott) moved up the western coast. These two armies had made rapid progress north once Rome fell, but found themselves stymied by the strong defensive positions of the Germans along the Gothic Line. Three attempts, in the fall of 1944, had been made to dislodge the Germans from Mount Belvedere, the linchpin in this defensive line and the principal obstruction between the Allies and the Po River valley. All three attempts had failed. This, then, was the situation when the 10th Mountain Division (under Brigadier General George P. Hays) arrived in Italy. As American forces, they were assigned to the 5th Army for Operation Encore.

My father arrived in Italy on January 13, 1945. The war in Italy would be over on May 2. Three and one-half months, or 109 days, does not seem like a long time; however, of the 14,500 10th Division troops that landed in Italy (of whom more than half were support, and so not as exposed as the combat troops) and of the 4,000 replacement troops, 992 would die in combat and over 4,000 would be wounded—one of the highest casualty rates based on time spent in combat for any unit in World War II.

The 1st Battalion, to which my father as a member of C Company was attached, shipped north from Naples on the Italian freighter *Sestrie* on the sixteenth. The following day they disembarked at Livorno (Leghorn), and were trucked to Staging Area No. 3, three kilometers west of Pisa on property that had formerly been part of King Victor Emmanuel III's hunting grounds. It was from there, on January 18, that my father first wrote from

Italy to my mother. On the twenty-first, the regiment moved into a bivouac area in the village of Valpromaro, east of Camaiore. Twelve days later, on February 2, the 1st Battalion was trucked to La Lima, and then marched to Catigliano. They were now in the foothills of the Apennines, and their first combat mission was to defend a line of about three miles that stretched from one mountain, through a deep draw (the town of Catigliano), and up another mountain. This initiation to combat was generally quiet, though not without risk as six men in the regiment were wounded and two were killed during this week.

On the twelfth of February, the 1st Battalion was withdrawn to San Marcello to await new orders. Those orders arrived on the sixteenth, so the battalion was trucked to Vidiciatico in preparation for the assault on Belvedere—an attack that commenced on the night of February 18 and would continue, with only brief periods of rest, for eight days. By that time my father had been in Italy for thirty-seven days, and had been able to write my mother only eight times, suggesting that things were moving fast and that he was busier than he indicated in his letters.

༄

The first two letters in this section are from my father from Camp Swift in Texas. The next three are from Fort Patrick Henry in Virginia. You will note that, even then, he was unable to tell my mother where he was, or where he was headed. It was only on the eighteenth of January he was able to say he was in Italy.

December 11, 1944

Dear Mary,

I have an awful lot to say tonight, but don't know if I'll be able to as I'm getting awfully sleepy. I was up all last night getting back to camp just in time to shave before reveille and got very little sleep Friday and Saturday nights. I've got three of your letters to answer and the very good one from Mary, and I want to tell you all about the weekend. I'll have to write some of it tomorrow. We didn't come in at noontime, in fact got no lunch; so I couldn't write then either and this evening, I suppose because I was sleepy, it took me an awfully long time just to clean my rifle and hang up my clothes etc. I got three packages today from mother, and Uncle Frank and Aunt Louisa,[1] and from Aunt Minna and Uncle Walter.[2]

Well, Dick and Arnold[3] and I all met. I met Arnold just by accident in the hotel lobby, and it's awful, but it's perfectly true—he was standing so his face was rather in the shadows—that I didn't recognize him and would have gone right by, though I was looking for him. Luckily, he recognized me. He said he almost didn't recognize me, my cheeks are so much rounder. And the reason I didn't recognize him was that his cheeks have grown so much more hollow. His face dead white, his hat pulled way down to his big black glasses, and he needed a shave. He had a black suit and his hands are white and transparent, much smaller than mine. I suppose it's partly just that I've never got used to seeing him wear glasses, and partly of course that he was never indoors so much when he was at home, and partly that I still expect him to look as he did five or six years ago, forgetting he's growing older. But it really gave me quite a shock. He says he weighs less than he ever did since he grew up and he looks awfully, awfully thin. Of course, everybody I ever see has a healthy, weather-beaten face. I remember even in Peterborough I was shocked at how pale city people looked, and I'd never noticed it when I'd lived in Wellesley. So I may be exaggerating and don't tell Jane or the family how terribly I thought he looked. His face has become very mature looking, almost too much so and deeply lined. He'd been up all night. We met at 3 p.m. Saturday and we sat up till almost 2 a.m. waiting for Dick, and all that time we kept asking for him or a message from him at the hotel desk. Dick got there at nine p.m. and sat up alone till 2 a.m. waiting for us. He hadn't slept the night before either. He also kept asking at the desk. Also, all

---

1 My grandmother's brother and sister, Frank and Louisa Hunnewell.
2 My grandmother's brother, Walter Hunnewell, and his wife Minna.
3 My father's brothers. Dick served as an army artillery officer on Okinawa; Arnold was an army doctor based in Colorado.

three of us had each paid for a double room and registered Dick in both the ones we had; in fact, Arnold had taken the room that Dick had originally reserved, by wire, at the clerk's suggestion to hold it for him, and after all that they kept telling both sides there were no such names on the register and had been no one in looking for us. We found Dick about 10 Sunday morning and had a very good time, thereafter, until 10 p.m. when we separated. That was awfully irritating, though in a way I'm glad I spent an evening alone with Arnold.

Today, the coldest so far, is 32. This morning was 45 and has been very windy all day; it kept me awake and felt good after the sun came up. The Austin radio is talking about the cold wave. It went below 30 somewhere.

I love you an awful lot.
Sydney

∽

December 16

Dear Mary,

Well, it's Saturday night and I was thinking of trying to go to San Antonio to take a look at it, but I'm still in camp. It was the same as once before: only a certain number of passes, and a boy with his wife in town, and no pass; so I had to let him go instead of me. The only trouble is that I see by the passbook that he went on my pass instead of getting another for himself. So I hope he treats the name with the respect it deserves. The platoon sergeant told him to do that, which shows the attitude everyone takes towards such things. If he should get into trouble with someone else's pass he'd be out of luck.

Today was warm, like midsummer at home in the afternoon, when I had a chance to go out on the range with only a few others and use up boxes and boxes of ammunition. We made such a noise, it was a noisy kind anyway, that my ears started ringing, something I'd never experienced before I was in the army, like a lot of telephone bells right by your ear, drowning out every other sound. I used to think "ears ringing" was just a sort of indefinite phrase. After a while the ringing stopped, but now 6 hours later I still can't hear much. I went to the movies tonight and could understand very little. But it was very good fun and really good practice. Usually any firing on the range is conducted very formally to make it safe with lots of people, but this was perfectly informal and we just fired away as we pleased.

Were things broken too much to be exhibited in Wellesley, or could they patch them up a little and show them? Seems to me there was something funny about the head on my figure anyway. I've a vague idea it broke before, or for some reason I cast it separately or made a new one or something, but I may be thinking of my dancing marble figures. Anyway, since it's plaster, I don't think it matters much. There are several things that should be changed on the figure anyway. I don't believe you packed them badly—they were probably treated unusually roughly. I'm glad Alec[4] made a new milking stand for you. You certainly must have needed it. And I wish "Judy" hadn't stepped on your toe. In the movie tonight the newsreel part was all about horse races with slow motion pictures of them starting and running. They were really wonderful. I was surprised how much their shoulders moved. They were beautiful.

It's a funny feeling not being able to hear very well. It shuts off all natural conversation. I can see how deaf people must be awfully lonely. No other disability could so completely cut you off. I think too that's why father's letters, and even sometimes conversations, sound occasionally a little formal. He misses lots of the little inflections and asides, and what might be called monosyllabic grunts that are a part of easy, intimate conversation and are such an important factor in natural understanding.

It's Sunday morning now and a beautiful day again. It was 45 at sunrise and now 60 on the north side of the building. When it's not raining, winter here seems very much like October at home. Everybody is full of rumors and speculation and it is amusing to see how much significance people try to see in the smallest events or phrases that some officer, or person who might know something, lets fall. As yet I've found no evidence to substantiate anything I've heard; so we are really as much in the dark as ever. I think I get less and less reconciled to being away from you instead of getting used to it. Intelligence can go on explaining the necessity over and over till doomsday, but instinct stubbornly maintains that it's unnatural and therefore unreasonable and also claims the more realistic point of view. All I think about is you and the children and it's hard for me to concentrate on what I'm doing just as it is for you.

This morning I've been reading *Anna and the King of Siam*, which Mary Fyffe sent me. It's very good but I wish there were more direct quotations from the book it's taken from. You're never sure whether it's the way Anna felt or the way the author thinks or hopes she would have felt. The difference

---

4 An Italian-born handyman who worked for my grandmother.

between a fictionalized biography and a real one is that in the former you save effort by using the author's imagination instead of your own, and you get the facts pre-masticated and comfortably delivered to your belly. The author's stock in trade is his understanding, imagination, and judgment, and is as good or as bad as a doctor's might be. You trust him instead of finding out for yourself.

I'm surprised how much feeling the British troubles with Greek elements seem to arouse here. As I said there's lots of anti-British feeling which, as far as I can see, is based on nothing but ignorance and prejudice but nonetheless real and strong. People consider isolationism foolish and outmoded which it is, but don't seem to realize that the only alternative is to assume responsibility and "interfere" as they call it with other peoples' affairs. The same people who call themselves internationalists, and contrast themselves with isolationists, are the ones who wanted us to give the Philippines their unprotected independence long ago, and now worry about "interfering" with other countries internal affairs. They want us to see that justice is done in the world to all, but without taking any measures to ensure it; they're all crazy.

So far I've done nothing but sit around all day. There's nothing you can do outdoors for entertainment except walk up and down, which I did for a while. So I guess the day will just be spent reading and writing letters. Now I feel the need of exercise, but I suppose eventually I'll get more than I want. Just because I remember the last war stopped pretty suddenly, I keep thinking this one may. Both the Germans and the Japs are the kind that would put up a pretty good show till the very end, and, unless they had a good reason to make you think the opposite, will probably look stronger when they are in the final stages. Mary, I wish I were with you. I love you so much; it seems as if it had been a lifetime already and it will be so much longer even.

Sydney

⁂

Christmas

Dear Mary,

I meant to ask to speak to little Mary, too, on the telephone, but I worried about the time limit and didn't. I was afraid getting her to come and everything might take too long. We had a large meal with turkey and everything at noontime, and that was the extent of my Christmas celebrating. I went to the movies last night and tonight. I've certainly gone to them mighty frequently of late for one who doesn't like movies too well. They seem to be almost all in the escapist style nowadays, which I'm afraid is exactly what I want. Didn't get any letters today, but they seem to have followed us in a rather mixed up order and anyway I guess now I'll have to get used to not getting them so often. We have to stand in line to get in and out of the mess hall; at noontime yesterday, I stood an hour and ten minutes to get in and about fifteen minutes to get out (we have to rinse off our dishes as we go out), so that altogether dinner took about two hours. It's the same with everything else.

After I get more used to writing in this kind of situation, I'll try to write more and better. I kept wondering all day how Mary looked when she saw the new pony, did she really have no idea she was getting it, and what did "Judy" think? How much does Frank understand about Christmas? I guess he doesn't remember the last one. Was there any snow on the ground?

I love you an awful lot.
Sydney

December 26

Dear Mary,

I got two letters from you and father, and your mother and father's Christmas card today. It's an awfully good picture but when was it made? With two grandchildren too few, it's way out of date. I can see how an up-to-date picture would hardly be practical, but it's too bad to have everybody think that that's all they have to show so far. I'm awfully glad you sent me the picture of Matt Hale's children. They are awfully cunning. I feel as if, or rather I know, I've been losing touch with most of my friends which I don't like at all. It's ten years since I've seen very much of Matt and seeing pictures of his children is a big help in maintaining some sort of picture of his life now.

Your description of the snow persistently blowing back into the lane and covering all signs of traffic makes me homesick for New England, Peterborough, or East River. Maybe Mr. Harris[5] could do a real job on the car so it'll start when you want it to start, or don't you use it enough to keep the battery charged anyway? I thought too that it was exciting when the snowplow would come through by our house in the middle of the night connecting us again with the rest of the world after a big storm, and seeing that light in the kitchen window of an evening meant as much to me as anything in the world. I'm glad

---
5 A neighbor.

the staff have snowball fights through the kitchen window. Why doesn't your mother join in the fun too? Or does she? She wrote a very nice note to me on the Christmas card. Your mother is a remarkably nice person.

Yesterday, the 25th, I heard a K. P.[6] in the mess hall say that if one more guy said "Merry Christmas" to him he'd kill him. At least that's one thing I escaped. The only really sadistic people in the army are the mess sergeants. Other noncoms are just subhuman, curious survivors of the original genus engendered in the primordial ooze. Harmless souls with hearts as soft as their brains. I think, too, that "Judy" should be restrained most of the time, except when she's out to exercise; otherwise I'm afraid she might grow up to be a horse like "Wenny" with characteristics more admirable in the human rugged individualist. I think I'm still getting fatter everyday but I shall be careful to at least stay recognizable.

I love you.
Sydney

December 30

Dear Sydney,

Today I got two letters from you, written Christmas and the day after, and now I feel badly for the letter I wrote last week in which I bemoaned the fact you hadn't written then. But those two were postmarked the 28th. I gathered from one of your references that perhaps I am right as to my surmise of where you are.

Gosh, Sydney, I feel low tonight and I shouldn't because I got two letters from you, but I feel just about sunk and very, very sad. Sometimes it is overpowering and everything everybody says makes it worse. I love you such an awful lot and I don't know how I can stand it, but I must try. I'm glad you didn't have K. P. on Christmas Day at least, but the standing in line must be terrible. I have ordered *Reader's Digest* for you as a present, because I'm sure you'll like it. If you want, I'll give you *The New Yorker* too.

I wonder where you are tonight. Tomorrow is the last day of this year and let us pray for reunion in 1945. I don't know how much longer I can exist in this life of apathy and over-wrought emotions.

This morning we hitched "Mitzi" up to the pony cart. The children were thrilled, and she went beautifully, though the ice and snow made it definitely not buggy weather. Her feet slip and when we hit snow it pulls so heavy, but "Mitzi" just buckles into the collar and gallops forward! Not like

---

6 The Kitchen Police were those assigned to help the cooks with the preparation of meals and the cleaning up afterwards. All enlisted men served on K. P.

good old "Nona" who stands still and backs up! The cart is fine. It has a brake on it, and everything. It is very light. Mary pulls it around with Sydney and Frank in it, so I think "Mitzi" can do it. I can remember taking Mamie and Baby Joe[7] to drive with "Honeymoon" in that same cart.

I'm enclosing a card I got today from Joe, as I think it will amuse you! He really is funny, isn't he? Apparently, he's through with Greece now the shooting has started, and said in those ruins, wherever it was, he'd seen more action than he'd seen since Elba.[8] So we don't know what's next on the cards.

This afternoon we went to Guilford and saw Jane[9] and the children for a few minutes. When I was at the goat food store the man there said they should be moved (from one feed to another?) once a year anyhow. It's a Purina Checkerboard store. Ours never have been and I don't think they need it, but I wonder. What would you suggest?

The children have all had little colds but are mostly over them. I have escaped so far. I don't know how Sydney doesn't seem to have it. Mary started it, mildly, and gave it to Frank and Betsy. Frank is the worse, but perhaps that is because of his age. He can't sniff or blow, or rather won't, so it shows more. Betsy is a little rattley but not bad.

Nat gave B. Anne[10] a pair of four-foot hickory skis for Christmas from Sears Roebuck; so, I have taken the information and I think I will get Mary a pair because you said you'd like her to have some. They only cost $2.16. Mother gave me a new, four-quart milk pail for Christmas, and it's come and looks very professional, like a cow pail. Also, she gave me a flashlight that attaches to the chest, leaving both hands free. It is very useful and will be wonderful in Peterborough.

I guess I better not write any more than the rest of this page, as I want to enclose Joe's card and must write a few other letters if I can, which I doubt. When I have written you, I am ready for bed. I love you such an awful lot, honestly, and I'm still praying something will keep you in this country!

I sent the Hales a picture of our children too and I write Cathy Farlow fairly often and Franny too. So I will keep the contacts for you as best I can while you are gone.

I love you an awful, awful lot,
Mary

---

7 Baby Joe was my mother's youngest brother, born in 1919. Mamie was hired as his nurse; she stayed with my grandmother until she died in 1961.
8 German occupying forces in Greece withdrew in October 1944, as Russian forces advanced. The invasion of Elba occurred June 17–19, 1944. The invasion was conducted by Free French forces, supported by British and American ships. My mother's brother Joe commanded an LST (Landing Ship, Tank).
9 My father's sister, Jane Greene.
10 My cousin, B. Anne Greene, Jane Greene's daughter.

December 31

Dear Mary,

The nuts came today but no letters. I celebrated New Year's Eve by drinking a quart of milk at the service club. Since then I've been looking at a book by Lincoln Rothschild, who apparently has no aesthetic sense whatsoever, called *Sculpture Through the Ages* or something. His only interest seems to be in social trends of thought as shown by art of different periods. He understands the trends pretty well, but it seems incredible to me that anyone so completely artistically blind should have written such a book in the first place. How did he ever get interested in the subject? It has lots of good pictures in it, though, which make up for what is lacking in the text.

    I don't suppose it's a very practical suggestion now, but didn't Hollis[11] and M. F. show us a nice two-wheeled basket or governess pony cart that they were anxious to get rid of? Maybe it was too heavy anyway, but I don't think so. The idea of living in that distant future called 1945 still seems pretty ridiculous, but I ought to start getting used to it tomorrow, I guess. I think I'd better just leave all my hopes and aspirations in mothballs, for the time being; so that they'll be in good shape to dig out for 1946. Wrap me up a package for next Christmas. We'll just scratch this year off the list. Tear some pages out of the book and change the number of the next chapter. My life away from you is just a break in the movie reel, no matter the time in fixing it, the story is renewed just where it left off. But that's my part of it. I'm missing ages of the children's life and eons of your love.

I love you.
Sydney

December 31

Dear Sydney,

Here it is the last day of this old year—a year that has brought us a great deal of sadness, but also happiness in Betsy and the rest of our children; so I guess it about evens out, and let us hope that 1945 will bring us together again for good—that's all the resolution I am going to make! I love you an awful, awful lot—I wonder where you are and where you are going—it preys on my mind and terribly—whenever I open a paper or listen on the radio—my feeling is that of all my brothers and yours, you are in the most dangerous

---

11 My father's cousin, Hollis Hunnewell.

position and I don't see why it should come to us this way—but my Faith is still unshaken—I wish to God you'd be kept in this country—well—I am not going to celebrate tonight—not even stay up till midnight! How well I remember all the carefree New Year's we've celebrated! New Year's—in Tamworth and last year at the Dodge House—I love you an awful lot, and may God see to it that there will never be another with us apart!

It is warmer here tonight and foggy—45—and mother and daddy were to go to New Haven to celebrate but I think they have weakened! Betty[12] is staying in town, coming out on the 8 a.m. bus tomorrow. Today we had more pony rides—I really am 100 percent pleased with "Mitzi"! She is all I could ever ask for—I had her staked out on two goat chains today to eat dried grass—she is very clever at that—the staking out I mean—not the eating—she's good at that too! I wish you could see Mary and Sydney and Frank all trying to pick up her separate feet at the same time. Mary picks them up as easy as anything. She gets on and off completely alone and is learning to bridle and saddle her—she is so looking forward to when she and I can go for long rides together! Me on "Judy"—she on "Mitzi"—she wants to go to the post office! She just loves that pony! She still gets a great kick out of pulling the pony cart around with Frank and Sydney for passengers! Jean's mother and sister came over this afternoon—Jean[13] is in the state of Washington. Her husband's still in this country and he's been in the army almost 3 yrs. now—they expect her in Madison in the near future for a visit, at least her little girl. Sue is with her mother.

I just wonder if I'll get any more letters. Gosh how I hope and pray so! Wouldn't it be a miracle if for some reason you didn't go—I think I'd die of joy! I've heard of so many breaks other people have gotten but I fear it's not in the cards for us—I just pray nothing happens to you—I guess some people come back safely but it seems like such a long chance somehow—Dear God how I pray for you.

Mother is going to Ambler, Pennsylvania, this week or next to be with grandma for about 10 days before she—grandma—goes to Washington, so I will be alone again for a little while. I wrote you last night too and am mailing both separately this time, as they'd be too heavy and also you might not get one of them—why don't you tell me the dates of the last letters you get—I wonder if any of them ever get lost—they say sometimes the mail bag gets run over when the old man doesn't hook it on right—I wonder if that's happened to any of my letters—I love you such an awful lot I feel as tho I'd

---

12 My grandmother's cook.
13 My mother's best friend, Jean Kaiser.

burst honestly and I feel so helpless—such a wisp in the winds of fate—I think that's the worst part really. There is nothing one can do—no one to call up and tell them to send you home!

I have ordered a pair of skis for Mary and ones for Sydney too! Maybe they can learn to just walk around on them—if we ever get any more snow! What we had for Christmas is almost all gone—just ice—mud and slush left! Give me a good old Peterborough winter any day! I must say the lack of daylight this year—with electricity—seems negligible compared to last year! People don't know when they talk about the dark mornings down here! But I wouldn't exchange any other home with electricity for our home without it! I feel as tho I could hardly wait to be going back—but when I feel that way I think how much more so you must feel it, away from the children and the animals and your parents.

I must go to bed now—this living room must be 90 in the shade, its terrible! I feel the heat more than the cold so far this winter but I'm not kicking! It certainly is different, a winter in Conn. from one in N. H. I never really realized it before—I love you such an awful lot. I have to go, I cannot listen to the radio any longer—it is terrible—the actual news is more encouraging. I love you an awful lot

༄

January 4

Dear Sydney,

Today I got three letters from you—two this morning and one this afternoon so I guess I may not get any tomorrow—they were written Dec. 30th, 31st, and Jan. 1st—I have a pretty good guess as to what you are doing from something Ombo said way back early last summer—it is potentially dangerous, I would say, an[14]d I hope to God I'm wrong—tho it is all earmarked that way. I suppose since you must throw my letters away anyhow I could tell you, but it might be wiser not to—my guess is you are in the vicinity of where Joe was for so long and practicing what is up his alley. If you can say I'm right or wrong—say so. Of course I haven't mentioned my surmises to a soul and never would for your safety.

You are wonderful in finding things to write about and as I said your letters aren't a bit stiff or unnatural—in fact I am overjoyed because you had me scared when you warned us beforehand—so keep it up and never think for a

---

14 Osborne Day was a friend of my mother's youngest brother, Joe. He was a 1943 graduate of Yale and later served in the CIA.

moment they aren't wonderful letters just as full of you as they ever were! It's like hearing you talk to us for a few minutes to get a letter! I worry too about the anti-British attitude, and you know what a Tory daddy is! It is a thing that will be difficult to override but as you say, no future hope for peace and unity can ever be achieved without an acknowledgement of the fact that the Anglo-Saxons are the superior race and must always be united in purpose and ideals to uphold themselves and the rest of the world.

You said the nuts came—did you find the knife in the box? Or haven't you really looked? I do hope it isn't lost but you didn't mention it so I wonder—maybe you looked in the wrong end tho I only opened one end—do be sure and tell me as soon as ever you can as I'm anxious to know! I'm afraid I'm ignorant about Lincoln Rothschild—I never ever heard of the guy so I don't know how he ever got interested in art! I guess I'm dumb but it seems as tho I hadn't learned much! I'm going to write your ma and pa tonight and I shall ask about the governess cart! It would be just the thing!

I feel as tho the clock stopped too—when you went away and all this is just a question of endurance and existence but as you say, it is life to the children and so I try my best to keep you in close contact with their little everyday doings—but I always feel at the end of a letter I have failed miserably. I cannot do justice to their expressions, their little mannerisms—as fleeting as time itself—so I see no way to encourage you in that line—it is just a bare, hard, given fact and we will pray you will be home soon enough to get in on some of it at least! After all, their lives are always full and interesting and their development a constant source of pride and will be ever after they leave babyhood—so we should have years together to share with them. As for my love—God knows I pour it out to you every day in every letter and I exude it all day long—It, and God's protection are what I'm counting on to keep you from harm—If love can do it you should emerge unscathed—tho I must confess at night I sometimes lie [awake] and think of all the dangers—the anguish—the suffering that is about to confront you, and if I pray awful hard and believe with all my power, I succumb to moments of such horror as I hope to God none of our children will ever have to bear.

I thought I'd told you that as far as Mary's letters go, she tells me what she wants to say. I sometimes edit the wording and then spell the words for her, tho she's beginning to recognize words that begin with different letters, like pony (p) and papa (p) and can get quite a few, tho only the first letter. She knows how to make every letter when I name it. So, I think she's as good as any nursery school child, don't you?

I don't get cold in the morning; don't worry about me! It hasn't been to zero yet! And the barn is warm and remember how it felt in Peterborough? Or I guess it was the evening you said you felt perfectly warm milking at below zero. But only once or twice have I really wondered is it worth it? When the north wind and snow have driven over the meadow as I walked across—biting my face and neck— then the barn feels really warm—tho the pails are frozen and "Judy" and "Mitzi" whinny and the goats bleat and I know it's worth it! So don't worry about me! Worry about yourself!

This afternoon was like spring! So we hitched "Mitzi" to the pony cart and the children and I drove over to Charlotte's![15] They weren't up from their naps. Charlotte sleeping off 2 cocktail shakers for 3 before lunch! I asked Mary to go in and call Charlotte—she said "Sydney will do it." I looked at him and he said "I will!" Whereupon he proceeded to go in and wake her up calling "Charlotte!" I was surprised. Mary was embarrassed, but Sydney never hesitated! And Frank stomped in demanding "Where's Barbara?" Finally, they all appeared. Charlotte still feeling her cocktails, and we loaded the five children in, and Charlotte and I walked alongside, down to where Ruth used to live and back. Barbara and Frank on the front seat, looking too cunning, and the other three standing behind. It has high sides of wicker and a high back. Frank kept glancing at Barbara to see how she was taking it, and she was just beaming. She is just like Harpo Marx—doesn't say a word but just makes expressions. It only took about twenty minutes to get over there; on the shoulder of the road the cart goes so easily, and "Mitzi" trots along, not a bit even curious about the great trailer trucks that rumble by! She does want to turn in every driveway, but not seriously. Coming home Mary was talking about their going out in the storm the other day and she said, "We're tough Gods aren't we?"—I did have to laugh! I wish you'd seen her yesterday. She didn't know I was looking—she was trying to see the back of her head in the mirror—so she stood with her back to it and whirled around quickly trying to see it! Then she tried holding the back of her head and turning! It was very funny and when I laughed she burst into gales of laughter herself.

The colds are all gone, only Betsy still rattles now and then, as tho she should just clear her throat. She is so cunning. When she sees me coming, she beams and wiggles all over and throws her arms around, so happy to see me! I

---

15 Charlotte Lage, one of my mother's oldest friends and her matron of honor.

still pray that something will keep you in this country. I shall certainly be interested to hear what you have been doing. I gather you are not idle—not just sitting and waiting—which makes me think I am right. Well I must stop if I'm to write your family and I should write to Anne LaFarge.[16] I feel so sorry for her, honestly. Do take every care of yourself and always remember how much I love you. Let that give you strength when you feel you might falter.

I love you,
Mary

January 14

Dear Sydney,

It is a wonderful snow. Storms here, big flakes, and Katherine and Mary have been here building a "fort"—it's just a column sticking straight up—I wonder how much snow there is in East River.

    I telephoned Arnold last evening and they are fine. He seldom writes—the circuits were very busy and I had a long wait. We here just heard that Mr. Wilson wants cash for grain for the horses that isn't paid by the farm. Hay there and here is $44.00 a ton. He didn't write anything more so I suppose all is well. Jennie Hunnewell is getting ready to move into the big house, and is never going to leave it again. She could not have been more decided. Betty expects a baby in February. Lucy White expects one soon too, number four with her. George Sargent's wife has just had one, a boy this time. Frank Sargent's wife is living with her mother, Mrs. Fay—have you met them? Bye-the-way he is called Francis. Mary D. is expecting a baby too. Her second. Also, Grenny Jr.[17] has a son.

    I went to my sewing circle the other day at Susan Garfield's, Zeke's mother in law. The Garfields have gone for years to Falmouth on Cape Cod. The hurricane last summer took every single tree on their place. They are right on the sea shore and have a place of 10 or 15 acres—mostly fields etc., with trees all around the house. Some they tried to push up again, but since then we have had bad storms and now everything is flat. We have been fairly lucky with servants this year, except our cook has broken or rather broke her leg, so she went home last week and we have another coming tomorrow. She did not do it here, but on her day off and as it was a small bone and did not hurt after it was bandaged, we had a time preventing her walking on it. She had no faith in x-rays!! I liked her, but Mrs. Coffey says she had a terrible temper in the kitchen.

---

16 Another close friend of my mother.
17 Grenny Jr. was the son of Grenville Clark who helped draft the Selective Service and Training Act of 1940. His wife Fanny Dwight was my paternal grandmother's first cousin.

George is out at present with Biddy and they can't roam away for they are on the terrace and I have had part fenced in—we really had to. Putting 5 dogs out, one by one—two at a time go off—was quite a job.[18]

Lots of love,
Mother

January 15

Dear Sydney,

Here it is the middle of January—almost Sydney's birthday. He says you are to come home as soon as you get across the water. How I wish it could be so!

I dreamt a lot about you again last night. This time I was with you. We were in England, heading for the front lines, and I was beside you, where I belong. We marveled at it but put it down to the fact that in times like that they weren't so particular! I dream a lot about you, almost every night, and I'm glad. I hope I always will. I worry so much about you. You have come into my unconscious thoughts, as well as usurping all my waking moments. I love it and I hope I shall continue to dream of you.

Aunt Helen gave me a little off-the-record dope and just in case. Joe's ship is the USS *LST 601*. I do hope I can get a letter before too terribly long, and I'll be awfully curious to know how and when my letters reach you.

This morning, Alec had to go to a mass for his son, reported missing a year ago today; so, as we had to meet Betty and take Daddy to his bus, I had to bundle all four children into the car and be up at the post office at 9:00 a.m., quite a feat, as it necessitated getting breakfast first as well as all the chores—nursing Betsy, milking "Becky" and feeding the other animals. Both busses were late due to last night's snowfall. We have a fairly respectable snow cover now.

This afternoon I had a time catching "Mitzi!" I had "Judy" in the paddock and "Mitzi" loose. She flung up her heels and galloped in circles. But I finally got her with a little grain. She's smart. I thought she and "Judy" would get used to each other this way, because she goes up to "Judy," but "Judy" can't hurt her.

We hitched up the pony cart and drove to Madison to give "Mitzi" a little work. She needs some real exercise once in a while. I wish we'd had a sleigh, as the roads are perfect! The children love it and so do I.

---

18 In this letter, my grandmother refers to numerous cousins.

When we got back and were doing the evening chores, we got right close to old Jimmy Skunk![19] Sydney was fascinated and trailed him all over. The skunk moved slowly in the snow, so they got a good close look at him. Mary was quite nervous, but not Sydney and Frank. "Mopsa" bearded him once or twice, but he didn't squirt her, as she stayed a respectful distance. It was funny to see.

I love you an awful lot. I am alone again. Mother won't be back for another week.[20] Daddy will be home Friday. I enjoy the longer evenings and the freedom to indulge my thoughts and actions, without having to think of anyone else, after the children are in bed and asleep. They are so good, really, and so full of life. Sometimes I have to quell their exuberance when they are dressing or eating. And Mary looks reproachfully at me and says: "But don't you like us to laugh? You always scold us when we cry." And then I feel mean. But sometimes we'd never get anywhere if I didn't make them attend to what they are doing. All three of them, so young and so close together is wonderful. They have such a good time, and now Betsy will soon be joining in. People marvel when they see me trailed by all three—so small! But I am glad they are so close and that we had no inhibitions about having them. I thank God for them every day.

Mother wrote me today, a pathetic sort of letter, trying to find some way to help me bear my loneliness and anxiety. It's since she's gone that I knew you had gone.[21] But there is nothing anyone can do or say. It is in one's self that one must seek comfort and fortitude, and she is anxious too.

With Stu[22] in the Philippines and Joe not heard from for some little time now, you and I have a special sort of intimacy, I think, and no outsider can hope to penetrate the walls of it. I love you such an awful lot. Take care of yourself in every way you can and write me often! Write me every chance you get, won't you? Letters are like lifelines to a drowning man. I wish I could be anesthetized—like the final throes of giving birth to a baby—and wake up exhausted but supremely happy.

Someday that time will come. In the meantime, my hair gets grayer daily and I suffer as I've never suffered before—in mind, body and spirit. But there is bound to be a dawn somewhere after these wee, small hours of waiting.

I love you. I know my suffering is nothing to yours.

I love you,
Mary

---

19 *The Adventures of Jimmy Skunk*, by Thornton W. Burgess, was first published in 1923
20 She had gone to visit her mother in Ambler, Pennsylvania, and then on to Washington, DC, where she had a home.
21 The 87th Regiment embarked on the USS *West Point* on January 3 from Newport News, Virginia, headed to Naples, Italy, where they landed on January 13.
22 The second of my mother's three brothers.

January 18

Dear Mary,

Can only say that I am in Italy, seeing it rather differently than you did. It's a beautiful country; I can see why people used to get so enthusiastic about it. I just hope, but without much optimism, that I'll be able to see some of the things I want to see. It's going to be very tantalizing. The boat trip wasn't too bad, though even a sardine would have called it cozy. I'd breath once morning and evening, and not bother the rest of the day. I'm very curious to know if I'll see John Farlow.[23] We are allowed to number letters, so this is number one. Being in Europe seems about ten times as far away now as it ever did in peacetime. Haven't had any letters since I left, which doesn't make me feel any too gay. I keep dreaming about you every night lately; before I left I hardly ever dreamt at all.

I love you,
Sydney

January 19

Dear Sydney,

We are hoping to hear from you soon. We have heard from Dick saying he has arrived somewhere "after a comfortable voyage even though through a fairly rough sea. Mail from home has arrived. The train took us from Camp Hood to Seattle, Washington, where we stayed over Christmas. At the present time we are living in tents and have running water. Within a short time it will be possible to tell you where we are." He says he doesn't know your A. P. O. N. Y. address, but I have sent it to him in my last letter too. Here is his address: O-1168137 Battery A749 F. A. Boston, A. P. O. No. 345 c/o Postmaster, San Francisco.

Here is Arnold's: 1325 Olive St., Denver. I wonder how much time you will have to write. Besides writing to Mary, Jane wrote that they had been over to the Hotchkisses and the children had had a ride on "Mitzi"—who was quite lively. But she didn't blame her as it was a very cold day—Mary hopes to see Joe again when he gets back from his shakedown cruise and then he leaves, probably, for the Pacific.

---

23 John Farlow was a Belmont School and Harvard classmate of my father.

Have you met Harry Stanton—I wrote to you about him—Stephen Stanton's younger brother? I talked with Arnold on the telephone the other day about his news and he said he knew lots of boys in your regiment, also John Pierpont in the 86th. John Farlow is still in Italy, also Walter is in the Mediterranean. Willard[24] is home from Norfolk, Virginia. Walter home for a leave and then probably to the Pacific. All well here—a wonderful day just what you would like, cold and still sunny and a lot of fresh snow.

Lots of Love,
Mother

∽

January 26

Dear Mary,

I got a bunch of letters from you and one from Arnold—your last postmarked the eighth. I'm not able to write so often now. I'm glad you had such a good time with Naomi and the Shattucks; I wish you had a few more chances to be really gay. I'm glad my children appreciate the thrill of being out in a storm. It's the right attitude and I'm awfully glad you got them skis. We've had a chance to see a little of the country around here, and it's some of the most beautiful I've ever seen. I don't see why I never went to Italy before. I wish we were seeing it together. I like to think that it's familiar to you. I wish I could say what part I'm in and ask if you've been here. We are more comfortable than I expected though it's a little damp right now. I've really rather enjoyed it so far because the country interests me so much. I keep forgetting I didn't just come to look at it. Mail doesn't come and go as often as I hoped, but everything else is better than I hoped. Mary is a very good girl to write to her Papa so often.

I love you.
Sydney

∽

January 27

Dear Mary,

I got another letter from you dated the tenth, when you guessed correctly that I must have already left. It was an awfully nice letter. There isn't any more news that I can write than there was last time. Mother said in a letter

---

24 Walter and Willard Hunnewell were my father's first cousins.

I got the same time that Jane was very excited about the pony. Has B. Anne had a chance to ride it? I've met a friend of Arnold's that he had told me about, as well as two others in this outfit that I haven't found yet. I wish I could see Frank riding "Mitzi" and holding onto the "grass" on her neck. I keep reading in the paper about extra cold spells at home, and I think of you going out to the barn before daylight and hoping you aren't too cold. I don't think you need to worry about me; I feel very sure of myself.

I love you an awful lot, I wish the mail came a little more often. Today I saw an old woman milking her sheep, they were better trained than our goats, they just stood, they weren't tied or anything. The milk was yellower than goat's milk.

I love you.
Sydney

January 30

Dear Mary,

I got six letters from you today and one each from mother and Mary Fyffe. The postmarks ranged from the sixth to the twentieth. Was the picture of "Judy" or the pony? If it's "Judy" she's certainly grown a lot of mane and put on weight around her tummy. You said it was "Judy." Betsy, I'm afraid looks like a stranger, though perhaps something like Mary or Frank. Seems to me we ought to have a car that will run in winter as well as summer. I hope someday we can get a new one. Are "Mopsa" and "Rollo" really used to each other yet? I should think they would be. I'm writing this by the light of a lamp somebody made by sticking a rope into a bottle of oil. It works pretty well, but makes the atmosphere pretty thick. I feel very hopeful now that maybe it won't be as long as we thought. I'm glad the children want to go home to Peterborough, but I hope they like East River too.

I've been reading A. E. Housman's poems in a serviceman's edition. I've never more than just looked at them before. I like them pretty well and am interested but not as enthusiastic as some people get.

I hope Mary gets a chance to try skating some this winter as well as skiing. I hope I'm not too anxious and impatient to have them learn everything. I hope to God that they keep on being healthier and huskier than other peoples' children and I think they will. I hope they are always gay and laughing. Tell them Papa feels happy when they laugh and are happy.

I suppose that if Sonnichsen[25] were a prisoner they would have heard by now, but I keep hoping; it sounds just like him to be rescuing children. I'm afraid that describing my feelings to you under censorship is about as hard as building a fire under water. It just won't work. I wish I could see you all driving with "Mitzi." I haven't heard any news of Henry[26] for a long time; is he still in Cairo? Mother's letter was mostly a long list of cousins who've had babies. The more the better say I, but I'm losing track fast. I would like to keep them all straight, but I'm truly glad to know that my friends and relatives, the people, verily, that I respect and like the best in the world are multiplying as fast as possible. I wave my hat and give three cheers and pray that they will all inherit innerspring mattresses. I got a card saying father had given me the *Reader's Digest* for Christmas which was a good idea, so don't send ours or is it the same one. I'm confused.

I love you.
Sydney

February 2

Dear Sydney,

Brother ground hog must have been blind if he didn't see his shadow today! But personally, in spite of cold spells, winds etc., I still have that feeling of "where is the winter"—It hasn't been a bit like Peterborough—and now a letter today from Mrs. Adams[27] and Anna Mary says it's been the snowiest January in 16 years up there! The drifts pile in as fast as the plow clears the roads, and now Mr. Gleason of the Hancock snowplow says he can no longer see out of his cab windows over the snow heaped beside the road. But I feel I shouldn't be writing to you about snow. I should let you write me what snow really is. However, any Peterborough news is interesting, I hope! Mr. Adams can't even get into the woods to cut wood! Poor Mrs. Adams doesn't sound as though she'd been too well—is taking liver and vitamin injections—but still seems willing to have Anna Mary come to me next summer provided I don't confine her too closely from her young friends!

Well, the excitement here now is Betty! She was off this morning to meet her M. P. who has 24 hrs. to spend with her—she hinted they may go to N. Y.! She was to take Allan[28] to her cousin's in Wallingford. As she said, "don't ask me what we're going to do!" It all depends on whether

---

25 Warren Sonnichsen was from Madison, Connecticut. My father met him during basic training at Fort McClellan. Sonnichsen was sent to France and fought in the Battle of the Bulge. He was taken prisoner, but survived the war.
26 My mother's oldest brother.
27 Mr. and Mrs. Adams and their daughter Anna Mary were neighbors in New Hampshire.
28 Betty's baby son.

his intentions are honorable—hers certainly aren't. Now we are wondering when we'll see her again and for how long! I'll write you tomorrow what transpires! The baby's father is still undrafted—to Betty's chagrin, and I imagine the N. Y. idea was to escape him! It is very interesting and we are on pins and needles to see what happens. We may be minus a cook. He may, of course, even marry her tomorrow. Who knows!

Well I had to get a new battery for my car, or rather our car. The children think of it as ours and mostly yours. I'm only driving it while you are away! It has a new heavy-duty battery costing $13.95. I can't remember just when we bought this one, can you? And also how much it cost or how loud it was supposed to be. But I heard Mr. Harris telling someone about a remarkable battery that lasted from June 1941 until now—that's not quite 4 years old and I'm sure ours is at least 3 years old. So I don't feel so badly.

The proofs of Betsy arrived and I can hardly wait now to get the pictures to send to you. There is one pretty good one of me holding her. I hope you'll like it but I probably haven't the expression you wanted—of when I look at you because I can't look that way without you to look at! But I hope you'll like it! I'm going to get the under-8 oz. accordion frame that holds 12 pictures and send that with one of Betsy and me and three other different ones of Betsy. Then if you want you can put the other three children in it too and have them all together.

I love you such an awful lot. I feel as though you were lost honestly. But I guess when I get my first letter I'll feel better. But this business of writing day after day for four weeks now with no reply is very disheartening.

Frank is so funny when he falls down on the ice, which is often, as he insists on "skating." He'll quickly—before anyone can say or do anything—say "it's not funny!" We walked up to Harrises this afternoon and came back by the Hoops' pond, which is windswept in spots but not skateable. We slid around for a while and Mary can finally to do that and very skillfully. We found an old cardboard box and had a lot of fun with them sitting in it and then my giving them great shoves. They slid and whirled around! Later on back at the barn Mary rode "Mitzi" around bareback inside the barn and with no bridle. I am going to encourage that as it develops their balance in a way nothing else will. She just wanders into her stall and "Judy's" and sniffs the goats and turns around and all. Frank's legs are really too short, but he wants to keep on trying! Sydney does pretty well only he instinctively reaches for the wall if he is near it and of course that might pull him off, but I think it's a sure way to get their balance. Don't you?

Mrs. Adams said she sent you a letter and a package just after Christmas and is now afraid you never got them, but you will eventually I feel sure. She says their trees will look like Alder Bushes if it snows again and that there is just one path shoveled down the Main St. in Hancock. Doesn't that sound like something?

I got a thing today from the *Reader's Digest* asking if your subscription was requested, so I wrote back and said it was! They said they'd already entered the subscription anyhow, so I feel fully justified because once before you said you would like it! So I hope you really do want it and do get it! Your father sent me a check for $5.00 for Sydney's birthday—Sydney is thrilled over the prospects of money to spend! Your father also said that little Mary Fyffe greeted him the other evening with the news that her white doll and her black doll were being married the next day. Your father said he asked her if their child would be gray. Mary said, "oh no, they have one already and it's a duck!" I think that reflects on the Planned Parenthood, don't you! I must write him about it.

Well tomorrow is Saturday. But now I'm weakening as to whether I will get the letter or not. Joe's last one took two weeks due to bad flying weather, so it may be next week, but I'm still convinced that you wrote one on the 24th! I dreamed again last [night] that I got a letter from you. Yesterday Mary had a wishbone and she and I were to wish on it. I asked her what she wanted to wish—not being sure if she knew just what a wish was—she said, "I want to wish about Papa." Of course, I did too and so the head flew off. Neither of us got it, but I say that means we both get our wishes.

I have to go to bed now—it's late. But as tomorrow is Saturday I wanted to be sure and get this off. I'll write you a long one Sat. and Sun, I hope! I do love you such an awful lot. You are always and always in my thoughts—heart, body and soul. My daily life is geared around you. Write you soon. I live for your letters to me.

I love you—Mary

P. S. Stu writes he did not get the Navy Cross after all but the Legion of Merit and a very nice citation! They did not give him credit for the submarine but the admiral did!

February 4

Dear Mary,

No letters since I last wrote, so none to answer which leaves me nothing much to say. Everyone is excited about the Russians' advance and I can't help feeling rather optimistic. I wonder if the family has heard from Dick yet; it seems like about time. I feel awfully curious to know where he went. They make it so it's really almost impossible to write a letter at all. I spend most of my time thinking about you and the children. I keep wondering whether you've been here. Tell me what parts of Italy you know and then, though I won't be able to tell you, I'll know whether you've been here or not. I love you an awful lot and miss you an awful lot. Except when I get out to see a little of the country, I'm leading a pretty boring existence which seems too bad in such an interesting country. It makes me almost sad to write, being able to say so little makes me feel so cut off from you and it seems so wrong.

I love you.
Sydney

February 9

Dear Mary,

You needn't worry on those cold nights when you are sitting in front of the fire, because I'm living now very comfortably in a house, and on cold nights am apt to be found sitting on a sofa in front of a fire like yourself. For awhile we did live in tents, but certainly without undergoing any hardships. My latest letter is a valentine postmarked Jan. 25. It was very appropriately adorned but, of course, I've no idea who sent it, though it was from East River. Perhaps it was Betty.

In our nice house, with good food and a beautiful view it seems a very pleasant war so far. Yes, Frank Sargent is my cousin, but I've only seen him a couple of times. Mother wanted me to look him up and wrote me about him, but he'd already gone, a couple of weeks before I shipped. I don't know where he is now. Thanks for John's new address; I wrote using an old one and got no answer. You needn't worry about writing too much, I doubt if that's possible. Your letters are wonderful! I'm glad Mary likes her skis so much; such persistence is certainly going to help her learn even if it doesn't help her language. I believe that, fortunately, God is a pretty understanding sort of fellow, and sympathized with her entirely. I think you probably did get "Mocha" bred that fourth time; I certainly hope so.

I think the smallest size pictures are best to carry around. If you send me a package, how about sticking in some candle ends. Electricity is one of the few luxuries we lack, and candles are hard to get. I would like to say all the same sort of things you do, but feel awkward under the present circumstances. Tell Sydney I dreamt about him last night.

I love you,
Sydney

February 10

Dear Sydney,

We were glad to get your letter today. Though we knew from many that you had arrived safely—we write and telephone Mary, and she writes and telephones us, so we keep in close touch with each other.

With your letter came two from Dick. He likes his country as much as you like yours, and he describes the flowers etc. at great length, ending with "Well, while here it's good to enjoy all these things, nothing could take the place of home—even if it were 20 below zero with the furnace out of order!" He also describes a number of places he has been to, and in each case the censor cut out the name with a knife or pair of scissors. On looking at the envelope, we find it stamped "R. Williams, Examiner"—so Dick is evidently up to his old tricks!

We have just had one of the heaviest snowstorms on record. Traffic has been tied up for 24 hours, and we aren't fully ploughed out yet. Willard is expected at nine o'clock this evening for a two-day leave, and they are wondering if he will get here. Uncle Frank came out and took a photograph of your Mother and me standing by the drifts in front of the house. If it comes out well, I'll send you a copy.

Well, the war news is certainly encouraging—I wonder how long it will last!

Much love from Father

February 12

Dear Sydney,

Today I got your letter no. 3 airmail and I dreamt I'd get one just a few nights ago! Gosh I was thrilled—you wrote it Jan. 27th but it wasn't postmarked until the 29th because I see the 28th was a Sunday. Gosh it was wonderful to actually see your handwriting again and the paper you really wrote it on—paper you had touched—you don't know what it meant to me! Can't you write me more about the trip over? Or give any hint as to what you are living in? A foxhole or a camp. I'm sure it's not a wolf hole! I was interested to have you say your mother wrote as though Jane was very excited over "Mitzi"! I wonder if that was before or after the one time they've been here since we got her, because that day I felt Jane was convinced of the futility of it all! It was snowing and cold and "Mitzi" didn't like it and was quite a handful to lead. But the children didn't realize that and loved it! I thought, in fact I knew, I wrote you about that day. You said you'd just gotten my letter of the 10th and in the letter written the day before you said the latest was postmarked the 8th. What happened to the two of the 8th and 9th? I wonder because I've written you every single day—haven't missed one, since you went away last March, except the day Betsy was born. So, though mine aren't numbered, the dates should show if any are lost.

We have had a cold spell but its nearly too hot now. Don't ever worry about me going out to the barn. I haven't been cold yet. After all, a cold spell here is average winter weather in Peterborough! It's all very well for you to tell me not to worry about you! You know darn well it hangs over me night and day and my hair is fast turning gray. The things we don't know are the things that worry us most. Just suppose you were here and all you knew was that I was somewhere in Italy—more than likely in some sort of danger and you can visualize how I feel. It is almost beyond human endurance. All I live for are your letters now and the day that you come home for good. It's nothing tough physically, but mentally—dear God. I hope I'll never have to go through it again! As I said before, I don't think people give half enough thought to the one at home praying constantly. I'm not grousing. Don't think that, but I don't believe the soldiers feel any more homesick than their wives because home is not home without our husbands and letters from the boys mean even more, I think, than letters to them! Except perhaps in cases where the men may think their wives are running around! But you need never ever have a qualm along that line!

How much milk did the old woman get from her sheep? It's being yellower sounds as though it were richer than our goat's milk. I'm glad you feel so sure of yourself. I wish I felt sure of you too and sure of myself. But I feel all befuddled and all I can try to do is put myself in a sort of mental coma. I can scarcely read the headlines in the paper. I see by the *Peterborough Transcript*, which I read tonight as I ate supper because mother was out, that Sally Stearns[29] is with the Red Cross in Italy and she spoke of having just seen two Peterborough boys. Maybe you will run across her!

I love you an awful lot. I feel quite depressed tonight; it all seems so interminable. And even when it's over, how soon I can have you back with me and the children? All the red tape etc. The best years of our lives will be over, and we will just have our decline together and so much we can never catch up on. Though I feel as though writing you every day you are up on all important little things. It will be your experiences that will fill the gap. However perhaps we can eventually close that chapter and start life over again.

Well I'll try to be more cheerful and tell you today's little "features"! Frank is so funny. I spend quite a lot of time checking up on the goats. Usually that consists of lifting up their tails and examining them. Well, now Frank has taken the habit and I wish you could see him lifting up "Mocha's" tail peering under and muttering something, then going on to "Gay!" It is very funny honestly! Then he has a hat he wears that can come way over his eyes. Every time he pulls it down he says now I can't see him! If by any chance it slips down by mistake, he yanks it up and says "too dark"! This morning in the P. O. a woman and a little girl came in. I didn't pay much attention to them, but I did talk to them. After we left Mary said, "I don't know who that woman was but we've seen the little girl." I said I never had, where had she? So she said she was one of two that were playing outside Mrs. Beiseigle's[30] house one day last summer when we got a chicken there! I do think her observation is extraordinary, don't you? Today, the child was dressed in a snowsuit and cap! Also this afternoon she recognized a child that she'd seen just once before. I didn't recognize her at all until Mary told me! Yesterday at the party Mother had shrimp for hors d'oeuvres and Mary and Sydney each had one. They loved them! So I said I'd save one more for each when I went down. They were all gone of course. So Mary, this morning, asked me about them and when I told her they were all gone and I hadn't

---

29 The daughter of the owners of the Peterborough Players.
30 A neighbor.

even had one, Mary said "I only got one and that's all I've had in my whole life!" It was quite pathetic!

We had Peterborough blueberries for supper. They are wonderful! How I wish I could somehow send you some! I feel cruel eating them and the blackberries. We picked them together and canned them and we're, by all that's right, supposed to eat them together! Mother bought some cookies for you which we are sending off and I hope you'll get them all right. I'll put in a couple of flash lite batteries if I can find them. Your mother's letter asked for them, so I know she is sending some too, but I'll only put in 2 this time and more later, that is if I can find any to send you. None in Madison but perhaps in Guilford? Here is another letter from Mary! Do send them cards if you can and Sydney too! He does so want mail from you. Joe has sent Mary nine cards from Italy.

I love you an awful lot.
Mary

February 13

Dear Mary,

I'm now in a town behind the lines. When I last wrote you, I was on the front where I was living very comfortably and safely, but it was the front lines though I had no adventures whatsoever. I was afraid to tell you that for fear of worrying you, and now I'm worrying because I kept something back from you and have decided after a lot of thought that I should not have done so. I spent my first day on the front lines sweeping floors and moving furniture purely for housekeeping reasons. The rest of my combat experience consisted of sitting in front of a fire in a nice fireplace and eating and talking. There was always a slight possibility that my peace might be disturbed, but it never was. You can tell Mary that I didn't have to hurt anybody and nobody hurt me. I think her idea that people fight each other to kill each other to eat each other is perfectly logical. I can see that to a child it would be much the most plausible explanation.

I got a letter today postmarked the 26th of January which is the latest so far. In the house where I lived at the front there were some nice stone carving tools which I was tempted to steal, and which reminded me that I should take advantage of being in Italy. I should think there would be better stone chisels here than at home. Can you think of anything else like that?

I finally got a letter from John Farlow in answer to the one I wrote from here, and though neither of us knows just where the other is I'm sure we'll be able to meet up somewhere sometime. I got the pictures of you and the children riding "Mitzi." They are very good of you and I don't think your hair has got any grayer. It's nice to see a new picture of you and see that you are still you and real. In the picture, anyway, "Mitzi" looks very much like "Mousie," the pony we had when we were little. I think maybe he was even smaller. You wanted to know what I was doing when I was waiting to leave: I was doing literally nothing. You'd be surprised how much time we spend that way, and nevertheless, often or almost usually, with the time not our own. Seems to me that patience is the virtue most put to the test in the army.

I love you an awful lot.
Sydney

FEBRUARY 15, 1945—MARCH 2, 1945

Mount Belvedere had to be taken. It overlooked Highway 64, which runs between Pistoia and Bologna, and was the principal north-south supply route for the German army. As mentioned earlier, three previous attempts, in the fall of 1944, had failed. The division's plan called for the 86th Regiment to scale Riva Ridge, which they did, on the night of February 18, and overpower German guns that were aimed toward the heavily mined, gentle, western slopes of Belvedere. The operation was accomplished in one of the most daring and successful feats in military history—a nighttime rope-climb up the steep face of Riva Ridge by 700 men of the 86th Regiment, which, in its audacity surprised and overwhelmed the German defenders. Meanwhile the rest of the 10th Division assembled in the mountain town of Vidiciatico, about three miles from Belvedere. On the night of February 19, at ten o'clock, the 87th Regiment marched to Querciola at the foot of Belvedere. By midnight the regiment was heading up through mine fields, under shelling and machine gunfire.

Orders called for the 1st Battalion of the 87th Regiment to take and hold the summit "at all costs." By dawn on February 20, C Company had secured its objective, a ridge above the little village of Valpiano. During the attack, near the town of Corona, C Company's commander, Captain Alfred Edwards, was wounded and was evacuated. Lieutenant Morley Nelson replaced him.

A German counterattack hit C Company at 6:10 a.m. the following day, February 21. Soldiers in C Company waited until the German scouts were about thirty feet from their forward foxholes. The order to "fire" was given, the Germans were routed, and that became the final German counterattack on Belvedere. The next few days were spent patrolling and securing the area until, on the evening of February 27, the 1st Battalion, relieved by a Brazilian regiment, moved to a rest area at Lizzano, where my father was finally able to write letters again.

While still in the vicinity of Valpiano, PFC Juan Barrientos of C Company was killed by shell fire. The significance of that death, as it pertains to

The grave of Juan Barientos in the American Cemetery at Castel Fiorentino, south of Florence

my father, can be seen in two letters from him: in the first, written on March 1, he acknowledges being nicked by a shell fragment; and, in the second, written on March 22 (in response to a query by my mother), he tells my mother that a man standing behind him had been killed by the shell fragment that nicked him. There is no doubt in my mind that the man behind him was Juan Barrientos, who is today buried at the American Cemetery at Castel Fiorentino, south of Florence, and whose grave I have visited.

February 15

Dear Sydney,

Nat [31] took these pictures last June when we were all in Wellesley. They are pretty poor pictures, but I'm sure they are the only ones with so many of the family. Nearly everyone looks all right in at least one of them.

I haven't seen Mary [32] since Sydney's birthday but hope to tomorrow or the next day. M. H. F. and two girls are going to come for a night or two then. B. Anne keeps busy fitting us all in and I'm sure if K. B. F. sleeps in M. W. F.'s bed by mistake, the whole visit will be ruined.

B. Anne had Susan Whitehead to lunch today. I think you met her father and mother once over at the Shattucks' in Branford. She is one of the most obstreperous children I've ever seen. I'm all worn out. B. Anne thinks she is perfectly marvelous.

Walter is getting quite big. He has now decided that the more he can eat the better and goes on and on—at least twice as much as the other two ever ate. Now that his two lower teeth are in he's very cheerful. I never believed much about fussy babies at teething time. But he certainly felt sorry for himself about that time.

Mary has probably written you about all the wonderful snow we've had in Conn. More than I ever remember. It seems ages since I've been anywhere when winter was winter and you could use the season as such. A Mrs. Jamouriez, who lives up the road, tells me that part of it is unplowed with drifts 4–5 feet high. I suppose once it gets packed like that you can't get a plow through and I suppose shoveling is too much work. Actually, the snow isn't deep at all and it sounds pretty silly, as lots of places must take drifts like that for granted and provide against them. There have been beautiful pictures of drifts, with snow thrown up on top to get through, in the papers. Most are in northern New York State and piles are twice as high as the cars.

Nat says the army is going to get some more tramways, but their company didn't bid. They seem to keep busy on coalmines etc. which can't be half as much fun to make.

Sandy thinks it is time for a new baby and while wise about it we'd both get two and also two mammas.

"John" seems livelier than he did last autumn. He'll see his sister this

---

31 Nathaniel Greene, married to my father's sister Jane. B Anne is their daughter; Sandy and Walter are their sons.
32 M. H. F. (Mary Hunnewell Fyffe) is my father's and Jane's sister.

summer. It is remarkable how well he gets around being both blind and deaf. It doesn't worry him at all the way it does some dogs. Of course, he sleeps 95 percent of the time.

Love,
Jane

February 16

Dear Mary,

I got your letter postmarked January tenth; the latest I've got was the 26th. They certainly do not come in even halfway chronological order. That boy Kent, whom you said Naomi knew, was the same one that is a friend of Arnold's, I'm pretty sure. I've already tried to look him up several times but he's always been away somewhere. This letter I just got was the one that had the picture of Mary on "Mitzi" in the paddock, with Sydney just appearing in the corner of the picture. It's awfully good. I'm still in the same place behind the lines and today got a much-needed shower. The principle recreation is drinking martinis (sweet, unfortunately) and such in cafes. We have a certain amount of independence and life is very pleasant. I got a long letter and a box of candy from Mrs. Adams, some of the latter is homemade fudgelike stuff with butternuts in it and it tastes wonderful. Her letter was nice as could be too, but just a little bit more formal than ones she writes you. Did Sydney have a birthday party?

I love you.
Sydney

February 24

Dear Sydney,

Today I got your letter of Feb. 9th written before the one I got yesterday. So when you described your house I knew you were at the front. I'm glad that you were that comfortable there. I wish it would always be so! I'm glad you got the Valentine! Sydney says he remembers reading it to you! But I was alone all by myself the night I addressed it! It didn't come from Betty at all! It's funny you mentioned the candles because, as I wrote you a few days ago, we just decided that's what would be welcome!

In today's paper there was an article on the Italian front that starts off: "Swift and well-timed one-two punches by U. S. mountain troops and the Brazilian Expeditionary Force have pushed the Germans off the last heights from which they had dominated for months the long stretch of highway 64 from Pistoia to the battlefronts southwest of Bologna." Then it says "American doughboys took the summit of 3,500 ft. Monte Della Toraccia." I wonder so much if this meant you? It's the first actual verbal reference I have seen to the mountain troops. But of course you must not actually have been there. Can't you just answer yes or no with no other reference and I will know what you mean. Just start the first letter after you receive this with the word yes or no. This article is datelined Feb. 23rd. Dear God, how I pray for you Sydney. Do give me that little clue and it won't prove a thing to anyone but me! This is Saturday night so I will add more tomorrow.

Today was a red-letter day. "Blondie" finally came out with her first egg, in the doghouse, after trying for three days! Mary is so excited because now she says we won't have to sell her! It is a red-letter day in another way. Frank and Sydney just went berserk while taking their rest! Sydney got into Frank's room and between them they ripped up Frank's mattress—tore the cover off and spread the entrails high and low. When I came in Frank stuck out a pencil at me and positioned on the end was a large wad of stuffing. He said so cunningly, "want some mama?" Well we stuffed it back and with the help of my old straw adhesive plaster patched it up some then turned it over. I haven't dared tell Mother yet. Of course then they were like dogs who had just tasted blood. They were on the rampage. They really feel so good that every few days they just can't help themselves and break loose. Anyhow I was going to buy them all ice cream cones as we went thru Guilford and I didn't. That's all the punishment I inflicted, as it was the first such offense. But that displeased them considerably. Of course, Sydney was most to blame—he should and does know better, but egged on by Frank he couldn't help himself, I guess. Frank is really a handful and he's so funny. He was helping me this morning cleaning the stalls. He had his shovel filled with manure and spilled most of it. He looked at the pile and then at me and said, "Who did that?" I said, "Well, who did?" "Thought Frank did," he said, "I did not," so I said, "who did"? He quickly said, "Mary did!" She was down in the hen house with Sydney! So I said, "Why, Mary is not even here." Then he said, "No, she isn't. Well, maybe I did it because if I had to I just had to!" He is potentially cagey, I think.

This morning when I got back from the barn, I found Mary and Sydney had given themselves baths and were all dressed and they hadn't even flooded the floor! It's been a week since we planted the orange and grapefruit seeds, so far no signs of life. I wonder how long they should take to germinate. I hope we get something out of the three pots! Today I was suspicious of "Sweetie." It's been 6 weeks since she was bred, so I took her back again to Moose Hill Inn and left her for a few days. I like that man so much and he is so nice to the children and loves animals. His goats look so fat and happy. He's got four little kids—the oldest a week old. I had a time getting Mary and Sydney away. So I told him they loved them. He looked so sheepish and said, "so do I." He sits with them he says and they just climb all over him and cuddle up on his shoulder. They were with their mothers, but aren't with her all day. He strips her out at night. If only he wasn't deaf! I would ask him so many questions. He is always so interested in you. He's got a goat there I like very much. If "Sweetie" wasn't Mary's, I'd be inclined to see if he would trade her plus a little cash. He wants $25 for this goat and I paid $5 for "Sweetie" but I don't know, "Sweetie" may turn out to be pretty good at another freshening. After all she was only a year old when she kidded and I got her when she'd been milking over 5 Mos. She is 7/8 purebred—purebred sire and 3/4 dam. So perhaps I'd better keep her another year. I wish you were here to help me decide.

I love you an awful lot and just can't get the thought of you, out there in real or potential danger, out of my mind for an instant. My dreams and my sleep are all sort of a nightmare of horror. I must stop for tonight, as the radio is saying "Good Night! Sweet dreams, sweetheart."

I love you such a terrible lot.
Mary

Sunday, February 25

Dear Sydney,

This has been without a doubt the worst day I've put in so far. Twice today the radio has referred to the 10th div. of the mtn. troops, repulsing counter attacks and strengthen[ing] their positions. Dear God, Sydney, how I pray for you. I suppose there is a chance that it's not your part of the 10th division but it is a slender reed for me to cling to. I am almost sick with anxiety and will be until I can hear you are safe and well. For God's sake Sydney, write every single little chance you get, won't you? You cannot even begin to imagine the hell that is my days and nights. All I can do is try not to think, and pray.

Well, today we went for a buggy ride and as we were starting off Sydney was near the wheels and "Mitzi" started forward and the hind wheel knocked him down and went over his leg. Luckily he wasn't hurt, though he hollered. But it went fortunately went over the outside of his upper leg. If it had been the inside it might have hurt him badly. I was helping Mary do something to the seats and didn't notice where Sydney was, but he's all right. He's even forgotten which leg it was when I undressed him tonight! But I certainly was scared and we will all be terribly careful in the future, you can bet! We went down the Neck road, looking, as mother said, like Cinderella's coach pulled by the mice! Daddy said he would get in between "Mitzi's" hind legs and the cart and help pull. Mary said he'd better not because he'd get his suit dirty! A little boy paced us on his bicycle the whole way. The children were intrigued. Sydney kept talking to him, calling him "Boy." He was 8 years old, but big for his age. He wanted to know why the children had on snowsuits on such a warm day. So I said they got so wet in every puddle. It's like Peterborough in the late March here now. And he said, "Oh, I didn't know they were that kind of puddle timers!" I was amused.

I wish you'd seen Sydney take two mice out of the grain barrel—just reached in and grabbed them by their tails! Daddy said he wouldn't do it! Mary was too nervous too, but Sydney was pleased as could be! I called up Charlotte today at 3 P.M. and she and Bill[33] and the children were eating lunch. I really think their schedule is something! Tomorrow is Willie's[34] birthday and they are invited for supper. I hope Charlotte is a little more on the ball! As I have to get mine home and in bed before 6 o'clock or around then, as I don't want to keep Betsy waiting too long! It is awful funny to see Frank catching hens. He just walks up and grabs one. He has no fear of their flapping, no more than Mary or Sydney have! Mary dresses Betsy now completely except for the diapers. She really just adores her and this is just wonderful, I think, to see how she looks at her—so lovingly! Betsy is so cunning. When we had the party for Charlotte and Bill two weeks ago Betsy finally was overcome by the strangers and started to cry. Then I took her upstairs to say goodnight to Mary. I wish you'd seen how happy she was to see Mary. She beamed and gurgled and cuddled up to Mary. I think it's wonderful.

---

33 Bill Lage, Charlotte Lage's husband.
34 Willie Lage, son of Charlotte and Bill Lage.

I love you such an awful lot and it is so wrong for you to be missing all this. *Please* be careful! I just cannot visualize the future if anything happens to you! I just plain haven't any courage as I told Betsy tonight. I'm afraid I'm not very brave! I want you as I've never wanted anything in my life. How long must this go on? I feel pretty close to the breaking point. Can't you tell me even vaguely where you are, now they've started mentioning the 10th division? Today was the first time the news said it had been announced that the 10th division was over there near Mont Belvedere. How many regiments are there? Didn't you say 86th, 87th, and 88th? I love you an awful lot. I hope you have more courage than I have. I love you an awful lot. And I am just praying I have a lot of Faith in God and you, so I know you'll be home some day. But dear God, make it be soon!

I love you,
Mary

February 26

Dear Sydney,

Today's New York paper carried an editorial on the boredom afflicting the army in Italy, a very good one it was too, showing how tough the going was. Gains gauged in yards and looking spectacular enough to even get the headlines. Though this man, John Chabot Smith,[35] says God knows the slugging is tough, as tough or tougher than where everything is more spectacular. It also carried an article about the U. S. troops of the 10th division and their week-old assault in Italy. I am worried sick, honestly, and I will be until I get a letter from you dated around now. In other words, if I get a reassuring letter about when you get this one perhaps I will relax a little, though who knows what lies ahead. It says the 10th division is specially trained on snow-covered mountains in sub-zero temperatures—I could tell them of one who wasn't—and how proud they are of their toughness! Well, may God keep them tough, for they will need it and I guess that means you? The paper says they made their first appearance in the lines Jan. 9th. That must have been the 86th wasn't it? What other regiments, or can't you tell me, comprise the 10th division? Dear God, how I pray for you and an end to this insane murder. If you love me, write me as often as you possibly can!

Today was little Willie's birthday. It has been a fiendish day—a real

---
35 John Chabot Smith was a reporter who covered Europe during the war for the *New York Herald Tribune*.

southeast storm, wind and sea and rain, not snow. We were invited to Willie's house and the children had supper there. I told you of the plans last week but I always fear a letter may be lost. Mary said, as we were getting ready to go, "isn't it nice we have somewhere to go instead of just out in the rain?" It sounded as though I was so cruel to them! They all wore their best clothes and Sydney looks wonderful in his little short pants suit! His tummy is so big he almost pops the buttons on his coat! The coat is large across the shoulders for him and the sleeves had to be shortened two inches and still it hardly buttons! Mary's hair looked lovely. It was just the way you would have loved it. We brushed it for almost 15 minutes and it all stood out with electricity and looked so pretty! They played for a while first. Frank walked right in the living room in front of everyone and removing the lid from an enormous chest of toys nearly dropped it on big Billy's toe![36] No one invited him to or said, "now find something to play with." He just knew what to do! They were all awfully good. There were 7 children—our 3, Charlotte's 2—little Billy Low and Mr. Pope's little girl Marshall. She is a little older than Frank and not half as self-possessed, though she is quite pretty.

Mary just seated herself at the opposite end of the table from Billy's Mama and Papa—it was too funny to see her! She and Sydney ate almost all the sandwiches! Frank ate 3. They all drank all their milk and they each had a large piece of cake and a dish of ice cream. Frank had ice cream twice yesterday (Sunday), so he turned his down today! Willie and Barbara ate nothing but candy! I must say I was proud of them, especially Sydney. He is so cunning and so good and sort of gentle and his eyes were so bright and shining and he was shivering with excitement when the cake appeared! He wasn't cold. I felt him, just excited. Frank is cunning too in his deliberated, independent, man-of-the-world way and everyone says he's the most beautiful child they've ever seen. But you can see he'll never have the wool pulled over his eyes! Sydney has a completely different look, a sort of trusting simplicity like a dog and you know when I say that that its high tribute! He loves to see people happy and just likes to watch them, while Frank is out to make the most of the good time himself. Mary was the oldest there, but she was very good, not bossy or indifferent. As they were getting undressed here at home, she said, "we did have a good time, didn't we?" Just getting dressed up and going somewhere thrills her. Anyhow our children were the handsomest and the healthiest ones there! Billy Low and Patsy[37] arrived in the midst of it. Big Billy, I mean, his ship just got in

---
36 Billy Low, brother of Charlotte Lage.
37 Patsy Low, wife of Billy Low.

a day or so ago. He looks well, but thinner than ever. He said they'd had a rough trip this time and a wave washed in on one side of their superstructure, gun emplacements etc. Charlotte and her Billy looked pretty well the worse, for their two weeks of being out till 2 a.m. every night! But Billy is wonderful with the children and does so much more for them then Charlotte does or ever did! He really is almost as good with them as you are with ours! I felt awful lonely. Charlotte with Billy and Patsy with her Billy and me all alone, with the thought of you in the thick of it. They all asked about you and as I'd start to tell them they'd dash off and say "I've got to get a drink," so I gave up and just felt even a little bit more unhappy! They don't know, either of them, what it means to be anxious, though Patsy has a little more idea, but she is about the most selfish person I know. Charlotte is just wrapped up in herself and sort of thoughtless. Well, anyhow it was a welcome diversion and we got home about ten minutes of 6 and the children were undressed and in bed 20 minutes later. So I wasn't so late for Betsy. Betsy was asleep anyhow and not a bit concerned over where is Mama! Well, I hope I've given you a fair picture of the party. Frank had to wee-wee in the middle of supper and so as I took him, unostentatiously I thought, Sydney saw us and bellowed out, "does Frank have to wee-wee?" So then everyone knew and looked around!

This morning Alec was getting wheelbarrow loads of stones to cement up the hole in the side of the old manure pit that Julius[38] made, trying to bust it up. He is going to make a sort of root cellar out of it, build up double walls about two feet high, fill them with sawdust and then put in 3 levels of shelves. I should think it would be fine. Anyhow Mary and Sydney and Frank all went along. Mary and Sydney on each side holding the barrow and Frank perched on top of the rocks! Thirty extra pounds! He is so good with them and seems to love to have them around too. When they come down in the morning he is usually in the kitchen and Sydney and Frank rush at his legs! They certainly need the companionship of a man, but you needn't worry. I won't to go out and get one for them! Like me, they will have to wait until you come home again.

Frank's grapefruit seed—at least one of them—has sprouted! Isn't that exciting? It is just a tiny little twig now—I do hope some of the others do too.

Mother got a letter from Joe today. His ship now has three stars on it, for 3 engagements, also he carried out an idea of his which he says was conceived in gin, then invited the admiral to dinner on his ship! He came and had, as

---

38 Julius was an older handyman who worked for my grandmother. He died during our time at Wyndham.

Joe said a jim-dandy time! The first time he'd even been invited for a meal onboard any of the boats! Joe does that sort of thing in a way few others could, I think!

I love you such an awful lot. My heart bleeds for you and I long for news! I love you such an awful lot!

I love you,
Mary

February 28

Dear Mary,

I'm behind the lines again after spending another week on the front. This time it wasn't quite so comfortable, with foxholes and shells landing round about and that sort of thing. But the weather was nice and it wasn't really too bad. I'm afraid I didn't write any letters all that time. I was in the attack on Mt. Belvedere, which is more like a hill than a mountain, but I certainly didn't play a very active part, and never even fired my rifle nor had any hair-breadth escapes or adventures to tell my grandchildren about. I've got a lot of letters from you, three yesterday. I get letters on the same day that were written three or four weeks apart, so it's rather hard to get a consecutive picture. In the last mail I got letters from mother, Jane, Dick, and Arnold as well as from you, that's pretty good for my family.

There were crocuses in bloom on Mt. Belvedere and the view was beautiful, both day and night, a strange setting for a battle. I like the story about Sydney's seeing the woof that woofed. That proves it was a woof.

I'm now sitting in the sun drinking beer after an enormous meal and feeling so sleepy I can hardly hold the pencil. Today we took showers and shaved off our beards, which last act seems to have used up all my energy. I think when the papers refer to the changes in returning servicemen they mean people about fifteen years younger than me. I guess there's no fear of my being changed in any way you would not like, or hope for improvement either. I've been to Naples, Leghorn and Pisa, but seen absolutely nothing of them. The only towns I've had a real look at have been very small ones in the mountains, but they are certainly fascinating.

Your letters average two to three weeks in transit. I think V-mail does come a tiny bit quicker, but other things considered is certainly not worth it. I'm glad the children didn't think that Bill Lage was their idea of a Papa. As a climb, Mt. Belvedere just about corresponds to Skatutakee and reminded me of it in other ways too, but of course I never climbed Skatutakee with someone shooting at me. I fell asleep during the attack and dreamt about you.

I love you,
Sydney

お

March 1

Dear Mary,

I forgot to put an air mail stamp on yesterday's letter so I don't know when you'll get it. I'm in the same place, a little ways behind the lines, today. I think I'm allowed to mention its name; it's called Lizzano, a former mountain resort. We sleep on the tile floor of a large and dreary orphanage whose meager plumbing has ceased to function, and most of the glass has been blown out of the windows. I told you yesterday about the attack and living in a foxhole, etc., which in all wasn't too bad. I got three letters from you today, the latest postmarked the fourteenth. I've had no adventures but for a piece of shrapnel which sliced a few hairs off my cheek, but I needed a shave anyway. I think the henhouse playhouse is a wonderful idea, and I should think your attitude toward the paint would satisfy the most extreme of modern educators. I've had lots of letters from Mary and one from Sydney! Tell them their letters make me very happy and I'll write them some as soon as I can. I understand that the whereabouts of our outfit is no longer a secret; so perhaps you can get some little bit of news of us from the papers. The sun here is very hot now even in the daytime and I'm now sitting in it almost roasting to death. The temperature changes very suddenly at sunset and then I freeze to death.

I love you.
Sydney

お

March 2

Dear Sydney,

Yesterday I asked Mr. Hotchkiss to lunch at the club, and invited Jack Richardson to meet him. As I expected, they got along splendidly together.

I suppose you have heard how Joe Hotchkiss was giving a dinner party in the landing boat of which he is in command, and thought it would be nice to ask the admiral of the fleet, who came with all his staff, and the dinner was a huge success!

Milton Bracken, the war correspondent, has him sending dispatches from the Italian front, and says the different Army units can now be identified, and mentions the 10th Mountain Division, and the 87th Reg., which he says had spearheaded the landings in Kiska, Alaska some time ago. They must have put you into a veteran outfit!

He gives the names of the mountain and villages captured, and mentions the Brazilian Troops taking part.

From what we can make out Dick is still in Hawaii. We hear from him every two or three days.

All well here. We have had a lot of snow which is just beginning to go, and it looks like a better hay crop next summer. Hay has been $53 a ton lately.

If you find air mail or V-mail quicker, please let me know which.

Much love from Father

March 2

Dear Sydney,

Today I got a letter from you dated Feb 16th—You were still there behind the lines and I gather living very pleasantly! I hope you don't come home a rum hound? You're spending your time at sidewalk café's drinking martinis! Maybe you should write me another page to each letter! I love you an awful lot. I hope life isn't so pleasant, or wasn't so pleasant, that you don't want to come home! I like to hear you're having a good time but you didn't say anything about missing us! I guess you do and it goes without saying, but I like to hear you say it! I'm not complaining Sydney because I love you such an awful awful lot. I feel about to burst with my love for you and I keep telling myself that damn censor stands between you and me and what you say and so I read between the lines.

I just called up your mother to tell her I'd heard from you. She said Dick has seen quite a lot of the Livingstons and has been doing a lot of swimming! The mail certainly sounds most irregular, but I think the Airmail is worth the price because Joe said 67 percent went that way. I wish you'd seen little Sydney pitching hay this morning. He was up on top of one of the salt hay stacks pitching it down into his wagon. He looked wonderful! Sydney is so funny. He was quite disturbed over the smell in half of the hen house! This warm weather has aggravated all the barnyard smells. You know how it can! Betsy is so cunning now. She reaches out for everything, grabs at things and is so gay and laughing. Her pictures won't be ready for another week, I am disgusted! She won't look anything the way she did then, when you get them. But perhaps that won't matter too much. I will take some more snap shots anyhow.

This afternoon we had "Mitzi" on the beach and Mary and Sydney cantered! They just love it, especially Mary who is getting very good! But poor Mama! Mary said, "we must get papa home. He can run much better than you can!" And that's true! However, I guess it's good for my figure to gallop over the sands. I feel very stiff tonight, but I guess I'll get used to it. The trouble is that they don't realize what I have to go through! Mary rode "Mitzi" back to the barn alone—no rope attached, and once "Mitzi" jumped forward when "Mopsa" popped out behind. Mary was as calm and collected as could be!

I thought Daddy said that on the 6:00 o'clock news it said that the 10th division had launched another offensive—they hoped their last. Now I can hardly wait to see tomorrow's paper. This morning's paper said all was comparatively quiet there. I am terribly anxious. I fear I may not hear for days now. If you were in on the last offensive, I figured that began a few days after your last letter was written. Do write every chance you get, won't you? I'm going to put in some extra sheets of paper in this letter. I notice your paper is nondescript and wonder if you are short. I will send some in the next package. I guess the packages will take at least 6 weeks to arrive. I must go to bed now, and get ready for Charlotte's party tomorrow night! I guess the weekend letter will have to be written Sunday night. I love you an awful, awful lot. I feel as though this letter wasn't very much, but all the love anyone ever had for anyone else and then double that is in it anyhow!

I love you!
Mary

P. S. I'm enclosing this letter from Sonny Wilson—the drawing is so amusing and when I showed it to Mary her first remark was "But I'm really much prettier than that" and then she said "and Sydney never wore a hat like that!" But its darn good isn't it?

March 2

Dear Mary,

I got your letter today postmarked the seventeenth. I'm still sitting in the same place in the sun and trying to thaw out a bad cold I picked up somehow. Two *Life*s, a *Reader's Digest*, and the *Peterborough Transcript* came yesterday. I wonder if you and father haven't both given me *Reader's Digest*s. Anyway I have lots of reading material at the moment. Enough people subscribe to magazines so that there are always quite a few lying about. I read *Time* while I was in my foxhole.

I think the worst thing about this war is the dirt. I get most unbelievably dirty. Every once in awhile we are herded through shower baths and given clean clothes, but usually there isn't even opportunity to wash your hands and face between times. If you thought I came home dirty after a day's battle on Miss Perry's[39] manure pile, you should see me now, and a runny nose and no clean handkerchief doesn't make me any nicer. In fact, I think if I came home looking the way I do most of the time now (I also have a long, droopy, and absorbent mustache), you'd probably send me right back saying someone had made a terrible mistake. I use and appreciate the airmail stamps you send, as I haven't always been able to get them, but don't send too many at once as everything I carry gets pretty grimy and they don't stay good very long. I love you an awful lot, I hope you aren't too worried, I'll probably be able to appear a little more attractive by the time I get home.

On a day like today when I'm feeling rather grumpy, I find my companions a pretty childish and stupid lot. It's hard to find anybody I can really talk to. Most of them will return to the small, narrow-minded little towns they came from with no more wisdom or knowledge than they had when they left. They have no intellectual curiosity whatsoever and they shed intellectual opportunities as a duck does water. There is good comradeship but no good talk; the former may be the more essential, but grows wearisome eventually without a little of the latter. I certainly hope "Mocha" is bred; if not it's awfully disappointing, not only because of the hopes we had for her, but also because of all the trouble it has been to you.

I love you an awful lot; this separation is more horrible than I ever imagined it could be.

I love you,
Sydney

---

39 Margaret Perry lived in Hancock, New Hampshire. My father worked for her for a couple of years.

Castel D'Aiano after being shelled, early March, 1945

Soldier shaving in the shell-blasted church in Pietra Colora, March, 1945

MARCH 10, 1945—APRIL 13, 1945

On March 3, the second offensive began for the 87th Regiment. After having spent three days in Lizzano resting up, they received orders to take taking Castel d'Aiano, located approximately four miles to the north and east of Belvedere. All of the military maps of this area show numerous mountains, some identified by their Italian names (such as Monte della Vedetta and Monte della Spe), and others by a number such as 997 or 813 that referred to the height of the mountain in meters. (This region of the Apennines is filled with steep, rugged hills 2,500 to 3,500 feet in height.) The approaches to the crests were usually across open fields broken up with downed trees and rock outcroppings. Most of the trees had been destroyed by heavy shelling and machine gun fire. Those that remained would have been leafless in this late winter period.

By the third day of this second offensive, March 5, the 87th Regiment was ready for its final assault on Castel d'Aiano a thousand yards north. The 1st Battalion was given the order to attack; C Company's objective was to take Hill 813. To reach this target, the troops had to first head down a slope with German defenders firing up at them. The attack began at six-thirty in the morning. During this action, 2nd Platoon messenger, PFC Glenn Bailey, was killed running across an open field. The regimental history of the 87th Mountain Infantry describes the situation that day: "The 2nd Platoon, passing the 1st, continued down to the left of Monfenaro to the mouth of the draw where it came out at the foot of 813. Here they were in full view of the enemy on 813, and a barrage of artillery and heavy machine gun fire pinned them down." Later, under the cover of darkness and friendly artillery fire, the 2nd and 3rd Platoons moved up and occupied Hill 813.

The regimental objective was achieved, but at a high cost. During those three days the regiment incurred 155 casualties, including thirty-nine dead. The regimental command post was established on the eastern slope of Monte della Vedetta, near the town of Pietra Colora, and was maintained for the balance of March and into early April. There were frequent skirmishes during this time, but there was also time to rest, relax (including visits to Florence), and, for the officers, time to prepare for the major Spring Offensive—the final push out of the Apennines and into the Po River Valley. There was also time to write and receive letters. During this period, March 10 to April 13, my father wrote twenty-one letters to my mother. Also during this period, the first member of my father's original twelve-man squad was killed. PFC Prentice Davidson was electrocuted on April 3, when a high-tension wire was shot down and fell across the telephone line he was using while the 1st Battalion was training at Camp Tizzoro.

At two o'clock in the morning of Friday, April 13, word reached the 87th Regiment that President Roosevelt had died. The order to begin the final offensive, known as Operation Craftsman, had already been delayed forty-eight hours due to weather. The waiting, for what every soldier knew was going to be a difficult battle, was nerve-wracking. Roosevelt's death, to most of the men, would have been one more thing to worry about. To make matters worse, American soldiers were at this time reportedly only seventy-six miles from Berlin. The German position was hopeless; everyone knew it was only a matter of time before they surrendered. So there was a nagging hope among the 10th Division soldiers that the delay would obviate the need for their own expected offensive.

That hope was not to be realized. At 8:30 a.m. on April 14, the first troops crossed the line of demarcation. It would prove to be the worst day for casualties for the 10th Mountain Division.

March 10

Dear Mary,

I've got quite a few letters the last few days, when I wasn't able to write, and three more today. One was postmarked March 1st. That's the quickest so far. That was the one with the picture of men putting up the flag on Iwo Jima. It is a remarkably dramatic picture.

Since I last wrote you, I've been, most of the time, in and out of foxholes (I can get in pretty fast) and also in a nice thickwalled house used for the same purpose.[40] Three good-sized shells hit it without much effect and it had weathered a few of our own before that. I still haven't fired my rifle or any weapon at anybody, though they have taken a few shots at me. I find, rather to my surprise, that all that sort of thing doesn't interfere very much with my appreciation of the scenery, and, except for being terribly dirty etc., I haven't undergone much physical discomfort: a brilliant hot sun in the daytime and down to, I should judge, about 30 at night, sometimes not even that cold. There've only been two or three nights when I've really felt cold and that was when the situation did not allow any preparation to keep warm. So you mustn't picture me heroically enduring the elements. Also, the "mountains" that they refer to in the papers are hardly such. Just steep little hills, with lots of small spring flowers, only a few tiny "pieces of winter" in dark corners.

As for being scared, I certainly have been but still nowhere near as scared as I was after a bad dream when I was a small boy. I find that the kind of material they use for horror pictures in the press doesn't affect me very much. I seem to have developed a strangely impersonal attitude. Ruined houses with the former occupants picking over the remains is the sight that affects me the most. At the moment I'm comparatively clean and in a ruined village that is pretty safe and beautifully situated. I hope it'll get a rest now. I suppose spring has got started with you by now, and the beach must be pretty warm around noontime. I got another, very amusing letter from John Farlow, which I'm saving. It sounds just like Joe to invite the admiral for dinner; I'll bet it all went off beautifully. I wish I had as much opportunity for self-expression in my letters as you have in yours. You know the way I feel. The general war news makes me feel frightfully and probably much too optimistic. I can't believe it'll last much longer, though I believe there'll be a

---
40 My father had replaced PFC Glenn Bailey as 2nd Platoon runner, who, as mentioned earlier, had been killed on March 5.

certain amount of an unpleasantness for a long time afterwards. The children sound wonderful, you're the only person I know of that knows how to treat them sensibly.

I love you an awful lot.
Sydney

>

March 11

Dear Sydney,

Winter is definitely gone here now and spring is here. At least all the birds think so and we have one winter aconite. Some places look as if the grass was getting green, but that is my imagination.

None of the kale in the garden froze and neither did the Brussels sprouts or parsley, which was barely mulched. The kale is awfully good. I've been trying all winter to get some manure for the garden, from my cleaning woman's brother-in-law. As time goes on, she gets more and more explicit about why it doesn't come. It is because of the tavern on Water Street. Pretty soon I shall get some chicken manure instead, which is all right except the Kleins give us no bedding, and I get no compost with it. It is much cheaper, though.

Nat and I spent the afternoon getting stones out of the lawn down around the well. I'd like to build it up higher so you could definitely know what it was, and I think it will look very well. We found some old steps going down towards the road from it a little to the south. I suppose they may have been put there 200 years ago. That probably may seem recent in Italy. I suppose you haven't had a chance to see any of the villas. I've always wondered what the statues were like in them. From pictures and descriptions, the whole outlay of the places must have depended on them tremendously and I never could see how they got enough decent ones. Maybe sculpture used to be a more common means of expression.

Nat is working on the income tax. He's doing mine too. I used to help him but he got so mad at my figuring he's got to do it alone.

Walter continues to be very big and lively. He is much better natured than he was and he doesn't seem to mind being left alone so much. B. Anne still thinks he's wonderful and spends lots of time amusing him. She has a pile of salt hay outside already for him to climb on next summer. Sandy plays with trains and looks at pictures of them by the hour. He's going to be an engineer someday.

I haven't seen Mary since M. H. F. was here. First the children had a spitting up kind of grippe and then they had colds starting about a week apart. I hope to see her tomorrow and the next day. If there is any way we could help amuse her, let me know. Children are wonderful fun but a change is nice sometimes. All I can think of is going to the movies and that isn't much. Most women would get a change by playing bridge once a week. Maybe she doesn't want to do anything anyway.

Love,
Jane

March 12

Dear Sydney,

Today I got your first letter in nearly two weeks! It was yours of March 1st. You said you'd written the day before, without airmail. And of course, now I can hardly wait for that, as you said you told about the attack in it. I wonder if there's any other letter between the 16th and the 29th of Feb? Or was all that time when you were in a wolf hole? Anyhow, you don't know how happy I was to get this one! Your adventure sounded like too close a shave to me! Did it really cut the skin, or a near miss? The orphan asylum sounds pretty dreary but I guess it's better than a foxhole. I hope you aren't really awful cold. Have you had to use skis at all? I should think you could tell me if you had. By my clippings I see that there was a sort of lull between the end of Feb. and March 5th. I wonder if you were back in it again by then? You don't know how I worry, honestly! I called your mother just now to give her the news of you. She was fine, but I couldn't talk long as someone wanted the line. Jane came over this afternoon with her children and she said your mother had spoken of coming down here to Guilford for a visit, but I couldn't ask her as we were interrupted. The children all rode "Mitzi" in the paddock, and honestly Mary is getting so good! I wish you could see her dig her heels in and really make her go! Sydney insists on riding alone, too, and B. Anne, who always wants to run! But B. Anne can't make her go at a trot. However, all I have to do is say is "get up 'Mitzi'" from my position by the fence and "Mitzi" does!

Mary was so pleased that it made you so happy to get her letters. She is going to write you tomorrow again! She says, "Papa is a tough God." I forget why, but some one of the myriad things they have put aside for you to do when you come home that I can't do! Lizzie is really wonderful. She called up at 9:00 a.m. and told me to stop at her mailbox for a bag of greenery for the goats! Things she's collected from Charlotte's and various other of her customers! But don't you think it's funny? A large bag of cauliflower greens, lettuce, and carrot tops, bread etc. She's done it before too. This evening the children were talking about you fighting. They wanted to know what you fight with, so I said guns and mortars and grenades and knives. Mary immediately popped up with, "does he need a fork too?" I suppose she's thinking of your eating those Krauts again! I was very impressed with your fancy paper! Your company letter and all on it! You never said if you'd gotten the stamps I sent you, but this letter must have had one on it. It looked as though it might have been in your pocket for some time! "Becky" has bitten the billy goat's ear! Just a little place but I hope it will be healed when I return him. Have you gotten all my letters, do you think? Or are there gaps? As I write one dated for every day, you should be able to tell. I just wonder how many are lost in route. Tell me sometime.

I love you an awful lot. Some of my more discouraged ones might be better if you never got I guess. Though, I don't think any of them ended in the vein they may have begun in. Tell me if you don't like my letters, won't you and I'll try and improve. But some days are so black—always when I haven't had a letter for some time. I get up in the morning hoping there will be a letter and I live on that until I get the mail around 9 a.m. Then if there is no letter my day is blank despair until another morning comes around. This morning I was *sure* there'd be a letter. I had a feeling. Then I went and there was *none*. But Mrs. Werner[41] said she'd had two V-mail from Europe for different people that morning and often that meant there'd be more on the noon mail. So my spirits stayed up and then mother went to New Haven and stopped by coming home. Sure enough there was the letter! So she rushed it home to me even though she had to go on to Madison for a meeting. Jane was here then, so she heard the news too. She said she thought perhaps I'd find that the longer you were away the more used to it I'd get and the less I'd worry! I told her it worked exactly the opposite. The longer you're away the more I miss you! Every day is worse than the last one. She was trying to encourage me but it just proves how little one can understand unless one is suffering the same burden.

Well, there's not much news as of today except that I love you. If possible even more than ever! We are all fine—perhaps a slight cold going around

---

41 Postmistress for East River, Connecticut.

but not enough to worry about. Frank now has torn his mattress—pretty well shredded it, a little like "Rollo" and his. I've patched it with adhesive plaster but that's only temporary, and very temporary. I have spanked him, reasoned with him, cajoled, everything! But while he's taking his so-called naps that's his recreation! Mary goes in for furniture moving, as you remember well. I guess I better stop and go to bed now. I hope the vet comes tomorrow to see about "Sweetie's" horn. It bothers her quite a bit. Gosh, how I hope I do get "Mocha" bred! She's obviously not going to kid March 22nd. That was the second try, and she doesn't look to me as though she had it in her for May either! Keeping "Billy" the kid is my last resort! He's a nice black goat. But small—I wish "Mocha" was more cooperative! Well I've done all in my power. I love you! I guess your non-air-mail letters will take about 6 weeks which brings it to the first week in April!

I love you,
Mary

P. S. I predict: the war in Europe will be over sometime in April! You haven't referred to my intention of going to Peterborough this summer or haven't you gotten those letters yet? Anna May will stay with me. I live in hopes you'll get home perhaps sometime after this is over! I notice your letters aren't all censored by the same guy.

༄

March 13

Dear Sydney,

Well—this has been the thirteenth all right. Everything has gone wrong. Not seriously so. Just irritatingly so. It started with mother's car—when I went to go get the mail I noticed the car was hard starting and saw that the battery was discharging—not charging—so I left it poised on the hill by the barn and took ours—All of which delayed me especially as I had to go and get Anna too. Then someone nosed in ahead of me at the P. O. and I had to wait about ten minutes to mail a package for Betty, which by the way I think consisted of cookies she made with our ingredients and was sending her boyfriend! And so the day wore on. Anna[42] wanted to take the noon bus to Guilford. Just as we were by Crother's sheep yard, it went by! However, we chased it and caught it in front of the Surisses's! I had to run him off the road to stop him, which seemed to irritate him unduly, I thought! It all ended with my

---
42 Anna worked in my grandmother's house.

bumping my head on "Mocha's" this evening! I was discouraged!

Well—it's almost bedtime and there's a large and noisy leak from Mother's bathroom plopping into a bowl here in the living room by my left arm, as I write, that started today! Anyhow I love you an awful lot. I dreamt about you last night. I dreamt you were home and I wouldn't let you out of my sight. You wanted to go somewhere on a bicycle and looked for a flashlight you needed, and I put up an awful fuss! It all seemed so real. Today's paper also broke the bad news that Kesselring[43] has ordered his men to fight to the last ditch, not give up one foot without a fight, which blasts any hopes that had been put forward, about a withdrawal to Austria and Bavaria. I hope and pray you are safe tonight—that 13 was not unfortunate for you in any way major or minor. I hope for another letter before too long. Perhaps you could write again before going into action again. My clippings lead me to believe the 10th division started up again around March 5th or 6th. But, of course, I don't know where you personally were at the time. I guess the division comprises a lot of men. How many? Can you tell me? And is it the 85th, 86th, or 87th or 86th, 87th, and 88th? You told me once, and I can't remember. Anyhow I saw that the 85th and 88th have been in Italy some time. So far there has been no mention of regiments in your division. It speaks of the 10th as a whole. Do tell me all you are allowed to, won't you? If you know how I live every hour with you, wondering where you are and what is happening and all. You are, in absentia as well as persona, my whole life. God was good to you in that first shrapnel episode. May he always watch over you as carefully! That's what I pray Him to do fifty times a day!

This afternoon we drove "Mitzi" over to the Lages's again. I like to drive her about 3 times a week to really exercise her. She goes along just beautifully and is so pretty! The first thing that happened was Sydney and then Frank announced loudly to me that they were hungry! Charlotte looked desperate, but I quickly assured her not to pay any attention to them! Then Sydney and Frank disappeared. I looked high and low and finally found them in Charlotte's dump! Frank appeared with three enormous old cans which I had him redeposit in spite of Billy's saying they didn't want them! But as I put him in the cart to come home he was devotedly clutching a bottle of Four Roses. He insisted on carrying that home to the henhouse. Sitting there beside me on the front seat! I don't know what people thought! We came home the back way, up by the church and down by the graveyard, where we got stuck with the car. There was still a big hole where we'd been! As Frank says, the

---

43 Field Marshall Albert Kesselring.

day we couldn't get to Peterborough! He talks of Peterborough all the time. I wonder what he thinks it is for? I don't see how he can really remember, do you? It will be interesting to see when we get back if it rings a bell with him. I'm sending you some recent pictures! One of Mary and her family taken especially so you can see and recognize them! I will name them on the back. The one of Mary and Betsy on the steps, Betsy on her blanket I had to send, because Mary said she liked it best of all because she liked her head in that pose! She said she thought Betsy looked just like Frank used to look! Notice Mary's bare feet and the snow in the corner of the picture, the doll one!

Tomorrow we go to Dr. Salinger's,[44] Betsy to have her second diphtheria needle and this time I'll have Sydney examined. Mary wants to be last, because she likes it! I will ask him about having their eyes examined, I think. I think I will anyhow, sometime while we're here. Also, Mary has several times spoken of headaches. I hope that it's mostly to do with that fall she had off the porch. They only last a short while apparently, but I don't like her having them at all. It worries me a little tiny bit. However I guess it's nothing really. Maybe she had a short cold each time or something. But you never knew why you had them did you? Have you had any recently or some stomachaches or anything? I love you an awful lot. I hope you won't ever be like a stranger to me when you come home. But I have no real fears! We are too close to each other for that. But I do feel as though there's been a big piece sliced out of my life, and just when we need you most, when the children are little and need you.

I love you,
Mary

P. S. I won't want to remember these days.

I guess you know that Walter suddenly appeared at the door last Sat. March 10th—flown over and then walked up from the Wellesley station! Willard is being sent to O. C. S. All this you probably know, but in case a letter is lost it won't hurt to repeat! I love you. It won't hurt to repeat that either!

March 14

Dear Mary,

I have now been to Florence, and in some ways it was a most disappointing trip, as I knew that things I wanted to do and see were not at all what the

---
44 Robert Salinger, MD, was our pediatrician in New Haven.

others wanted to do and see. When I found that a lot of us could go I tried to maneuver around so that I could go by myself or at least go around independently after I got there. But I found there were about fifteen different people, each of which thought he was going with me, and as soon as I shook one I'd be with another, all fine fellows of course, but none of whom took the slightest interest in anything that particularly interests me. I finally ended up by going with Coates,[45] former professional skier, laundry truck driver, chauffeur, and hotel bellhop. He's a noble fellow no doubt but hardly one to add much to a discussion of the Renaissance, and I'm ashamed to say that until I became reconciled to the setup I felt terribly irritated with him and it probably showed. He has a brother in a town nearby and I kept asking why he didn't go to see him, but he was apparently afraid he'd be lost or something if he traveled alone. I'll be able to write more shortly.

I love you.
Sydney

March 14

Dear Mary,

I'll tell you more about my trip to Florence. If I ever get a pass again, I'm going to any lengths to fix it so I can go by myself. I like company and would probably feel lonely without it, but it's just plain an impediment in such a situation. I did see a few things I wanted to see, and none of the best things can be seen anyway. They are stored and bricked over etc., so maybe it doesn't matter so much. I felt rather sorry for the statues and things, I mean the artists who made them really, that they decided were not valuable enough to be given extra protection. At least they are having their day now as there's not much left to put them in the shade.

Do you remember the way they harness horses here, no bits, bridles like hackamores,[46] and two-wheeled carts with the ends of the shafts level with the horse's backs? There are practically no civilian cars and all civilian traffic is horses or donkeys or, in the country, cow-powered. We took a long sight-seeing trip around the outskirts of the town in a GI truck and a short one in the town in what I think could be called a Victoria (Carriage). I saw the David but am sort of mixed up as to whether it was the original. Some things they seem to have temporarily replaced with copies. I signed a New

---

45 PFC Clayton D. R. Coates from New York City.
46 Bridle-like horse headgear, with no bit but a strap over the nose.

Hampshire book at a place for soldiers, not far under the name of Walter B. Malley, Peterborough.

I love you.
Sydney

⁓

March 15th

Dear Sydney,

I love you. I've been thinking of you all day long. I saw in today's New York paper about some boy in the 10th division who'd been killed Feb. 20th. It's the first time I happened to have noticed such a notice and it gave me an awful shock honestly. I saw on a map of Italy that Alec has, just about where you are. He comes from near Bergamo, which is northwest of where you are in the foothills of the Alps. It's stupid of me, but I can't remember just how we went from Pisa and Florence over to Venice, but obviously we crossed the Apennines somewhere.

Your mother called us last night as I was about to go to bed and said they'd just gotten your letter written Feb. 28th, telling about your battle experiences. After you'd written me the letter I haven't gotten yet! I was so interested when she read me what you'd written then—imagine crocuses on the top of Skatutakee. Which reminds me, Charlotte has two orange trees in bloom in her yard!

You write wonderful letters! I wish mine would come out that way. I love you, so I hope you'll always keep as far in the background as you possibly can! Everything sounds grim for the Italian front to me—twenty-seven German divisions against you and no hope of their withdrawal. I only pray Germany will collapse very soon! Liquor seems to be undermining a few of them, including Von Rundstedt[47] I see. I wish someone would take them all on a binge!

Today we found 2 duck eggs! I don't believe it means a thing. This has been a very early spring and they start to lay March 14th! Last year was very late and they started Jan. 10th! So what? This morning under the faucet by the barn was a beautiful stalactite or stalagmite, whichever it is that grows from the ground up! It was made a drop at a time all night and was over a foot high! All gone by the time the children got over, to my disappointment!

Last night Sydney said he dreamt about you. He was riding "Mitzi" and you came up to him and he patted you on the head! Then you went on into

---

[47] Field Marshall Karl Rudolf Gerd von Runstedt had been German commander-in-chief in the West. He was fired by Hitler in March 1945.

the house, with his blessing I assume. But he was thrilled over it! I pulled a big gold inlay out of one of my teeth on a caramel Mother gave me. I suspect sabotage, as she immediately pounced on it and said she knew where to cash it in! Anyhow, it means the dentist for me before long, I guess. How are your teeth? I suppose you can't even brush them if you can't even wash your hands and face! Also, how is the food they give you? You told your mother they gave you everything you wanted. I am glad of that. Nothing is too much or too good for you!

We took "Mitzi" and went for a walk this afternoon along the beach to the Madison Beach Hotel and back across the golf course, the children taking turns. Mary, on "Mitzi," jumped over a little log. You ought to see "Mitzi" jump! Mary rode her alone, way ahead of us all the way from the Garvin's barn, down their back drive and back to our barn! As we were going along the golf course, Sydney riding and Frank holding my hand, Mary looked across at us from a little distance and said that would make a good picture. I was surprised at her observation, then she went on. "Of course, it would be better if you all washed your hands and faces and Sydney had on his new coat and Frank his blue pants and blue coat and you had on a skirt!" But don't you think that's pretty remarkable for a five-year-old? To think in terms of what would make a good picture? I do! I think they are all remarkable children!

Mother has gone to N. Y. again for the third time quite recently! Mr. Young is taking her to the theater tonight, and tomorrow she's going in to the auction gallery where the sale opens on a truck load of things . . . they finally have arranged to sell. It's depressing but a fact, to be faced. And they say now there is a good market for French furniture and a lot of such things that none of us could ever use. She comes home tomorrow night and so does Daddy. He leaves Sunday for a trip to Texas and Wessyngton. Grandma is at Palm Beach and finding it very hot. She sounds pretty well, but lonely and hot and a little depressed. Her last letter to Mother we could hardly read and she said she was worried by numbness in her right side. Mother is anxious now for the nurse's report. Grandma is apt to exaggerate her difficulties and disgusted when the doctor finds nothing wrong. She plans to come here this summer, so it will be as well if we move out for a little. The confusion would be tiring, I think, for the whole summer.

Betty is in New Haven tonight so I am all alone. Betty is something! Her telephone calls for just two days came to over $4.00 last week! The baby's father leaves for induction next Tuesday. She has had a row with him but still continues to call him and he her. He collapsed at his job the day after the final break! Now she has another man. She's a two-timer and still writing her "M. P." at Camp Atterbuty, Indiana, every day! She has a fit if he says he's gone out with a girl, and here she is living with one and about to live with another! She is really dishonest and I have less and less sympathy for her! She's appropriated about 12 of my precious diapers. I got most of them back today while she was away and have hidden them. I've noticed my supply dwindling, but didn't think an awful lot about it until I saw them all on the line with hers, which are different! She's been washing hers in her bathroom and drying them upstairs. But now the heat is nil in the radiators she can't hide them any longer. I am going to count the ones I wash every day and let her know I do it! Diapers are as scarce as cigarettes and hen's teeth! I know she's taken my hot water bottle. She thinks there's nothing like that slob Allan! Nothing too good for him! Even our children's silver! I've taken it all away now. The new doctor here told Mother Allan was a mess! She'd never seen [such] a mass of blubber. And Betty came home from a visit there saying Dr. Spencer had never seen such a wonderful baby etc. etc. He really is disgusting, and I think it's all Betty's fault. She doesn't feed him right. She stuffs him with desserts, sweet stuff and chocolate milk, etc. and cuts down on fruit and vegetables because she says the doctor said not to feed him too much and not to force him if he doesn't want to eat. So having a perverted appetite he won't eat what he should, but only what he wants. She's ruined his appetite now, I think. Ice cream on pie, chocolate cake etc. It's all because she has such a sweet tooth herself!

Oh well, I love you an awful lot. The way she trifles with love makes me mad and makes me feel sorry for her in a way. She has not the smallest conception of what love is and apparently hasn't the capacity to grasp what it means either. I'm beginning to feel like Daddy, that it smacks of the barnyard. I think she's over-sexed and that's the answer.

Betsy is so cunning now. When she smiles she screws up her whole face and looks so cunning. Her hair is very curly and has a real copperish tinge. I'll send you a sample when it gets a little longer. I must go to bed now, I guess. I hope my next letters I won't have to wait so long to get! I will send more stamps but fewer at a time as you suggest.

I love you,
Mary

March 16

Dear Mary,

I hope I didn't make my trip to Florence sound too unsatisfactory, because I really had a very good time in spite of all the things I complained about. I got the letter with Mary's tooth, it gave me rather an odd feeling. From the newspapers you probably now know as much general news about us as I do, except that whenever I've had the opportunity, I've studied the maps of our section as much as possible so that I've got to understand the geography of it pretty well. I try to understand as much of what is going on as possible.

You wanted to know who my companions are: they are the same as before, only I'm a runner from company headquarters to the platoon instead of vice-versa as you might think, so that I am more of the time with former than I am with the men I knew in the platoon. I see quite a bit of Harley Cass, from Peterborough you know. He's thinking, of all things, of setting up there as undertaker after the war or else of running a ski lodge in the White Mountains. On the whole my job is a little softer and safer than most peoples, and I have a chance to know a little more about what is going on. When I went to Florence, I probably could have gone to Rome to see John instead, but I had very little time and thought it might be wiser to wait for a better opportunity. But I was very tempted.

Your mother's V-mail letter did come faster than the one you wrote the same day but not much faster than some of your others, and I still think a regular letter by air mail is much better. I don't think I need or rather, perhaps, that I would have used the rayon stockings. I hope you don't do too much galloping; I'm sure it's good for "Mitzi" and the children and might be for me, but I don't believe you need the exercise. I'm flattered by Mary's opinion, but I don't know that my running would be much more spectacular. I hope Frank doesn't hang around "Mitzi's" tail too much, that worries me a little. Besides the danger of his being hurt, I wouldn't want him to lose that wonderful self-confidence. But he should learn to have a little respect for her heels at the same time. But I know you understand all that sort of thing much better than I do anyway. I got your letter with the clipping about Sonnichsen. I keep wondering if he could be one of those prisoners going home after having been freed by the Russians. I've seen enough to realize how much courage he must have had. In the "Talk of the Town", Jan. 27th *New Yorker*, is a piece about a former geologist naval officer from Iran. I wonder if he's a friend of Henry's. I love you an awful lot and am lonely all the time.

I love you.
Sydney

⤳

March 16

Dear Sydney,

You will never believe it but your letter about the first attack came today! Just 13 days after it was postmarked. I couldn't believe it. I was ready to wait a good six weeks! I love you! I hate to think of you living in foxholes with shells falling all around you, and the dirt and everything. I wish you could have told me how many foxholes you occupied and just how big they are and such little details!

    I'm so interested in everything because I really can't picture it too well. Though I've read several articles on ". . .with the U. S. 10th Mountain division in Italy" that give a fair picture, but not as good as you could give! How fast can you go up the mountains? I guess that all depends, naturally, on the resistance but I mean, for instance, do you go up spread out, or how? It must be truly beautiful country. Some day maybe we can go there and really enjoy it! Though I'd just as soon go to Skatutakee again with you.

    I'm awful sorry you couldn't see any of the sights in Pisa. I guess there's not much left of Naples. We spent a day in Leghorn walking all around, and it was especially interesting since we'd just all read *Anthony Adverse*! But there are some beautiful bronze doors on the cathedral in Pisa, out by the leaning tower, and also the baptismal font has some beautiful carving and some wonderful frescoes around the Camposanto Monumentale, the earth of which was brought by boat from the Holy Land. Maybe you'll get back before you leave and can see all these things. Joe apparently has been to Pisa recently as he sent me a postcard from there for Easter.

    Well, last night I was alone here. Mother was in New York and Betty in Wallingford. Sydney woke me up at 1:30; he'd been sick, not much, just a little, but then, when I got back to bed I suddenly felt as though I had a tennis ball in my stomach. I never had such a feeling. I ended by throwing up myself and then felt better. But I never did feel sick just this great lump, I guess a result of so much worry over you, undigested food. Anyhow, I felt fine this morning. I'm sorry my letters arrive so inconsecutively. Would you rather I saved them and mailed them, say once a week, all together? The reason I haven't is because I keep thinking some may get lost and this way even if some do you will surely always have some whenever mail arrives. But I'll do as you suggest. I couldn't possibly compress all I have to say every day into a V-mail! I'd have to leave out a lot! No one can fathom how I can think of anything to write to you every day! But the more I write the more I find to say. But you are the one; so I'll do whatever you want.

This morning I saw my first robin! And did I tell you; Mr. Scranton planted peas the night before last! I'll be interested now to see how early he harvests them. Certainly the ground is thawed and dried in most places. So I don't know why more people don't start in now. We are going to try to plow Man's Folly, in part anyhow. That's one thing about Alec; he's open to suggestions, not hide-bound like poor old Julius! The grass is really getting green and the songs of the birds sound so cheerful in the morning and evening. The vet came today and cut some of Sweetie's horn off; but it still seems to hit her over the eye. He says he's afraid to cut any further from fear of hitting the artery or whatever. Anyhow he cut my finger at the same time, but, not badly. I had my finger protecting her eye. He says he can take the whole thing off when the weather gets warmer. I don't know why, but anyhow when we discussed the fact that she's to freshen in June we decided to leave it because before she freshens he says she may lose the kids and afterwards it would affect the milk flow. So I'm to watch it anyhow.

I love you such a lot. I can think of nothing but you. I imagine now you've been in another attack since there are letters that have just come, and from the papers I gather there's a lull there, now. So perhaps tonight you are again behind the lines. I wonder if they're planning a major push now this spring if Germany doesn't collapse beforehand. I hope not! Though the reports sound as though that was in the cards. I pray to God to watch over you constantly. I wish I could just hold your hand even for a short time. It would give me a world of courage and I need it! It would help you a little too! This afternoon we drove "Mitzi" up Stony Lane, up beyond Mungers' [48] to the house where the geese scared "Rollo" and then came home that road and back thru Stony Lane again. It was wonderful and so warm and spring-like and the children were so happy. It reminded me of the walks we used to take before Mary was born and we were living in the cottage, just about this

---

48 A neighboring family.

time of year. I'm glad you dreamt about me when you fell asleep during the attack. You must have slept more than once during that week, didn't you? How do you find the training you have had show up? You haven't mentioned any of the men by name. Are you still with the same squad? Do you share foxholes? There are a million things I'd like to know, but most of all I want is to hear you are well and safe. Alan Banister is home and he and his family are in Portsmouth, N. H., until about May 1st, when he reports back to New London and then the Pacific.

I love you an awful lot,
Mary

P. S. I sent you two goat journals this morning for you to peruse.

❧

March 16

Dear Sydney,

We were glad on the 14th to get a letter from you, written the 28th, and to hear the same day that Mary had one mailed the 2nd. So we were only 12 days behind. Mrs. Pfeiffer in South Natick heard from her son at the same time.

What color crocuses grow on Mt. Belvedere? There is one purple one out here, and quite a lot of snowdrops and aconites.

There is a paragraph in the paper almost every day about the 10th division. Mary saves the clippings for you.

Mother has had Mrs. Faulkner from Keene here for a few days. It has been very pleasant, although Father and Mother and I spent almost all our time working on income tax returns! I'll be so glad when Joe comes home! I heard from him day before yesterday, but I can't guess where he is. You can be much more specific.

Walter is home, did anyone tell you? He and Willard each have 30 days, most of it over-lapping. Isn't it wonderful for them both to get home at once? And Jane P. H. has mumps! She said she looked forward so long to when Walter got back and when he turned up and surprised them all, she not only had mumps, but she was in the bathtub and couldn't find any clothes! The news looks good, doesn't it?

Katherine is almost a girl scout. Mary is as cocky as ever. We are all going tomorrow to the Audubon lecture and taking Morgan Palmer and Lisa and Francis Hunnewell.

I didn't know I was stealing when I took this paper. Now I have to put "George" and "Chips" in the pen.

Love,
Mary [49]

∾

March 17

Dear Mary,

I've been able to write every day for the last few days; so I hope it'll make up a little bit for the times before when I couldn't. I got a letter from Mary Fyffe today, V-mail, written on March 4th and one from you, air-mail, written on the 5th and postmarked the 6th. There's no postmark on V-mail. Yours was a wonderful letter. I wish I could write to you the same way, you know I feel the same way. I love you such an awful lot. I remember seeing the Haakons somewhere or other and thinking that he was much more attractive than she.

I've only seen about three or four goats since I've been in this country, just sheep. The goats must be in some other part; but sheep are everywhere, so that the hillsides are like lawns, like the top of our hill in Peterborough.

If Sydney is the least shy, that doesn't sound much like me. I'm awfully glad he is. Being as he is I should think that shyness would bother him more than the others. Mary's such a determined character that I'm sure her shyness will never get her down.

I haven't got any packages yet, but maybe it's still too soon to expect them. It does seem that spring is the worst time of all to be separated. It's beautiful here which makes it seem all the sadder. But I keep feeling that such a beautiful spring must signify something or other. If the flowers and trees have so much faith, why shouldn't we.

I'm glad that Charlotte's children are such a handy distance for pony cart excursions. It's too bad Ruth isn't there and other friends of yours that you could visit too. You could have a wonderful time. I suppose Jane is quite a bit too far. I wish you could see some of the horse drawn contraptions that they have over here. Though maybe you have anyway. Do you ever see Mauldin's cartoons in the papers, much the best soldier cartoons? It all seems just like that; they describe it much better than I ever could.

I love you.
Sydney

---

[49] My father's older sister.

March 17

Dear Sydney,

It's Saturday night, as the song says, "the loneliest night of the week."[50] But one night is just as lonely as the next to me! I wonder where you are tonight and how you are. Today's paper gave an account of the ski champion, Torger Tokle, who was killed in Italy, March 3rd with the 86th. Did you ever hear of him before? From the write-up, I gather he was quite a skier and not quite 27 years old. It seems awful and every time I read of someone in the 10th Div. killed it makes my heart sink. I wonder if you were in the same attack, beyond Monte Torraccia. It said he was a platoon leader, a Technical Sergeant. I've cut it out to save for you because of his being the champion skier of the western hemisphere. I thought you might be interested. Today has been a rather disappointing day. First, we expected the Shattuck children here for the afternoon, while Janet went on to Saybrook to see Dick, who by the way is now in I. A.[51] Well she called up this morning and said they had colds, so I said, "nix." I don't want to start that now in this weather. It's so hard to keep [the children] dry and then if they're wet with colds and a wind blowing, not so good! Then, Mr. Pope was to bring his little girl, Marshall, over this afternoon, and Charlotte her children to ride "Mitzi" and see the animals. We scuttled around and got all the chores done and everything set and they didn't come until nearly 4:30! It really disgusts me. I think once in a while when they come over they might get here early, don't you? Our children go in at 5 and they have to because of Betsy and the goats and my desire to be through with everything at a reasonable hour. Of course it's disappointing to the children, to all of them. They only get started playing when it's all over. Marshall looked so beautifully dressed and all our children looked normal. Pope said to me, "it's grand here the way the children just rough it!" I was amused. Could he but see us at home! I couldn't resist showing him the henhouse playhouse. Marshall looked very interested but he hurried her out! "Some other time, dear!" Barbara just loves to ride "Mitzi."

I wish you'd see Frank join right in any roughhouse between Mary, Sydney and Billy! He sticks out his lower jaw and charges right in! We were in "Judy's" pasture. "Judy" was in the barn. Mary really rides "Mitzi" very well, trots and canters by herself. She said she almost fell off twice but pulled herself up again! She loves it! I have got to try and find a pony snaffle bit.

---

50 The song "Saturday Night," sung by Frank Sinatra, was published in 1944.
51 An Individual Augmentee is a member of the military under temporary assignment.

The only bit I have is a curb and that's not so good. "Mitzi" has a very light mouth and if Mary holds her in too tight she doesn't like it, naturally. But "Little Joe," my horse, has none! We've invited Jane's children and Charlotte's, and the Shattucks and Marshall to hunt Easter eggs, Easter morning. They're all very excited over it! They all came over this afternoon after riding to see Betsy, and Betsy had a lovely reception. She sat up in her carriage and smiled at them and gurgled and waved her arms and then looked at me to see if it was real! She is so cunning, honestly.

In this week's *Peterborough Transcript* there is a letter from Dick Price thanking them for the Xmas box. The letter came from England, but he didn't say anything about what he was doing. It seems to me he was sent into the artillery. All those that went from Peterborough, where you would have gone. I wonder if that's where you'd be if you hadn't gone from Wallingford. But I guess you'd be where you are in spite of all!

I'll enclose a few more stamps in this letter and try putting them in a used stamp folder and see if that makes it any easier for you. I hope you can write as often as possible, because I worry about you constantly, naturally. But I do see how you might not have the time, or inclination or chance to write when you're in a battle. But don't forget how much just the words "I'm alright, I love you" mean to me back here! I bet it's pretty tough and you must get awful tired. I hope you got over your bad cold before you had to go again. I should think if you felt the least bit badly it would be a terrible handicap. You'd be much more likely to be less careful and more apt to get hurt. So I pray that was gone. I can see how you might easily pick up colds! So many men getting very hot and tired, and then suddenly getting cold. I have some wonderful vitamin pills called Adek that have kept all our family cold free all winter while everyone else had them. I think I'll send you a small bottle next time I pack a box. Try these anyhow! I wish I'd done it sooner!

Is it muddy where you are now? I guess there's a spring offensive in the air, now you have arrived. The rest of the news sounds more and more encouraging. As I said before, my prediction is it will be over in April! Mrs. "Monty" gave her hubby until March 23rd. One more week! But I feel April! This is Saturday so I'll write more tomorrow night. Daddy goes to Texas tomorrow afternoon. Mother goes to Wessyngton, April 4th.

Sunday, March 18

Well, the gas coupons expire the 21st of this month and I have 3 left out of six! I think that's pretty good, don't you? I'm going to fill the car tomorrow and try to keep ahead so I'll have enough to go to Peterborough on about the end of this period or beginning of the next. In other words, around the end of June. That proves how little I've gadded around! Because every time I've gone to N. H. in Mother's car I've either given her gas, or else we've had a special allowance like taking Betty to the doctor. I'm just mailing Alje Holt the application for a new license and for my driver's license too because they expire, April 1st. As usual I'm on the late side.

Well today has been another spring-like day. So far this month we've had none of what I call typical March weather—high, white, billowing clouds and a wind, but instead mild breezes warm air, hot sun and the smell of fresh earth full of earth worms. Remember the day we brought the buggy and took lunch up to the Jacquith house? It was so warm when we set out and we found drifts of deep snow and it was cold before we got home? I so often think of that day and Mary remembers it vividly too! We've had no days like that. This afternoon we went for a drive in the pony cart taking "Mopsa." She got lost from us, and spoiled our drive because instead of going on around the way I'd planned we had to turn around to find her. I was mad! Anyhow it was fun. The children just love it and clamor to go every day! Today we got 5 eggs from 7 hens and one duck egg. That's not bad, is it? Though the other ducks better hurry up and start to lay! I still have the billy goat—almost two weeks now. I must go and see his Italian owner this week and beg to keep him one more week. If "Mocha" doesn't get bred this way I give up! He's jumped up on her a number of times, but it remains to be seen. I'll probably find she'll freshen in May anyhow! But I don't care. This is worth it. Obviously she wasn't bred either time at Moose Hill Inn. The next two tries were to a Saanen billy in Clinton. A registered buck. This one is just a nice ordinary billy goat!

Betsy is really starting to bite me. She clamps those two teeth down and it hurts like blazes! Luckily she doesn't do it every time I nurse her, just once in a while and then she smiles up at me and laughs and laughs! She's the laughingest baby I ever saw and screws her little nose up and her eyes! Her eyes are the color of Frank's—real blue, not like Mary's and Sydney's. Her hair is getting very curly and soon I will send you a sample. That darn photographer hasn't yet sent those pictures! Two months now. I am disgusted. I've called her once and will do so again if they don't come tomorrow. I hope I get a letter sometime this week. I can't bear to think of a whole week again without one. But last week I got 3 to make up for none the week before. I've never gotten two the same day, yet!

I love you an awful lot. You may get this around Easter. Happy Easter anyhow! We're going to have an egg hunt. I've told you, I think. I wish you could be here too! Maybe next year! I got a letter from the *Reader's Digest* and what they do when two subscriptions are entered in one name is to extend the subscription, so now you'll get it for two years. They said Stu had it paid for through 1948. Someone must have subsidized him! I love you. I'm going to answer an ad now for a governess cart I saw in the paper. This cart is a little big for "Mitzi" and the rubber tires are coming off in pieces! I love you and I want you, and my life is a constant prayer for your safety. Be careful won't you.

I love you,
Mary

҂

March 19

Dear Mary,

This is your paper that you sent me. Yesterday I got letters postmarked the 7th, 8th, and 9th. That seems pretty quick and I guess I must have got about all your letters so far. I'm sorry that you think it might be a good idea to sell "Judy," getting her was all your idea, but it was still one of the last things that we both did together. But I can see how it would be much better if you had something that you could use riding with Mary, and how training "Judy" would be quite a problem right now. I know that what you decide to do will be the most sensible thing. I keep hoping and thinking that I will be home before the year is over, but maybe I'm too optimistic.

I'm sorry you got stuck in the place by the graveyard. Seems to me we turned around and retreated once at that place before, a long time ago. Digging yourself out with your hands seems like too much; I haven't even had to dig a foxhole that way and hope I don't. I'm now living pretty much a life of ease though I can hear machine guns occasionally. As for all the exercise you talk about, I still get very little even in combat itself. Nine-tenths of combat consists of sitting in a foxhole or somewhere and waiting for something to happen. You can spend several days in a hole only getting out for a few minutes at a time. The only exercise is when we move to or from the lines or advance, and, of course, that is always at night and over rough ground so as not to use the obvious routes. At such times it's useful to be in good shape, but most of the time it seems to me that a man with the physique of a policeman that just stands on a windy street corner all night long is the best off.

I'm disappointed that you think that maybe "Mocha" still wasn't bred, because I really think that she's a most unusually good goat as you know. But I'm glad you could find a billy goat that had evaded the pot and that you brought him home. I think that's the best way, at least it worked once. At this point I'm not worried much about his size, but it might help matters some if there were a few Peterborough boulders for him to stand up on. You've certainly tackled the problem with determination. Anyway, if it worked now it would be the best time for plenty of milk next winter and she's the easiest because the quickest to milk when it's cold. I hate to think of your hands getting so cold that they cracked.

I love you.
Sydney

March 20

Dear Sydney,

Today really has been like midsummer. I don't know actually what the thermometer said but it must have been near 80°. I got a letter today from Mrs. Adams and one from Pat.[52] It makes me so homesick just to read their letters! Mrs. Adams was glad to know you'd received her second box. I hope you'll write her yourself! She sounded a little funny about it, I thought. She said and I quote "I am also glad Sydney did not trouble to write me. He needs all his energy and leisure to acknowledge his family's gifts and messages. It was nice to know it arrived because you know how difficult it is to get a package into the mail, and one does like to know if the person for whom it was intended received it."

I can't quite make out from that whether she means what she says or if her feelings are a little bit hurt. What do you think? She is such a funny brusque and abrupt sort of person. I can't always understand the tempo in which she says things. She writes a very good letter, but I'm always conscious of money with her and though she comes from N. Y. State she's more New

---

52 Pat Holsart, a friend from Hancock, New Hampshire.

England than Charlie, I think. Anyhow she is so nice and friendly and says Anna Mary will come here if I want and make the trip up with me. However, I think Mother wants to go as far as Wellesley, so maybe Anna Mary can join me there. I'm getting so excited about going, honestly! She says to tell you she's begun the woodpile, though it isn't sawed yet and the heap of snow in the ell is still five or six feet deep! She really is so nice. I asked her if she had any syrup to sell, but apparently not. It hasn't been a good year. The spring has come too quickly. She's cagey. There's a ceiling on gallon tins but one of the ways she sells it is in glass quarts! Well anyhow she's a real friend to have for such a near neighbor, but I do feel as though I should have on kid gloves when I handle her! She's confused and thinks you're in the 10th Army and says she can't find any references to that!

 Pat wrote a nice letter too. They are now looking for a couple—relocated Japanese Americans! Well anyhow she writes very friendly letters and full of messages to you and sympathies to us both. I always like her better after reading letters from her. I'm sorry about last night's hasty letter! You probably won't get these two consecutively, but still! I love you an awful awful lot and I pray you are safe and well. No letter today either. I fear you must have gone to the front again with that bad cold. I long to hear now. The papers sounded as though things began again around March 3rd or 4th or in there. It seems to be fairly quiet now except for patrol clashes, which have involved casualties. The Germans, they say, are very sensitive to your probings! The daily account sounds like a page out of a dentist's diary. I think the reporter must be an ex-dentist! I should think I might hear the end of this week. I hope so!

 The air is full of peepers in every puddle—flocks of robins about and iris shooting up their arms. No daffodils yet, but it won't be long, I know. This afternoon we went to the Hammers' stable in Branford. I wanted to see their horses and talk to the man about "Judy." They've got five saddle horses, one imported from England and the rest from Virginia. They are all jumpers and the stable man is very nice, English, and he says his job used to be breaking colts. He agrees with me two people are better than one and assures me "Judy" won't be too old when you come home! He says he prefers to work on a 4-year-old. He'd love to train "Judy," but says he can't. He's employed privately and the 5 keep him busy. Too bad! But anyhow he says to just handle her and wait for you to come home. He said one thing that interested me. The Hammers had a colt they raised and made a pet of and all and that colt got so it stood on its hind legs and lunged down on you. Just what "Judy" has done a few times. Though I'm getting her over that, and just as I deduced he said it came from spoiling them with too much affection—letting them feel their superiority. He says you have to be kind and gentle, but firm and not make too much of a pet out of them because they soon grow too big and strong. Anyhow it bore out my theory, which I deduced too late to forestall, but as I say I am overcoming it. If I can get Ethel Wilcox to come over two or three times a week, I may tackle teaching "Judy" to drive, but I'd rather do nothing than bungle it and make her so she has to unlearn things first. She is lovely, honestly, and I've about decided I can't bear to sell her after all. She's exactly what we want and so strong looking and healthy. I know when you come home we can manage her. She's not a bit nervous, very sensible and used to all sorts of confusion, children screaming etc. and responds to discipline without getting a bit crazy. So I guess I'll keep her another year anyhow. I have all the harness we need but nothing to hitch her to except the buggy which I don't want to have busted up.

I don't understand "Becky." She looks enormous now and isn't due until June 9th. She's certainly fallen off in her milk! The Keatings were playing the Ouija board the other night and it kept saying "goats, goats, goats." So they asked it if it meant my goats and it said "yes." So they called up to see if our kids had arrived! So you see even the local Ouija boards are interested in our goats! I love you. I want a letter so badly! Mother had one from Joe Blagden today. He is en route to Honolulu Beach, commander on some sort of landing ship. He's captain of a platoon of 45 men. All have been trained in digging fox holes, small arms mortars, grenades, etc., and infiltration under live ammunition. It sounded like your training. Anyhow he's not a bit keen on any of it. Says he hopes all they have to use of the above is the foxhole digging, and, as he's the one to order them out of there, he says they'll probably stay in there as long as possible! He really sounds disillusioned and says he's afraid he's too old for this sort of thing. His heart just isn't in it and he has an absolute horror of West Point and Annapolis and never ever wants any children to have any contact whatsoever with the above or their graduates! He says the mention of Iwo Jima brings horror to them and they've all voted for a beachhead on Bali! His experiences really haven't been too happy and the final removal of him from his ship for nothing other than prejudice, I think, which hasn't helped his attitude any! He says he thinks he's physiologically unfit and I think he is too!

The children have been wading quite a bit and wanted to go swimming today, until they felt it! They are fine and just as gay as can be. Sydney said he dreamt about you last night. He dreamt of a trainload of soldiers and it stopped and you got off! I guess he was thinking of the troop train we saw go by a little while ago. That impressed them immeasurably! I must say it's a terrible sight to me. It makes my heart sink into my shoes every time I see one go by. I think of all the desperate depressing sights a troop train embodies all the feelings one has. I can't tell you what it does to me to see them go by when we stand by the bridge in Stony Lane, and it makes me think of your mother more than ever. And I suffer for you knowing you were on one not that long ago. So alone—so friendless, no one knew where you were, the future? I think it's grim.

I love you an awful lot.
Mary

P. S. I sent Betsy's pictures airmail today—let me know when they arrive. She was 6 months old when they were taken.

∽

March 20

Dear Mary,

No letters for a couple of days, but your mother's package came and is already half gone. I mean the cookies. I'm going to save the sardines for awhile and will use the soap every once in a while, I hope. I've rather got out of the habit, though I washed my face the day before yesterday and again today. I've been in the same place the last few days and nothing at all ever happens and I don't do anything whatsoever; so it doesn't leave much to write about. Like most of the places, it's a very pretty spot and I wish I could show it to you after the war. But it's too far up for me to be able to just wander around and see very much, and my job as runner means that I have to just hang around in one spot all the time anyway, in case I should be needed to take a message to my platoon. I stay all the time in a house with no furniture or roof and sit and smoke and talk and read old magazines and sweep the floor once in awhile and run silly little errands and that's about all. I'm situated so that I practically can't open my mouth without saying "Sir," and I'd probably make a very good butler or something after the war.

I forgot to say that I shaved today too and combed my hair, and mustache of course. So you can picture me as looking quite presentable at the moment.

The goat journals came too and I've been reading them. By the way none of those cookies even cracked in transit. The ordinary box of cookies that arrives here is nothing but a finely pulverized dust, very good of course, but hard to eat without sneezing. When I have nothing to do I find that I'm almost always thinking about the little details of some repairs or improvements that should be made at the Dodge house. I don't know why I should keep thinking about such things. I love you an awful lot. I don't think I'll even want to cut wood out of sight of the house when I get home. The studio is far enough.

I love you.
Sydney

March 21

Dear Mary,

Well the wise men decided long ago that on this day spring would really begin. It seems as if it started here some time ago; but I'm sure of course that they must be right. For the next six months there'll be more sunlight than darkness and I'm praying that it'll be true figuratively as well, and that the sunlight will be in such quantities that it can be stored in our hearts against next winter's night as it was before the war. I guess I'm getting rather sententious; that sounds like a high school essay, but I've reached an age where I don't mind appearing adolescent. I wish I could. I'm sitting in the aforementioned sun now with nothing to do but twirl my mustache and sharpen the pencil once in awhile. I keep planning to shave the mustache off, but it's so useful in straining the grounds out of my coffee, it's always full of them, that I can't bear to do it, besides I think it's rather cute. I was trying to mold it into a regulation villain's mustache, but it seems to have developed into an amiable handlebar. During those extended stays in foxholes it got out of control when I wasn't looking.

I sleep in a room with some of the officers, who are gentlemen of course, but unfortunately there are privates in the room too; and though the officers most politely only took one cookie at a time this afternoon, your mother's box is empty and serves only as a writing table with sweet and slightly crumby memories. I'm going to try and wake up a couple of hours before dawn and quietly open a can of sardines. You can see that Sydney doesn't get his generosity from me. I'm a very selfish person, as I've often been told. But at least I don't think I'll come back any more selfish than when I left, so you needn't be alarmed. I guess the only change will be that I'll want to stay closer to home than ever. That's another reason why I want to do nothing but work on sculpture.

I hate to think that by the time I'm home Mary will have to be away at school all the time. But I guess I'm pretty lucky to be able to be with the children as much as I was, so much more than most fathers. I want it to be that way again. I like especially to think of when we had tea on the grass behind the house with the children eating supper, and all I had to worry about was just which gray birch trees I should cut down so we'd get a little more evening sun and still not spoil the effect of the moonlight in the goat pasture. I still think that such problems are really more important than some of the "realism" I face nowadays.

The whole situation on this side of the ocean is ridiculous and completely unrealistic and unnecessary. At the height of the worst shelling that we've undergone so far I heard the 1st sergeant say that if he lived through this he was going to spend the rest of his life writing books on the futility of war. The remark and the way he said it tickled me so that I didn't worry much about the rest of the shells. He lived through it alright and I hope he starts writing. He's a very remarkable fellow that I would have liked to have known in civilian life. I've got to know him since I've been a runner. He's rather an intellectual, but surprisingly like Forrest Wilson in appearance, sense of humor and mannerisms. He's Scandinavian.[53]

I hear some good talk now once in awhile. The other night there was a really good bull session on the state and needs of the world in general which lasted from suppertime to 1:30 a.m. I didn't contribute much of any, but I really enjoyed it. Of course most of it was the kind of thoughts I had about fifteen years ago and which one is apt to smile at a bit as he gets older, but there were a few good ideas too, and the brave thoughts of men who are not so very old harmonize most smoothly with the season and are beautiful to listen to. I think I must find at home a suitable tree in whose shade a seat can be arranged where a few of my friends can rest with me occasionally and indulge in useless but delightful philosophical discussions which won't fool the children at all.

I love you.
Sydney

---

53 He is referring to 1st Sgt. Lester S. Ersland of Ames, Iowa. Sergeant Ersland was killed on April 15, just beyond the town of Torre Iussi. That was the second day of the Spring Offensive, as they fought their way out of the northern Apennines and into the Po Valley. According to the *History of the 87th Mountain Infantry*, compiled by Captain George F. Earle, Sergeant Ersland was blinded from dirt thrown into his eyes, as snipers targeted him and the soldiers he was leading. He stepped on a Schu mine, stumbled, and fell on four others, dying instantly. The story is familiar, as I had heard it several times, but never realized he knew the man killed so well.

March 21

Dear Sydney,

I got two letters today! One written March 10th and one the 14th, just a week ago! And both postmarked the 16th, just five days ago. Thank God you were safe and well there and I guess your cold didn't seem to bother you too much as you never mentioned it! I'm glad you're good at jumping into foxholes, but I don't like those guys who aimed at you. For a rifleman you have kept your gun pretty clean. Is that so you don't have to clean it too often? I hope you never do have to use it, but I hope if you do have to you won't have forgotten how! I'm glad the scenery is so beautiful and you really can enjoy it, in spite of being disturbed in your appreciation. I'm glad you haven't been too cold. The papers do make it sound more than uncomfortable, and I bet it is too for those of less-rugged constitution than you. The spring flowers must make a weird setting but also they must lend inspiration. I am thankful you have developed such an impersonal attitude toward the "horrors," because that is something I think no one could foretell one's reaction to.

It was wonderful you could get to Florence. I hope, in spite of the company, you could see some of its treasures. There is so much to see there that is beautiful. Did you see Michelangelo's David, or have most of those things been removed? The bronze doors on the baptistry are wonderful too and the statues of the Medici. I wish we could go together! Mrs. Werner in the P.O. this morning greeted me with the news that I should be very happy today—two letters and she was right! It was a grey, rainy day and it seemed to me as though the sun shone right through it all! Tonight's paper speaks of an impending offensive in Italy, coordinated with a Russian drive to isolate the Germans in Italy. It fills me with apprehension but I know God is watching over you and I have faith. The news really gets more and more encouraging, so perhaps it won't be long now!

This morning Mary and Sydney and Frank were playing goat. Mary was the owner, Sydney was the billy and Frank was to be bred! I waited with bated breath for the next move. Mary led Sydney up to Frank, they touched noses and Mary announced, to my relief, "there, she's all bred!" Later on in the day I overheard Mary explaining the facts of life to Sydney. She began "You know how you get kids?" No, Sydney didn't. "Well", said Mary, "you get a billy goat and he jumps on "Mocha" and then he does it again the next day and the next day, and then in a little while Mocha has kids." They were both thoroughly satisfied! This business of exposure may have its embarrassing moments. I keep my fingers crossed, but it seems to me to be the most natural form of sex education. There is no mystery, no whispering and gradually they will realize, I think.

This afternoon we went over to see Mr. Pellegrini, who owns "Billy," to see if we could keep him another week. He said "yes" and then we saw three of his little kids. They are adorable! But something is wrong with his care of his goats. He's lost two in childbirth and one kid. They look like they never get any exercise for one thing, and I don't know what he feeds them. But I suspect something is lacking. I am getting very nervous about "Gay." She's due in a week. She seems fine so I don't anticipate any trouble, but I feel exactly like the grandmother! I can sympathize now with Mother! We stopped in to see Charlotte and Willie and Barbara. Our children just love to go there and get into their toys! As we drove up the lane we saw Arthur's sheep standing in the rain. Two of them, or rather one was lying down and when we came home there were two baby lambs! Tiny little soaking wet things on wobbly legs and trying to nurse. We were gone about two hours. The children were thrilled and I must say they are adorable and close-up to the fence we got a wonderful look at them! But wouldn't you think he'd have taken them in? A fairly cold drizzle and east wind, and those little things. They must have thought it a hard, cold world alright!

Mary has started on the salt block again! She has a piece of "Mitzi's" she carries around and generously gives Sydney and Frank licks when they get hungry!

Charlotte said Bill called up last night and says there's to be a big Coast Guard party Saturday night in New York. He told her if she didn't come down he'd have to get a floozy but then she said he paid her the highest compliment by saying there wasn't one in N. Y. he'd rather have than her! She said, "You know that means a lot because there are beautiful people you or I don't know. Not at all like they used to be 5 or 6 years ago." I must say there's a good deal of life that I am ignorant of and my pride makes me refrain from asking all the questions I'd like to! I have to wait for an opening. I am awfully curious as to whether he's ever slept with any other woman since they've been married! I shouldn't be surprised either way, but I'm dying to know. Some time the opportunity will arise for one to ask a lot of things. I could have if we hadn't gone to the movies the other night.

Our love for each other seems so much more real and genuine and simple! I know you'd never do anything like that to me, would you? I wouldn't bear it, and that's why I'm curious about them.

I love you,
Mary

March 21

Dear Sydney,

I have just been talking to your wife and your letters of the 12th & 14th had just arrived so as usual she called me up.

It's a great relief to hear from you. It has just come in over the Radio that we have made some gains in Italy today. We all hope you are behind the lines.

Katherine has just had her tenth birthday party—few children due to gasoline—Francis Hunnewell, Hollis's boy, came, he told Katherine, because his mother made him. He didn't want to come. We can be frank at the age of 6. Katherine didn't mind and he seemed to enjoy himself.

Tony Parker's boy came. He told us they had some milk goats now—I think you set the fashion. Uncle Walter and Willard are just coming over to borrow the floor machine to wax floors. They had it yesterday and want it again. I wish for real I could ask them to do one of our floors. Old James who works for us, he is 73 and can't do very much, so lots of things don't get done.

The lawn is getting green, and red silver maples are in blossom, crocuses in bloom too.

Father saw Mrs. Forbes, Sandy Forbes' mother, yesterday and she asked where you were—then said she had spent much time in those Italian hills, an uncle had had a house there and she was going right home to look up Mt. Belvedere etc. in the geography—many of my friends ask for you.

Small Dick is very curious and friendly—making all kinds of noises, repeating a noise like boo boo but not talking yet.

Lots & Lots of Love dear.
Mother

P. S. Just now Mary F. can mail this in Natick, so she can bring children home from school.

March 22

Dear Mary,

I got four letters from you today postmarked the 10th, 12th, 13th, and 14th and one from Jane. I guess a good many of the questions that you ask have now been answered by the papers. As far as the special training is concerned, that you keep worrying about, I haven't needed it anyway and if I had, I know more about it than nine-tenths of them anyway. I'm glad you saved the news clippings, I would like to read them and keep them. I've seen some sent DeWick[54] from the *Boston Herald*. I thought the accounts rather exaggerated and silly. I'd rather you kept them at home to see later than send them to me. If a period, like those you mention, goes by with no letters you rightly guess why, but you needn't worry because by that time it's a week or so later, and if anything were wrong you would have already heard; that sort of thing only takes a few hours, and you can be pretty sure that by the time you've stopped getting letters I've started writing them again. I'm glad you don't pretend in your letters; I don't either.

I went for a long walk today with Bob DeWick and spent most of the time telling him about "Nona" and "Wenny" and "Jill," with a particularly long account of our attempts to drive "Jill." I think I bored him but I enjoyed myself walking and talking. It's the first time since I've been in the army that I've gone on such an ordinary, informal walk independently. He knows a lot more about horses than I do and explained to me what I never could understand which is how a horse could get hot, drink too much and then, getting foundered, have that affect its feet. The drinking gives it a cold in the chest and to relieve pressure on the painful chest it stands with its legs in that peculiar position which puts an unnatural pressure on its feet and if it lasts long it becomes foundered. Bet you didn't know that.

Don't send cigarettes. We wade up to our knees in them, and are given pipe tobacco too and enough candy to make the whole world sick. I suppose it's supposed to be full of quick energy. Mostly it's not the kind that I like anyway. I'm certainly not surprised that there's a cigarette and match shortage at home, or chewing gum. We leave a trail of cans and papers wherever we go. After we've stayed two or three days in one spot it looks like the city dump and smells worse; it must make a fine impression. Enemy positions that we take look pretty neat, I suppose because they didn't have much anyway, and lived off the natives and potatoes which are still in the fields and such. Whenever convenient, we are given beer as well as cigarettes. We pay for that.

---

54 PFC Bob DeWick of Topsham, Maine, was in my father's squad and the closest to him in age. I met him in 1999 when I first began working on my father's letters.

It's a little odd if, while I'm drawing an allotment for you and the children, your father is also deducting you from the income tax. He should be getting it back from me. I suppose if it's summertime when I come back I'll find "Mitzi" lying with the rest of the family on the beach under the big umbrella drinking a bottle of beer and talking politely to the guests. Today I saw the congresswoman from Connecticut who stopped at this company during her "Eleanoreal"[55] travels. She really looks young and pretty and attractive, and a battery of cameras appeared from nowhere and she was photographed in every possible attitude including sitting in a foxhole, not mine. I live in a house with the upper crust but there isn't room for everybody. People were stepping all over the accompanying, very impressive, brass, crying to get a good look at her. She had on rather a silly looking outfit that I'm sure was designed for the trip and that she considered "practical."

Yes, the shrapnel did cut my cheek just barely, but enough to bleed quite a bit, and killed a man nearby.[56] It was several days before I got a chance to wash my face so I was going around with blood down my face looking quite impressive. All that was the first time before the lull you mention; the next times they missed me. You know damn well I like your letters and don't think they should be written any differently. I hadn't heard that Walter had been home. Don't let Kesselring's order worry you. I've seen how little affect it had. The pictures are wonderful, especially the one with the dolls. I agree with Mary that, in the ones she liked, Betsy does look like Frank. In the family group I think she looks as Mary did. The ground is covered now with violets and other small flowers that are unfamiliar. Leaves are just barely beginning to come out. The countryside looks most serene and peaceful where it's not damaged too much.

I love you.
Sydney

March 22

Dear Sydney,

This morning we dug out parsnips, the children and I, and I was pleased and surprised to find so many! We had some for supper and they were wonderful! Yesterday we opened Mary's goat barrel and I'd forgotten we'd stored kohlrabi[57] in it! There were a number spoiled, but a lot that were

---

55 Clare Booth Luce was a Republican congresswoman from Connecticut's fourth district, which encompassed Fairfield County. "Eleanoreal" is a reference to Eleanor Roosevelt.
56 As mentioned earlier, PFC Juan Barrientos of Slaton, Texas, was killed by shell fire near Valpiano on February 27.
57 A type of turnip.

very good and we had some of those ourselves last night! All making a great impression on Mother and a welcome variety to carrots! The goats weren't as enthusiastic as I'd hoped, so maybe we'll eat more of them ourselves. They love the mangels[58] best of all! But anyhow I feel as though we'd contributed a good deal in the vegetable line, plus our canned beans and tomatoes and of course the fruit which we've eaten right along, but still haven't finished!

Did I tell you how Alec is going to build a root cellar out of the old cement manure pit? With double walls, sawdust filled like our pump house and a low roof, then banked up about 2' all the way around. He is a wonderful worker and you would 100 percent approve of the way he works. He isn't satisfied unless a job is well done and not just knocked together any old way. He could do so much for us—our barn and the red shed, and he'd do it right. I'd give anything if we could borrow him for a couple of months! I know you'd like him too. He listens and discusses and is open to suggestions, and if something turns out wrong like the sieve he made me for the drain in the barn, he's willing to try again! He likes to visualize a thing first and then start in. He's really all I've dreamt of in a repairman! And I can't help but think how he and you could fix up our place in no time. When he starts a thing he goes right at it until it's done and done right. We've been so used to poor old Julius who'd start something and stop and start something else and say you can't do it that way etc. etc. This place looks like you must look after a shower and shave and clean clothes when you come out of the lines! It's a pleasure to watch him and see things really get done! Just this morning I was talking to him about the hinges—three broken sets on the board that covers the gutter behind the stalls. When I came back this afternoon he'd put on the other ones he'd found around and removed the broken pieces!

This morning when I was nursing Betsy at 6 or rather 6:30, I heard great moves in Mary's room. When I took Betsy back I found Mary had made her bed and done it very nicely! Betsy now sleeps in the crib in with Mary and they both love it! The girl's dormitory, and so far it's working beautifully. They don't bother each other at all. Mary just adores that baby. I wish you could see them together, and Betsy just grins from ear to ear and wrinkles up her nose when she sees Mary! It's too cunning, honestly.

I have a large and unpleasant sty on my right eye and it bothers me some because I can't open my eye wide and I'm conscious of always seeing it. I hope it will go away soon! One of the two little lambs of Arthurs' died. It's lying out in the field, and I feel like a murderer, almost, because I didn't tell

---

58 A beet variety.

Arthur they were there in the cold and wet. I think it died of exposure last night. They both looked healthy standing up yesterday afternoon and I feel so guilty honestly, but I thought, of course, he'd look for them knowing they were due soon, but I guess he didn't. He has no man to help him, but there are three or four females around. Someone might have taken an interest, I think.

This morning was the first time "Mitzi" whinnied at me when I came in the barn! "Judy" always makes a terrible noise, but this was the first time "Mitzi "said, "good morning!" She is so full of personality, you will love her! I really think "Judy" is beautiful and I've about decided I can't bear sell to her! You will love her too. She's so strong looking and well-built and very intelligent. Just what we want when we get home again! I think she'll get over her nipping. She doesn't do it as much now as she did, and really when I think of it she's pretty gentle if I can lead her up and back to that pasture no matter how cold the weather. She's not yet two and of course, she feels lively. When I stop and realize all that, I think she's very good not to try harder at times to jump around don't you?

Mary said last night she dreamt that you and I and your mother and father and my mother and father were all over at the barn and starting to walk back when a gust of wind came along and blew her away right through my legs! That's all she remembers! When I told her you were in Italy—this was a long time ago but I forgot to tell you—and then explained more or less what Italy was and how Alec was an Italian and that's why he talked so funny, he really talks very broken English, she looked quite worried and thought you would come home talking like that! So we wouldn't be able to understand you! But I quieted those fears! Barbara Lawrence says that her husband, who is a Major, and with the A. M. G.,[59] I think, is in Florence! His name is Major James Lawrence, but I guess with the caste system you probably couldn't talk to him if you ever did see him. But he is just as nice as he can be and I know you'd like him a lot. He's just as nice as Barbara. She wrote me today and is expecting her 5th child in two weeks. I will quote you what she wrote about it because I think it proves how nice she is. She says, "Well, I hope that 2 weeks from yesterday or today I'll have another son or daughter to write you about. It always seems incredible. The whole process, just beforehand, don't you think? And it's just as exciting and wonderful a thing as before one's first, I find, which is hard to explain." That's just the way I feel and somehow I have a special feeling

---

59 Allied Military Government occupation forces.

for other people who do too and who say so the way she does! Tonight at the children's supper Mary asked, "How do German's hold their spoons?" So I said, since they did everything wrong, I guessed they even held their spoons wrong. Mary thought for a moment and said, "I guess they really know how but just don't do it." Which about sums things up in every way, I'll say. Sydney says, he's going to have to hold his like the Germans until you come home and show him the right way, and Frank too. You showed Mary and she's never forgotten that fact, and so impressed it on the others that I'm afraid there's no hope here for me to show them. They are determined you alone can show them correctly!

Today has been more typical of March again. Rain, sleet, snow, wind, everything—a heavy snow in New Haven we are told by Betty who is there now and supposed to come home tonight, but has called once for permission to stay, which was not granted, yet. But I guess it must be if she calls again. We went to Guilford this afternoon and I did a little Easter shopping for our egg hunt! Also I looked at baby carriages. Betsy needs a new one. But they are so expensive. However I will have to get one and it's just a question of which one, the $18.95 or $29.95. I think the latter probably is the best, but then we'll just have to have another baby to use it for too! I love you. I must write Grandma about the fruit she sent me.

I love you an awful lot,
Mary

☙

March 23

Dear Mary,

I got letters from mother and father and Dick today, the latter V-mail written Feb. 27th, but though I got four yesterday I wish there had been another from you. Your mail and the family's often come on different days; they must come different ways. Your letters mean so much more than anyone else's that when I don't get one, I'm very disappointed no matter how many others I get. I feel much more let down on days when I don't get a letter than I do on days where there isn't any mail at all.

Absolutely nothing of interest has happened today. I've shaved and had a shower and combed my hair and arranged my mustache in an artistic fashion and that's the extent of my activities. I feel very respectable but rather futile. I got a *Life* and *Peterborough Transcript* yesterday and two more *Life*s today which have kept me busy. I'm now writing in a second floor room, which is very pleasant because one wall and part of the roof has been blown off and it is beautifully warm and sunny. It's about the only house in the village with any roof at all. I love you an awful lot, I feel as if I'd been torn in half. I'm awfully lucky that you can describe the children and what they do so well. I almost feel as if I'd been with them after reading one of your letters. But it's terrible not to really be there. With so little to distract me here right now, I think of home more than ever. In peacetime with a civilian's freedom, this would be a very pleasant place to stay, but now about all I can appreciate is the view, which is wonderful, but somehow seems to emphasize my lack of freedom. Last night I ate a box of your mother's sardines and went to sleep licking my lips and sucking the ends of my mustache.

I just happened to think today that a way to describe moving up when the enemy is firing artillery at you, is that it is exactly like playing musical chairs; you feel just the same way, each foxhole or shell hole or depression being a chair, you hesitate by each one and then quickly move to the next. I think when I was little I got more excited playing 'Going to Jerusalem'[60] as we called it, than I did playing it this new way. That's probably because I'm better at it now. I think I will try and bring home some sculpture tools if I ever get to a place where I can get them and I suppose there are lots of them. I'm afraid I'd have to start a war against the Germans to get any marble as I believe they occupy that part of the country, but, who knows, perhaps someday they'll get tired and go home, if they live that long. I notice they die very young; it must be an unhealthy race. I love you and think this whole thing is making me stupider and stupider, I've got only half a brain on this side of the ocean. I mean only half of what I had, if that was whole. I just noticed that I stepped on the first page of this letter. I don't suppose a footprint on a letter has quite the appeal of the other sorts of imprints they use on them nowadays.

I love you. I wish I could kiss you goodnight.
Sydney

March 23

Dear Sydney,

Well the war isn't over yet and this was "Monty's" [61] deadline, set not by his wife as I thought, but his Ma! Today's papers say that your friend Kesselring

---
60 A game similar to musical chairs.
61 Field Marshall Bernard Montgomery.

replaced von Rundstedt. Now I wonder who is in charge in Italy and what events will follow. Before I even read the headlines I scan the papers for news from your front. That's where the war is being fought from my prejudiced point of view!

The sty on my eye is much better! It broke today and now the tide will ebb, I think and hope! It doesn't hurt but I keep wanting to rub the thing away that's been hanging in front of my eyeball!

This morning Sydney was so cunning, honestly. At breakfast he pulled a stubborn fit, wouldn't bring his own chair to the table and he began to bellow. When I saw it was approaching deadlock I took him up to his room to get control of himself. When I went back about ten minutes later he was sitting on the floor reading. I looked at him and hugged him. He laughed and then threw his arms around me and then immediately said "I'm sorry." I hadn't said a word! So then I explained to him how now you were away he was the man of the house and how I knew you wanted him to do for me all the things you'd do if you were home and that impressed him and he came down wreathed in smiles and carried up his chair! But the readiness with which he said "I'm sorry" certainly got me! He is so cunning and affectionate even if he hasn't learned his prayers after nearly two years! Frank has learned "Now I lay me . . ." just by hearing me struggle with Sydney through the door! I have a premonition he won't be winning any scholarships for himself and probably won't even be a good student, but I hope Frank won't outsmart him too much! There are no flies on that one! He's as smart as a button. Sydney is definitely a dreamer. I think he's just like you in every way!

Well this morning Alec and I and the children took our car and spread three loads of well-rotted manure from the bottom of the pile on my goat garden! Last year it had nothing on it now I'm wondering if I won't just get it harrowed not plowed. We'll be away most of the summer, but I think I'll plant a few things anyhow. Mangels and kale and such, and get them well started before we leave. I am really quite optimistic about "Mocha" now. But my fingers are still crossed! It may be she'll freshen in May after all, but if not I do hope the billy has succeeded in making it August. I'm thinking I may keep a billy kid, if Gay has one, as I've no doubt she will and then use him next winter. By December he'll be 9 months old and I could use him for the one I breed late. Well there's time to decide that still.

This afternoon we hitched up "Mitzi" and went for a drive. The red maples back in the country are all in flower but not down here yet and I saw one man discing his field with a team. That field, I was interested to see, had not been plowed first. Another man is to plow and harrow here next week, then Alec will plant peas. Mr. Scranton's are already in! Alec has asked for a $10 raise, to Mother's extreme consternation; he's now getting $150 a month and wants $160. I'm sorry because he's so nice and as Mother says he's only been here 3 months, or a little more, and already asked for one raise. Where will he stop? We are all very upset honestly! Julius only got $100 as it was, so this is no laughing matter!

I don't know what's the matter with Betsy tonight she won't go to sleep and is fussing a little but Mary apparently isn't bothered! We had to have supper early as Mother went to a hearing in the town hall so I had to milk "Becky" afterwards. They thought I'd forgotten them from the sounds. I saw Arthur as we drove up the lane and I told him about the little dead lamb. He did not know so I feel more than ever like a murderer. He said he didn't see the one until yesterday morning. So they spent that first night out in the rain and cold. I thought, of course, he knew or I would have telephoned after I got home. Another time I won't think, I'll follow my first impulse. "Gay" hasn't long left to go now and I feel so nervous! I took her to Moose Hill, Oct. 24th and left her there about a week. I foolishly never asked which day he thought she was bred, but the 24th itself would place her, March 22nd. So it's any time now! I do hope all will go well and I guess it will. She has a nice bag. I haven't yet clipped any hair around her hind legs, but think I will tomorrow if it doesn't make her nervous!

All is quiet now. Betsy must have gone to sleep finally! I've decided to get the larger baby carriage and I think it will come tomorrow. I hope so because she's about to get out of the old Rolls Royce! We had a letter from Stu today at long last. He said he thought he might be in Honolulu when this letter arrived. I should have written him Dick's address. Your Father asked me to and vice versa, but didn't. But I think your mother thinks Dick has gone on. They had had no letter when I last called for quite a while. Anyhow she said they'd captured a Jap! Found him floating on a bit of wreckage. He said first he didn't want to be rescued but pointed at his head and said "boom, boom." Then he thought better of it and climbed up. They found a grenade in his belt either for them or so his ancestors would give him E for effort, as Stu said! Stu thinks he may get leave from Honolulu. He has the division commander aboard which keeps him up no end! I love you an awful, awful lot. I feel optimistic about the war's end and maybe another spring will find us in each other's arms where we belong.

I love you,
Mary

P. S. The radio just said Patton's men have crossed the Rhine!

March 24

Dear Sydney,

I love you. I got another letter from you today, from Florence, I guess, and the children got their cards! They were in 7th Heaven, honestly! I just wish you could have seen them when Mrs. Werner said, "Well, you ought all to be very happy today!" We knew what that meant! Letters from you!

I'd forgotten how they hitched the horses but now you reminded me, I do remember. I never saw any cow-powered vehicles! I suppose it's true most of the real treasures are stored away but there must be a lot of "second-rate stuff" that's worth looking at, after seeing nothing artistic for so many months! I wish you could get hold of some more chisels—wouldn't it be wonderful! I love you. I wish it were you [and] me seeing it together.

Well today's big event was Frank falling out of the pony cart! Frankly, I was terrified, but all is well. We drove up to Anna's via the underpass. Foolishly I never thought of "Mitzi" hesitating at that, but hesitate she did, and from a goodly trot, she jammed on all four brakes and Frank, sitting in front by me to be safe, pitched forward and out! He landed slung across the axle between the wheel and the body of the cart. "Mitzi" stopped, and I jumped to her head. Then I was able to extricate him, but honestly it makes me sick to think of all the "might have beens"! His arm or leg in the spokes, if he'd fallen thru and the wheel had gone over any part of him, I just can't think. All I can do is thank God and believe more firmly than ever in His goodness! He must be close to us as I know He is to you! Frank's only affects were a few grease spots, not even a scratch. It is nothing short of a miracle! He cried bloody murder until I had him in my arms, then all he wanted was to be put back in the cart again.

In lieu of a rabbit's foot I'm sending you his tail or a piece of it, I guess! For luck! The children just hope it's not the Easter Bunny's—so do I. This morning "Mitzi" was lying down staked out and so we tried sneaking up on her á la "Wenny"![62] It worked, we didn't sit on her but we were able to pat her, much to their amusement. This morning I trimmed up some of "Gay's" hair, sort of like the shave I get in the hospital, only I did it ahead so as not make her too nervous. She gets up on the milking stand and doesn't mind my massaging her bag. So I don't think she'll be too hard to milk. She didn't like the haircut, however! Last night just before I went to bed I took out a few of your letters and they made me so sad. You write wonderful letters. The nicest love letters anyone ever got, I know! It seemed strange your wondering where you were headed for when you left Devens[63] that time and all, and to think now where it's all landed you. It's short of terrifying. I can't exactly express what I mean, but it makes one realize how much better it is that we cannot foresee the future. "We lives in hopes, if we dies in despair" as the saying goes.[64] This last year has seemed endless to me and as far as I'm concerned futile. I have proved nothing, accomplished northing, given nothing. However, I feel I have gained in a spiritual way—a strength and courage from you and God. I wish I could feel I gave you the same fortitude you give me, but in all honesty to myself and you, I cannot! My letters have been selfish, telling you all my trials, worrying you with things other people would have left unsaid; so that sometimes I feel unworthy of your love. You are a wonderful person; there's nothing small or selfish about you (though I've accused you of it when you sat in the bathroom over long!), but that was my selfishness, not yours. I wanted you to do something else then. Anyhow you are a much bigger, finer person that I am. I know my faults and frailties, but they seem to be all tied up with my pride and I cannot seem to humble myself the way I should. But what's the good of my telling you all this. You know me as well as I do. I haven't a secret in this world from you and I never want to have one. Why is it I could never talk to Mother or Daddy as I can to you? I sometime think it's natural. There is only one person in the world for everybody and it's not likely to be a parent! It's more likely, I think, to be the person one is in love with and that's true love as I know it. There are a variety of loves. Love of one's parents, love of one's children, love for animals and growing things, love of inanimate things. But the only truly comprehensive love is in the giving of oneself body, soul and mind to the one person whom God made to receive it. And in my case that person is you and could never be anyone else.

    This all probably sounds pretty foolish to you and I am inept at express-

---

62 "Wenny" was a horse owned by my father's family that he and my mother rode.
63 Fort Devens in Middlesex County, Massachusetts, is where my father went when inducted in March 1944.
64 "Tell Joseph, he may live in hope, Ma'am," said the major, "or he'll die in despair." (From Charles Dickens' *Dombey and Son*.)

ing myself, but I guess you know what I mean, don't you? And whenever I say I love you it means all that and a lot more! There aren't idle words and I know the same is true when you say to me "I love you." So I look for those words in every letter! They are always there and I hope they always will be. There is something in the physical act of giving oneself to the one one loves that seems to fuse, not only our bodies but everything else and while the physical act must naturally come to an end, the rest of it never does. It's more complex than any chemical compound; it can never again be broken down to separate elements, and so it goes getting more and more complete until now I feel a part of you, and with you away it's as though half of me had been taken away. But someday, Sydney, you'll come home and we'll be a whole person again, won't we? This is Saturday so more goes into this letter tomorrow. Anyhow you know how much I love you. So goodnight and God Bless you. I kissed where you had sealed the envelope today and then I felt silly and thought probably the old censor had licked it, not you!

Mary

March 25

Dear Mary,

I'm back on the front or rather almost on it. There are other troops between us and the enemy, and this is about as safe a place as could be found. But it sounds well to call it the front and so everybody does. The news has been pretty exciting the last few days and everybody has been making rash prophecies that it will all be over in two weeks and that sort of thing. I wish they could be right, but I'm afraid it'll be a little longer.

I'm beginning to think that my mustache is sapping my vitality, I don't feel so strong lately, I'm getting rather decrepit, and the thing I can think of to blame it on is my mustache. I've been asking my friends and they all agree that—they've been noticing all the time—as my mustache grows longer the rest of me seems to be shrinking and deteriorating. Well, just for the sake of science I think I'll keep it a little longer and see what happens. I can always cut it off in a hurry if the situation seems to be getting really dangerous. Last night I got your letter written on March 14th with the enclosed from Mary and the mysterious ski track picture. I certainly don't see any sense in worrying about Sydney's diction. I think it would be ridiculous and probably harmful to do any more than occasionally correct his pronunciation yourself, and you certainly should never let him worry about it. I started writing late and I'll make it a short letter hoping that there's still time for it to get censored and go today, but there probably isn't. Jane wrote and asked me about the gardens of Italian villas. Where are the villas? I haven't seen a sign of one. Again I'm living in a house with the upper crust while most of the rest are in foxholes. The runners have to be close to the people running things all the time and that has some advantages. But while everyone else is getting sunburnt, I'm practically getting a nightclub tan. I spend a good deal of time as phone orderly, and of course I never can hear anything at all, so it's an easy job.

I love you.
Sydney

Sunday March 25

Dear Sydney,

Another beautiful day has gone and I saw the first crocus here on this place, an orange one that miraculously escaped the hurricane—the only one, I guess! This morning you'll never guess what happened! I was there with Betsy early, as we'd decided to go for a ride in the pony cart because we couldn't this afternoon, as Betty would be off and Mother out to lunch. Well Sydney was with me. He left Mary and Frank at the barn pretending to spread manure with the pony cart. They'd spanked him or something; anyhow he and I set out to find them and hitch up "Mitzi." We got to the barn, no Mary, no Frank; I called, no answer. So we went to the beach; it was a beautiful warm day. Hot sun and no wind early, typical of this time year—a wind comes up during the middle of the day—well anyhow there they were and Mary had been in swimming! "All the way in," she said, "it wasn't a bit cold!" She takes the prize! She went in, in November and now again in March! Anyhow it stung the scratches on her legs. She was yelling, but I guess she's a chip off your old block for toughness!

We finally got away and drove to Madison, saw Willie and Barbara, and came home down Stony Lane. It was lots of fun. On arrival here, I found Mrs. Gunther[65] had invited herself to lunch with me. Mother went to the Strode-Jacksons' to meet some English commander, this afternoon. While I was alone here nursing Betsy, the doorbell rang and I got Mary to go down and heard her say, "What's your name, what do you want?" Then she came

---

65 A neighbor. Her husband John was noted for his *Inside . . .* books.

up and told me he was Mr. Pellegrini and something about the billy goat. She thought it might have been the man who came out when we were talking to the old one and seeing his kids the other day. But she said she wasn't sure because he had on a grey suit and not the black jacket he'd had on that day. Well I asked her to tell him I'd be down in about 10 minutes. So finally I got there and it was the brother of the black jacket, another son and resembling him enough to confuse Mary a little. Well the old man was in the car and he wanted me to buy the billy! He said he'd sold all his goats this morning and didn't want him anymore! So I said I didn't want him but how much did he want? He said $7.00 and I should have a billy with 4 nannies. So I tried to explain I didn't want him! He said "$5. So, I said, I was planning to give him $3.00 for letting me use him and I'd do that and return the billy. After a lot of Italian sparring, the young man said I could have him for $3.00. I said I didn't want him! I'd give him $3.00 anyhow and he could sell him to someone else, all to no avail! So now I have that billy and I don't know what to do. I have no room for him after "Gay's" kids come. I think I'll have to sell him. I don't know what to do. I want a billy, I think. It would be much simpler for me, but I want a good one. This one's mother is a 3-qt. goat so he's not too bad, but I don't know what to do honestly. I think if "Gay" has a son and I'm sure she will, I'll try and sell this one and raise that one because I've found out that the billy at Moose Hill is a good one, not just a scrub. Well I'll just have to wait and see and in the meantime consult Alec about a place for this one to live. Oh dear, life is so complicated at times! I can't take more than four goats to Peterborough. But, Alec can take care of anything I leave here, in the non-milking line, of course!

 Mary had a dream last night that someone came and got her and took her up in an airplane. I tried to get her reactions, but she was confused. Apparently, they flew upside down and she got her head wet! She is so funny telling me her dreams. They sound silly to her when she tells me about them! This afternoon we saddled "Mitzi" and Frank rode her and Mary pushed Betsy to the point where we left her while we walked over to Mrs. Gunther's. I took off "Mitzi's" saddle and she rolled in the sand. Then I tied her to a ring in the wall and we went in for a minute to look at some alterations she wants to make. "Mopsa" and the children all streamed in. I said as "Mopsa" went in, "Oh, you don't want her in here, do you?" Mrs. Gunther said, not of sottovoce, "I don't want any of them, but what can you do?" I pretended not to hear, because I don't know if I was meant to or not or what. She's also so nice to the children giving them cookies etc. and asking them over, alone even at times, so I couldn't quite fathom it! Well, we came out soon! Then she started talking about some league of arts she and Alice Keating Cheney[66] are getting up here in Madison and said something about wanting me to teach sculpture! But she never got any further! I said I was going home this summer, and she said this might be an inducement to stay here. Anyhow, even though she came back to supper, I never got any more than that out of her. Nothing is going to stop me from going home anyhow. I know that!

I love you an awful, awful lot. I hope you'll get a chance eventually to read all this long letter. Do I write too often and too much, or have you any suggestions? After all, though it's my selfishness that makes me want to write you all the time. I should consider you! If you're like me, you'll want every letter I can write, but maybe there's a limit. Anyhow, there's no limit to how much I love you.

I love you,
Mary

P. S. Have you ever received Mary's tooth?

༕

March 26

Dear Mary,

I guess yesterday's letter didn't go till today and this one tomorrow. I didn't get any letters today. There's really nothing more that happened to write about. I think I've just about exhausted the subject of my mustache. I guess if I can't think of any more jokes about it I'll have to shave it off, though I'm getting rather fond of the thing and will be sorry to see it go. I'm still saving that can of sardines for an appropriate occasion.

This not being able to talk to you about what I please is terrible. All the things that first come to mind can't be said, even though they are all trivial seeming anyway. We're in a place that's very picturesque, as usual, and as usual I wish I could go all over the place looking at it all with the civilian freedom of peacetime. I think at least I'm getting a more intimate idea of the small places in the hills than I would have as an ordinary tourist. We live in the first really small house that I've seen, upstairs, with an Italian family downstairs. The middle-aged lady of the house seems to think nothing of having to go half a mile down the very steep rocky hillside to get water. Our

---

66 Alice Keating Cheney (1894–1981) and her husband Horace Bushnell Cheney Jr. (1899–1930) established the Jitney Players, a traveling troupe of actors, in 1923.

place in Peterborough is ideal farming compared to this, even if this weren't tilted up at about 50 degrees, and still they seem to be able to raise everything they need and must be able to sell something once in awhile too. It makes me awfully anxious to work in the garden at home, or at least to plan working in it. I picture it now with all kinds of fruit trees scattered around growing out of cracks in the rocks, always in blossom and laden with fruit at the same time, and grapevines and terraced plots in odd corners producing in similar fashion. In the evening the goats would all come and quietly stand in line by the kitchen door waiting to be milked. I find that to keep myself happy I have to keep thinking about home instead of here. I do anyway all the time without trying, of course. By now I've got to know everybody pretty well and there's plenty of talking and laughing and good companionship and all that sort of stuff, but while it certainly helps it doesn't really do very much good. I just plain wish to God all the time that I was home and had been all along. I take a certain pride in my present situation, but it seems pretty small stuff in comparison.

I love you.
Sydney

P. S. It is claimed that the lady of the house, while engaged in conversation with some of our men, made a lightening dive towards a dark corner and grabbed a rat by the tail, which she promptly skinned and ate. Roll out that grain of salt.

March 27

Dear Sydney,

Well, "Gay's" kids arrived today! A lovely little girl named "Little Mary" and a little white boy, named "Little Sydney!" Just before I took the children into lunch, I went over and looked at "Gay," who was tied out by the corner where the Garvins' drive goes up. I took her some water and some apples. She looked fine and I felt her bag, which was heavy—and she had milk in it, so I knew it would be within 24 hours, probably. Then, we came back and after their lunch, while I was putting them to bed, I again looked out the window and saw Gay apparently all right.

About 20 minutes later, the Monarch laundry man drove up and said, "You know, you've got two little goats over there." Betty and Alec and I all went right over, and sure enough there they were, all wet and slimy and "Gay" looking so pleased! The brown one is the biggest and she was on her feet and mostly dry. "Little Sydney" was still very wet and all sprawled out. I put him where "Gay" could see him and she licked him a bit but was much more interested in her daughter. Anyhow, he is fine! "Mopsa" came over and licked them too. And "Gay" didn't mind a bit! She's not a bit like old "Becky" and her young! The children were thrilled naturally and hugged them and patted them, and Mary even carried "Little Mary" in when I brought them in later this afternoon. They are still with her tonight, and tomorrow I will separate them, so I can milk "Gay" out, then pan feed them. We fixed up the little pen by the barn where the doghouse is, remember? Where Stu thought we could keep "Mopsa" when we came down before Sydney was born. I'll put them in there and then tie "Gay" where she can lick them, but they can't nurse her.

I saw Mrs. Fullerton in Guilford this afternoon, the person we got "Sweetie" from and she said the system worked beautifully for her. Let the mother feel she's with them but not let them nurse her. So, I'm going to try it and see. Then I can keep a check on "Gay's" milk and all. I feel so excited, honestly. I've gotten a bag of calf-starters' and am going to follow the Purina[67] schedule for kid raising based on conserving milk. I think I will keep both of them for a while, anyhow. The children won't hear of selling them! I'm going to advertise the billy next Sunday and then raise this one for next fall. I think Betty and Alec are only too anxious to take care of them this summer while we're in Peterborough. "Gay" is so good. Not a bit wild and so proud and pleased and so friendly.

And then I got a letter from you this morning! So, it's been a wonderful day! I'm awfully sorry about Mary's tooth.[68] It was her idea, but I shouldn't have sent it, and it made me cry, just a little when I read your letter, because I gathered it wasn't such a good idea. I won't do anything like that again. But Mary thought you would be so excited over her first baby tooth to come out! The one thing she wanted was to send it to you, but I should just have pretended to send it, I guess. I'm awfully sorry, Sydney.

Is the Cass [69] boy nice? I hope he is. Janet Shattuck wants me to ask you if you know a boy in the 10th by the name of Frank Smith from New Haven. She goes to a dancing class with his fiancée.

I should think being a runner might be a little more interesting. I hope it is, and by that I mean you can hear a little more of what is going on. Also,

---

67 A food used to transition newborns from milk to dry-feeding.
68 He had written: "I got the letter with Mary's tooth; it gave me rather an odd feeling."
69 The Cass family lived in Peterborough. Harley Cass entered the army from Beverly, Massachusetts.

I hope and pray it is just a wee bit safer and softer, as you say! I hope the opportunity will soon come to get to Rome and see John.[70] That really would be wonderful, wouldn't it?

Don't worry about Frank and "Mitzi," because he doesn't really hang around her hind legs. He usually does get her tail to brush, but that's all, and I have impressed on them all about horse's heels! They've all seen "Judy" in action, so they know. I may have exaggerated to you just to prove how gentle "Mitzi" is! They all have a healthy respect, really, for all parts of her! After all, she may be small, but she looks plenty big to them! So, don't worry. I don't understand these things better than you at all! But do believe me, with you away, I am much more cautious than normal, because, after all, the full responsibility is mine and I feel it very deeply. I'm taking care of them for you.

Your letter was written on March 16th and not postmarked until the 21st. Almost as long as it takes after that for me to receive it. They have come very quickly recently. That's six days ago and the last one was five days in transit.

Sonnichsen[71] has not been liberated yet. He is in a camp near Brandenburg,[72] which Mrs. Werner says is, I think, quite close to Berlin, maybe a little north. I'm not sure, but at last reports the Russians hadn't got there yet.

I love you an awful lot. I feel awfully badly about the tooth, but I know you will forgive me and it won't happen again. I promise! Charlotte just called up. She'd been to New York last Saturday with Bill to a Coast Guard party. Captains and Commodores up from Washington, and she said she'd never seen such a drunken brawl. Some of them arriving from Washington at noon were so drunk they had to have doctors revive them, so they could get to the party. It sounds pretty awful to me. She said they got to bed at *7:30 a.m.!* Charlotte is still feeling terrible—didn't even want to talk about New York at first. I think it is outrageous and it makes me sick, honestly.

Well Betty has stepped out tonight with another boyfriend—not the baby's father. I told her I was going to tell the M. P. that she's double-crossing him! Anyhow, this other one came up and got her in his car, and the moon is one night off full. I wonder! Mother practically made her take Allan[73] as a chaperone. Poor baby! I should think he would discourage an amorous swain. But Mother doesn't want Betty to start that!

Your mother just called up and told me what you'd written her! I wish I'd seen the barber combing your mustache. It sounds as though it is quite a soup

---

70 John Farlow, his college classmate.
71 Warren Sonnichsen was from Madison, Connecticut, (my mother did not know him) and had been in basic training with my father. He was taken prisoner during the Battle of the Bulge.
72 Brandenburg is a German state that surrounds, but does not include, Berlin. Wikipedia lists eight German prisoner-of-war camps that existed in Brandenburg.
73 Betty's baby.

strainer by now. Now it is awful late, and I have to get up extra early tomorrow to take Mother to the 7:00 a.m. train for New York. I love you an awful lot. I feel awful lonely too, all the time. I just can't get used to it at all and never will.

The news sounds good tonight! I hope it keeps on getting better and better! I see by the papers that there are five divisions in Italy, as against 27 Nazi divisions—I don't like the sound of that at all. Your mother says Mary's dog "Monday" has produced 7 little bastards. A gentleman from Wellesley is the villain. I must watch "Mopsa," as she should be interesting soon.

I love you; I'm just as hungry for letters as you are. Yours are such wonderful ones, honestly! Joe says all the Italian you really need is "God damn." That's all he's picked up so far.

I love you,
Mary

March 28

Dear Sydney,

We were all glad to hear from Mary last night that she had two letters from you written on the tenth or twelfth and the fourteenth, which had us only a week behind on news from you. What a time are having. We were so sorry to learn today that Charles Pfeiffer had been killed. Mrs. Pfeiffer told the family Sunday that they had not heard since the end of February.

Katherine had a nice party yesterday. She and Mary told Tony Parker's boy, quite proudly when I brought Dick down, that here was their little brother! He only said sadly, yes, we have one too!

I feel as if Mary would never learn to ride her bicycle. It is partly my laziness and partly my timidity. Joseph learned right off because his teacher thought he knew how and just put him on and started him down our drive and let go! But I don't dare let Mary go! I guess when Joseph comes home for his vacation I'll get him to teach Mary. He will not be so careful!

Dick has not written for quite a while now, so we think he may have gone off somewhere.

All well at home. Father is very busy with the Civic League. We had quite a record temperature on the 20th, officially 79. It melted the ice on the pond almost in one day. Do you remember the day you and Zeke[74] and Scotty and I sailed down the pond[75] on a float that had drifted to out from the college, the day the ice went out? It was March 10th, 1924, and that

---

74 Zeke Cheever, a cousin.
75 Lake Waban in Wellesley.

night I went to a party at Jane Prouty's. Did you know she had adopted a baby girl? She has one boy of her own.

Love,
Mary [76]

March 29

Dear Mary,

I got six letters yesterday, three from you and two from mother and one from Mary Fyffe. The news gets more exciting every minute and we feel just about ready to swarm down into the field and tear up the goal posts. Your last letter took just eight days. They must come quicker than they go. As they are almost all air mail anyway, I wonder if they don't just send the others, sometimes, along with them.

I went up Belvedere at night and, as most of the time I was lying on my belly and not moving at all, it took most of the night. That was when I was the most scared and when I fell asleep and dreamt I was home with you. I was in a bunch of bushes which 'Bush Crackle' Edwards[77] would have found most suitable. They were the noisiest ones I've ever seen. They were all tangled up in my rifle and between my pack and my back and pinning me to the ground by growing up through my armpits and between my legs. Meanwhile the enemy was shooting various things just over my head, including flares, which made it as bright as day making me feel most embarrassingly conspicuous. I saw no hope of moving in any direction and thought I'd have to stay there till the war was over. I still can't understand how I fell asleep, but when I woke up we moved on and soon came to some Germans who were busy surrendering. I stayed on top of the hill about a week and did nothing in particular. It was a fairly hot place for awhile, though, as the Germans seemed to think it belonged to them. The next attack was longer, a several days' affair with a similar week on the end of it.

Don't mail the letters in bunches, there'd be too-long waits in between. Unless it's too much trouble for you, every day is much better. I don't worry about the order; the news straightens itself out eventually. I don't like V-mail letters at all and nobody else seems to either. Some boys act insulted when they get one. I think Mr. Pope's daughter's name Marshall is the worst name for a girl I ever heard, and that whole outfit certainly doesn't appeal to me in the least.

---

76 This is my father's older sister Mary.
77 This could be a reference to Edward Hoar, a travel companion of Henry David Thoreau.

It looks like your prediction of April would be right. I hope you did get a chance to see Anna Mary. I hope you are getting more letters now. I've written almost every day lately. A governess cart ought to raise our social prestige; you can always say that the governess just fell out or got mislaid somewhere or was holding onto the hind leg of a pig and got dragged under a fence and got stuck, as once happened to our Swiss governess.

I hope Stu will let me look at his *Reader's Digest*s once in awhile after my subscription runs out. Everybody takes turns getting passes to Rome; so eventually I should get there, but it's very few at a time, and the way I figure it my turn comes last so it mightn't be for another six months. I wish I could go alone, but that's impossible. I'll always be with a big crowd of GIs until I get home. I suppose I might just possibly meet Joe sometime. He must be around Leghorn.

I love you an awful lot.
Sydney

March 31

Dear Mary,

It's still just the same as yesterday and before, I'm sitting around doing nothing. DeWick and some of the others have gone to take physical exams for OCS.[78] As I'm getting old and want to get home as quick as I can, and mainly as nobody suggested it when they made out the list, I didn't think I'd try. Theoretically anybody can try. But when such situations come up it always makes me privately wonder how I would do. I know I have really no reason to worry about being a private, but I'm afraid my pride is such that way inside I can't help being a little bit sensitive about it with all my friends and relatives in the service being officers. John Farlow is the only exception I know of, and he has the excuse of physical disability. However, I never had expected or planned to live a life where I had to order other people around. Today one or two people whose opinions I respect somewhat at least asked me why I didn't try, and very likely if they had asked me yesterday instead I would have tried to go.

I got a letter from you last night postmarked the 21st and a V-mail from Father written on the 19th. You say that Pat's letter was full of messages to me but you didn't say what they were. As for Mrs. Adams I'm afraid I'd forgotten all about writing her, for which there is no real excuse. At the

---

78 Officer's Candidate School.

time the package came writing wasn't too convenient, and afterwards I remembered I'd written her once, forgetting how long ago, and considered my duty performed. I guess when she wrote you she really thought she was glad I didn't think I had to write, but that unconsciously she was hurt that I didn't. I hope it doesn't discourage her from sending any more maple sugar if she ever gets any.

I remember thinking that "Wenny" got the way she is by being treated too much like a pet when she was little, but I don't see why that should do any harm if the horse is trained at the same time by someone who knows something, as you do, and who is master all the time. I suppose that would be one of the objections to waiting a year or so to train "Judy." It would be pretty hard not to let her get pretty independent in the meantime, and naturally she deserves and should have friendly attention all the time. I'm glad you think now that maybe you'll keep her, but I hope you don't if it is so much trouble that you shouldn't. I'm in no position to know. You probably think she should be driven first, but breaking her to the saddle I should think would be much easier if you haven't much help and I suppose that before too long she could be ridden very short distances occasionally without hurting her. Anyway you know much more than I do, but when people are talking about training people or animals or anything and stick out their chests, and talk about being master, and discipline and the rod, etc., I always think they sound a little silly as it seems to me that it has more effect on their own pride then on the trainee. There's a very great difference between teaching, which is what it should be, and having a contest to see who will be master. If it becomes nothing but that last, it seems to me that the larger and not necessarily more intelligent animal usually wins. As one sits reading by one's fire in one's easy chair etc., one thinks brain superior to brawn, but if once goes out and looks around a bit here and there he finds it a pretty good thing to have muscles and callouses well distributed instead of confined to the brain and hindquarters. Particularly now, when everyone has a theory but no one knows how to think.

Now for the day by day adventures of my mustache. People complain that it is not combed often enough, and all have different ideas about the most suitable style etc. Luckily it's still at the "retort courteous" stage; though there are a few rude people who claim to see cereal, old orange peels and such enmeshed therein. It's a big help in starting up a conversation. Then there are those who take it all very seriously, and that I can see would like to comment but dare not for fear of offending me.

I still can't speak any Italian at all, perhaps as I'm not such a good talker in any language, but I've got so I can read it a little and with the help of French and Latin can read most anything if I have plenty of time to figure it out, rather like a picture puzzle. The ones most interested in women are the ones learning it the fastest, so you should not be worried by my slowness.

I love you,
Sydney

April 1

Dear Sydney,

Here's the third conversation book.[79] Do you ever have a chance to try and talk Italian?

We are having an extraordinary and early spring. My purple azaleas in full blossom—grass on the lawn almost ready to cut. So hot that "George" wants to stay in the shade. We have let Mary's house for $200.00 a month. Isn't that fine?

No news still from Dick.[80] Your letter of the 19th came the day before yesterday. Radio news says we are landing on Okinawa. Do you suppose Dick is there? He and Joe[81] may be taking part. His last letter was long enough ago.

Uncle Frank and Aunt Louisa[82] were here this afternoon. We are going to Jane's if the little puppy is better. Mary's dog has had 7 puppies—father from South Natick—one week old. And one has had an abscess in the neck. Last night I did not think it would live, but today it is stronger. It almost starved. I fed it drop by drop.

Father is sound asleep. He has been working outdoors all afternoon.

Handkerchiefs are hard to get, even cotton. This is linen and absorbs water better. It seems wrong to send something so shabby, but it should be more useful than if new. Francis Sargent[83] has been sick in a hospital in Italy. I saw his mother yesterday in Dr. Lee's office. I was there for a check-up. I'm okay he said, but must not overdo again, so I'm continuing being lazy.

Lots of love, dear,
Mother

---

79 She is referring to a book of conversational Italian.
80 The invasion of Okinawa began on April 1. Dick, my father's brother—five years younger—landed on the second and was wounded a few weeks later on Okinawa, one of approximately 70,000 wounded over the roughly twelve weeks it took to conquer the island.
81 My father's brother-in-law, Joe Fyffe.
82 My grandmother's brother and sister.
83 Francis Sargent, a cousin of my father's and later governor of Massachusetts, 1969–1975, served in the 10th Mountain Division.

April 2

Dear Sydney,

I did get a letter from you today, this afternoon, when I went over to buy some cookies to send to you. I think God really must have been paying attention to my prayers in that shrapnel episode. It's a wonder to me it didn't get infected if you could not wash it for several days. I wonder if there will be a scar. I thanked GOD especially fervently for his protection.

    The papers haven't done much to satisfy my curiosity about you recently. They speak of patrol action, counter attacks, etc., but they don't say what you were doing. I'm glad you're the "upper-crust"[84] and live in a house, but how come? Your walkie-talkie[85] with Bob DeWick sounded like a lot of fun. I don't believe you bored him. If he really loves horses he'd be glad to listen to someone else talk about them too. At least I would! Tell him about "Judy" and see if you can get any suggestions from him. No, I didn't know how the drinking and foundering worked, or you can be sure I would have told you.

    I'm glad you get all the cigarettes and tobacco you want. I'd hate to have to send you any. Maybe you don't want cookies either, but I feel sure someone around will even if you don't. I have to tell a white lie and say they were requested. But it is not too bad because you did ask for candles and they are in the same box. I can just imagine the trail of papers and cans, but I am thankful you have the things that go inside them.

    Today's *Peterborough Transcript* said that Harley Cass had received a Bronze Medal for his "heroic activities." Carrying a radio strapped to his back, this on the point of physical exhaustion and maintaining the only form of communication with the rest of the bunch. Is he in your Company?[86] You spoke of seeing quite a lot of him. Were you in the same spot?

    I don't worry about the allotments and "Daddy's deductions!" The government gets enough as it is, so it doesn't bother me one little bit!

    I've got the picture of Clare[87] here for you. Maybe you can recognize the boy she's chatting with. It only says she's there, which is obvious, and that she's on the 5th Army front.

    The children certainly laughed over the picture of "Mitzi" under the umbrella drinking beer. I wish to God it would be this summer time when you come back. Somehow, I can't see how it will end. I don't know who is in a position to call it quits. It has all the earmarks of a terrific mess to me. I

---

84 As a runner for Company C to his platoon, he was housed with the officers and NCOs of Company C.
85 These two-way radio transceivers were developed during World War II.
86 He was.
87 She is referring to Clare Boothe Luce. As a Congresswoman from Connecticut, she toured battlefields in Europe and Asia, including the Apennines where the 10th Mountain Division was fighting.

hope Clare didn't look too "young and pretty and attractive" to you. I am relieved you didn't grab her and go to earth with her. Maybe it was lack of a suitable earth? Or perhaps the competition!

I'm glad you liked the pictures and especially the one of Mary's "family." Betsy really doesn't look exactly like any of them. Her hair is tight little curls now, about the color of spun gold and her eyes are as blue as Frank's—not grey or green. She really is beautiful! I hope you'll have her pictures by now. But she's grown up quite a lot since they were taken. She can almost sit up by herself in her carriage and she can turn around on her tummy and wriggle backwards, but so far hasn't gotten the idea of going ahead. All the children just love her.

Mary is still captivated by the little kids—she and Sydney. They are teaching them to lead. They drink beautifully and are so fat and furry. One of the hens has been laying her eggs in "Mitzi's" manger. The first time, "Mitzi" was in her stall, too, and it was funny to watch. However, before I could get there, after the hen had left, "Mitzi" had broken the egg! Now we have one sick hen; she's been ailing for two days and looked pretty weak this afternoon. However, I moved her and gave her food and water. The latter she drank and seemed to revive a bit, so I'll see in the morning. She's one of the ones Miss Perry gave us, with sore feet.

The forsythia is in bloom here now—daffodils, myrtle, dutchman's breeches and large buds on all the trees. The grass is very, very green, like a penny postage stamp, and around the barn there are hundreds of little maple seeds sprouting. It's awfully pretty. Cattails on the willows and luscious looking skunk cabbages. Daddy saw the first turtle two days ago. This morning Alec and I cut the billy's feet. We did the others before. Yesterday "Gay" gave a quarter of a quart less than three quarts and the same today. I have great hopes for her.

Last night I dreamt about you and it wasn't a nice dream. I was very odd—the way I sometimes am in dreams about Mother—and I hate myself for it. Then, a little later, I dreamt a strange thing—that I went in and gave some blood to the Red Cross. I've never done that, and I can't imagine why I should have dreamt it, unless it's a reminder that I should. But, honestly, I feel as though I needed all I have for the struggle I've got to just keep going. However, the dream preys on me a little. I hope I have a nice dream about you tonight because I love you such an awful lot. I can't imagine why I dream I'm mean to you. It hurts me when I wake up.

"Judy" is fine, and I really think she's pretty good. She doesn't wear a halter anymore. I lead her back and forth with a bridle. In the morning, she sticks her head over the stall door and I put the bridle on without even going into the stall, and, in the evening, when I go for her, it's the same. Now, I think that's pretty good! Sometimes she's just like the children. She comes up and starts to open her mouth and then whirls her head away. With no halter to grab, I have to wait. If she does it twice then I say, "Alright, 'Judy,' I'm going to leave you here," and I start to walk off. She then gets chastened and she whinnies. It's as though she understands just what I said. I don't want to sell her! But I do want you to come home and help me train her. I'm so afraid of making a mess of it. Do you remember how "George" went out at our first Easter egg hunt and found all the cookies? I don't know what made me think of it. The other day "Mopsa" was barking wildly. I said to Frank, "Look out and see what she's barking at." He came back in a few minutes and said she's barking at a green dog. (It was really black.) Mother has already seen the woodchuck! And just after Alec had planted the peas, beets and carrots. I am really going to fence my garden in this year, if I have to buy all new wire!

I love you. I must stop. Charlotte called and talked for 15 minutes just now, and I was mad! She said she likes the Shattucks such an awful lot and really sounded as though she meant it.

I love you.

P. S. Lucy White[88] was due to have a baby yesterday, Jane told me.

༄

April 4

Dear Mary,

Now I haven't written you for several days when I really could have done so several times but always thought a more quiet opportunity was about to present itself. I've got several letters, the last postmarked the 24th, and packages from you and mother. Mother's had some candles and tea which was a good idea and I've just about eaten your package all up. It took about six weeks coming but the journey had no effect on the contents which tasted mighty good. I like the feeling of holding something in my hand that you have held.

I'm now in a place further south, miles away from even the sound of artillery. I suppose it is supposed to be restful, but I have to get up much earlier in the morning than I did at the front, and I still have to take my turn at the

---

88 My father's cousin.

telephone for two hours during the night, and the countryside is a little less attractive. I have my duffle bag which is where all my extra things have been packed since I've been here, including my fountain pen, and all my pictures except the portrait photographs of the children which I had with me. So I've been enjoying myself looking at all of them and thinking an awful lot about home and therefore less and less of where I am now. I'm glad you bought the good baby carriage instead of thinking you should economize. I haven't got much to write about, but God, Mary, how much I wish I were home with you. I should think men away from their wives for several years would go crazy, and perhaps they do. I didn't get any letter yesterday.

Mail comes everyday but mine doesn't usually come more than every other day at most. I've been showing my pictures of "Judy" to one of the other runners named Carlton from Florida.[89] He's a tiny little mouse-like fellow that I hardly ever noticed, till one day I found that one of his former occupations was riding wild bulls in rodeos as well as bucking horses. He comes from an enormous farm that seems to be run on a western scale, and in like manner, with annual roundups and such. He has a remarkable sense of humor and knows quite a bit about horses and liked "Judy."

I can hardly wait till the new pictures come. I expect it every day.

I love you.
Sydney

April 5

Dear Mary,

I got a letter today postmarked the 29th, the one where you talk about teaching "Gay's" kids to drink. I haven't got the one describing their arrival, sex, number, etc. But I guess it'll come in a day or so. I guess Mary is really just the right age now to enjoy them most. I wish I could see her with them. I should think the 2 would belong to the billy goat's owner, or did you mean that anyway. I'm very curious about how much milk "Gay" will give. She should be better than any of the others, shouldn't she?

Now every kind of fruit tree is in blossom and leaves are coming out on everything but oaks and chestnuts. It's really beautiful, and it's terrible to think some people lie dying under the apple blossoms. There are big fat dandelions that remind me of home, and loads of violets that remind me of when I picked them for you after Mary was born. I keep thinking how nice

---

89 PFC Thomas F. Carlton of Perry, Florida.

it would be to pick you some flowers, as if I could bring them to you.

The grass was cropped by sheep last year, but it's getting longer now as there are very few of domestic animals around, the Germans only left them behind where we didn't give them time to take them. Whenever I've been in a house where the Germans have lived I've seen that they made the Italians, who had nowhere to go, live in the rooms exposed to our shell fire, while they lived safely in the downstairs rooms away from us. The Italians had to work for them and wait on them all the time, and the Germans tried to take all their food and they destroyed people's seeds when they left.

The paper I read is the *Stars and Stripes* which I guess you know about. It hardly ever misses a day getting to us, though usually a day old and is often delivered under shell fire and such. My friend Bob DeWick, the horse-loving insurance man with endurance from Maine, has applied for OCS. So I may not see him much more. Harley Cass was awarded a bronze star, and I foolishly don't know what he did; though I must have been close by at the time. More mail came in and I have to bring the 2nd platoon theirs. I just got your letter of the 27th telling about the kids. I'm glad the girl was the brown one.

I can't imagine what I said about Mary's tooth that made you think you shouldn't have sent it. I've been trying and trying to think and I don't remember anything. I must have left out a word or written something backwards or something. Or else it just plain didn't read the way I meant it. I'm awfully sorry. I should think that way of arranging the kids near "Gay" would be very good. I don't know the boy Janet asked about. I guess my letters travel part of the way before they get postmarked. I love you an awful lot, I wish I could tell you that in some better way. I don't know how much longer I can stand being away from you. There was a dachshund sniffing around out C. P.[90] today, we were very suspicious. Somebody told him to go away in Italian and he didn't seem to understand very well. It looked as if he had to stop and translate to himself. However, he really was a nice little dog. I haven't got my duffle bag anymore; so my pictures are packed away and gone again. I wish I could have them all with me all the time. Do you remember the one of Mary and "Beelzebub" and Sydney in the background? I always liked it especially.

I love you.
Sydney

---

90 Command Post.

April 6

Dear Sydney,

It's late now, just on to eleven, so I can't write a very long letter, I'm afraid. Your family have just left. I think they all had a good time, anyhow Daddy and I did! We had a good supper for them—native flounder, parsnips, tomatoes and Peterborough deep-dish blueberry pie! Betsy was awake when they got here—fussing with her cold, so they came right up and saw her. Betsy was too cunning. She smiled at them and acted coy—peeking around and really behaving beautifully. I was very proud of her! And, even after they left, she didn't seem to mind.

Mary is awake and sort of whining and says her ear hurts. Dr. Salinger said it looked a little inflamed and might bother her. I was hoping it wouldn't. I gave her a warm water bottle and an aspirin, and I think she'll go off to sleep now, in a few minutes—I hope so.

This afternoon, when we got back from a pony cart ride, "Mopsa," who had been shut up, was so overjoyed to see us that when I called her, she jumped right up! I think we'll have a circus yet! I wish you'd seen her!

I got your letter today from the front. How I wish you weren't there! And, now I see today's paper speaks of a new attack launched yesterday.[91] I pray for you every hour of the day and as long as I am awake at night!

I hope you weren't too serious about your mustache. Because, if so, you better chop it off and soon! I wish I could see you in it—or at least a picture of you! Can't you get one taken? My mental imagination pictures something fascinating—a coffee filter and long enough to comb. It sounds wonderful. I hope it doesn't preoccupy you too much, however, as I am fearful of its ever-changing prowess—couldn't you clip it, just a little?

I have to go to bed now. I promise a decent letter tomorrow. I love you such an awful lot.
　　　　　　　　　　　　　　　　　　　　　　　　　　　　Mary

P. S. The enclosed is a "calendar" Mary made for you.[92]

April 7

Dear Sydney,

Let me start right off by saying this is a news-less letter. But in spite of that we all do want you to know how all of us here in Wellesley think of you

---

91　She is referring to what was known as the Spring Offensive, which actually commenced on the fourth of April. This was the march toward to the Po River Valley and the Po River, which was crossed on the April 23.
92　Like so much, the calendar, sadly, did not survive the war.

often and are so anxious to hear your news. It filters through to us via Mary, then to your mother, and then on to us. Wellesley jogs along as usual, not so many of us here. Nothing looks too tidy or fixed up which really doesn't matter at all, especially now that spring is here.

Please don't think I am crazy when you read the three little clippings I enclose—but they are editorials from the *N.Y. Times* and I thought you might glance at them and realize that some people are still sane in this crazy world. I know I always enjoy reading them and would like to know the man who writes them.

Your family here are lively; your mother, I think, looks and seems better than she did years ago. She went in to see Dr. Rice a little while ago and he told her she was better and the result was she spent the afternoon digging wild grass out of the asparagus bed!!! They are down at your sister Jane's now and were looking forward so much to seeing Mary and your children.

At the moment we have had a nice time with Walter Jr. and Willard; both have time together on furlough. Willard is off again for more training and Walter goes in a few days to a new ship but it was certainly wonderful for their family to have them both home together. Caroline and Frank[93] are still in California, and are flourishing as far as I know. She is pretty busy, I imagine, with their children, no available help at all and no telephone. But every now and then she goes to the corner store and sits with the baby in her lap till she gets a call through and reports to her family that all is well.

Best love to you, take as good care of yourself as you can.

Affectionately,
Aunt Louisa[94]

April 7

Dear Mary,

I got the package today with the candles and all the other things. Tonight I couldn't resist being extravagant and lighting four candles all at once, making a most cheerful and luxurious light. One candle had an accident and melted down on one side and is almost gone already.

I got a letter from Uncle Frank with a picture of mother's and father's heads just appearing above the drifts in front of the house. I'm now living in a stone shed in back of a barn. The loft is full of chestnuts and the floor is

---
93 My father's cousin Caroline, married to Frank Blake.
94 My father's aunt, Louisa Hunnewell.

covered with straw. The windows have just narrow slits between sand bags. I'm living on C-rations again, which means cold food out of cans and not much variety. It always makes me feel as if I'd swallowed a brick.

As usual it is a beautiful spot, but this time I don't seem to be in such an appreciative mood. I love you an awful lot, and, though it always seems as if this being separated was as bad as possible, it still keeps getting worse and worse till I wonder how much longer I can stand it.

There isn't much news I can write about. I don't know much anyway. I guess this is another unsatisfactory letter or rather note, I'm afraid. I'm due quite a few letters from you now, and when I get them maybe I'll feel better. It's a dark and stormy night like the traditional opening of a story. It would be wonderfully cozy at home.

I love you.
Sydney

April 7

Dear Sydney,

Tonight is bad too! It's late again because Mrs. Gunther had supper with us, but I, being very rude, sat down at the desk right after supper. However, I'm so sleepy I'll have to go to bed pretty soon. The children have all felt pretty miserable today. At least Mary seems almost alright and Frank not so bad, but Sydney and Betsy have felt pretty grumpy. Sydney wouldn't eat any supper, and since he's been to bed he's fussed twice. He has a splinter in his hand that bothers him, too. So, all in all, these last few days haven't been too happy. Added to which I'm more than usually worried about you again, ince the papers have spoken of a renewed attack by the 5th Army. No specific mention as yet of the 10th division. But still I worry. I wonder where you are tonight and pray God you are safe. In one of Clare Booth Luce's articles she gave a good description of the occupation of one of those villages by your outfit. It gave me a good picture, if gruesome. She said the natives referred to the 10th division as "the laughing boys." So that's another nickname, that and the timber wolves.

I didn't tell you much about yesterday's doings in my letter last night. There wasn't much; we went pony cart riding in the afternoon and Mary took her lunch along that consisted of an Easter egg, pink, and a raw onion! First she ate the egg and then half the onion. The other half she gave to Frank when we got home and he ate it, in bed before going to sleep. I wish you'd smelt his room when I opened his door this morning.

I told you about "Mopsa" jumping onto "Mitzi's" back didn't I? The kids are growing enormous. I'm beginning to wonder about "Sydney kid." He has two distinct teats right by his balls. I must examine the black billy, because, as you know from the goat journal, hermaphrodites are common in goats and I don't know how it would appear; do you? If I plan to keep this kid as a prospective father, I want a whole man! But maybe as in dogs, that is natural. What is your humble opinion?

We took the kids for a walk over to Mrs. Gunther's house this afternoon. They were so cunning and just bounded about like puppies! Today "Gay" gave 3 quarts and 8 ozs. Her bag is shaped just like the ones they always picture, a great round protrudence seen from behind. Her teats are getting bigger. I can now get two fingers and thumb on them and can even use two hands when her bag isn't stretched too much. The children play with the kids all day long and they even pretend to breed them!

This morning we went "chopping," as Frank says, in Madison. In the First National, while I was buying stuff, they hung around the door. Sydney spied an old lady and went up to her with his most engaging smile and said "Hello Great Granny." She was old enough to be pleased, of course. Frank was pleased with the suggestion [and] incidentally took up the chorus. Sydney goes up and speaks to everyone, especially girls and is so pleased with himself! But that really did assure me! Now, every time I say anything in the form of a reprimand, Frank looks up at me and says "you nut"—not very respectful, you must admit, but I have a hard time keeping my face straight!

Tomorrow is Sunday. Daddy leaves for Canada at 7:00 p.m. so I'll have the whole evening to myself to really devote to writing you! So this letter should be fairly decent, I hope. I feel so dissatisfied these days when I can't really write properly to you. Now, I fear I'll have to stop and be polite for a few minutes and then go to bed!

I do hope your mother and father can come over in the daytime. So they can see our livestock and the children. I'm going to ask them Monday. They have to see "Mitzi" and I want them to see "Judy" too. I think she is very handsome! I love you such a lot. I wish I knew where and how you are tonight. The uncertainty is terrible and I just cannot foresee how it will end. If the Krauts retire to the mountains in Bavaria, it seems to me it will be one hell of a day to get them out. I hope they can be so cut to pieces they can't all congregate there. I love you an awful lot. I must go to bed now before I drop asleep!

Sunday night 8:30—

Well I've just finished a hectic evening! Daddy had to take the 8:10 bus to New Haven en route to Montreal. So we had a cocktail and roast beef on the kitchen table first at 7:30 and now I've just finished a hasty washing up so I can write you before I go to bed. I'm always about to go to bed when I'm writing you. It must sound very tantalizing to you, but I promise it's no fun! It's not the same as it used to be—there's a certain "je ne sais quoi" lacking, only in this case it's a "je sais quoi" that's lacking. I love you. I really hoped that today, April 8th would see the end of organized hostility. Anyhow but not so far! Another one of my premonitions gone wrong! Well, I still insist it will happen this month! I love you an awful, awful lot!

The children, especially Sydney, have been miserable all day with this cold. Sydney and Betsy and Frank, and I have passed the crisis and I hope Sydney will be better tomorrow. Mary is practically cured. But poor Sydney felt so badly this afternoon but refused to stay in bed. It's mostly a cough and eating is bad! He has lost his appetite and I can't blame him, he gags so. All he had was a glass of milk and a dish of applesauce for supper. But I'm not worried about them really, it's just uncomfortable, but I'm so sorry that they should have their first cold of the winter just when your family are here. Your mother and father came over on the 3 o'clock bus this afternoon as Jane didn't want to bring her children over, naturally and also Sally was there. They liked them all. Your mother says, "Mitzi" is about the size of "Mousie." So now you know about how big she is. They think "Judy's" very big. I think she's well developed and I'm proud of her. Also, with her winter coat shedding out, she begins to look very glossy. So I'm sure she's healthy. Only her feet badly need trimming.

I wish the blacksmith would come! I wrote him a week ago. Your father says he has a pony harness he resurrected from the Walter Hunnewell place with hope he can get hold of it. Also, a pony snaffle! I'm now listening to Gabriel Heatter.[95] He sort of irritates me but, I have to hear some news. The news sounds good, if not decisive, but I wish I could get news of you! Maybe there'll be a letter tomorrow. I hope so. I love you such an awful lot. My hair is all sticky on one side; as I milk "Gay" she sucks my hair continuously. Now she's gotten so I can milk her with two hands. Not at first in the

---

95 Gabriel Heatter was a World War II radio commentator, whose sign-on was "There's good news tonight!" His contemporary, Alexander Woollcott, composed the couplet: "Disaster has no cheerier greeter/than gleeful, gloating Gabriel Heatter!"

morning, but after I'm started, and at noon and in the evening. I've just been talking to Mary Clark[96] and she said she had just talked to a one-star general recently returned to the Island[97] who had seen members of the 10th Mountain Div. in Italy and he said the men in the ranks (that's you!) were vastly superior to the commissioned officers he'd seen in other branches! Never had he seen such a fine bunch! Love you an awful lot. I wish I could hug you all over right now and feel the sense of security again that comes over me when I'm in your arms.

I love you,
Mary

April 8

Dear Mary,

Nothing of note has happened since I last wrote you yesterday. It's been kind of cold the last couple of days, and, as there is nothing at all to do except when my turn comes on the telephone, I've been spending a good deal of my time just plain sleeping and reading the funny papers of which there seems to be a large supply. I can't walk around much here and it's just too cold to sit. I'm hoping I'll get a letter tonight. I got a package from mother with nothing in it at all, it looked as if it had been through a lot, but was tied up so nothing could fall out. Someone must have retied it without noticing that the contents were missing. This is much colder than it's been for a long time and I guess it won't last long. I keep thinking how wonderful it would be if it were you and I alone visiting these places and no war going on anywhere. There are such lovely spots for walking and such soft green grass for lying on.

Well, I got three letters last night and now it's the morning of the ninth. I read them while I was telephone guard from 2 to 4 a.m. I felt too sleepy and uncomfortable to write anything then. (I think the description of Easter day was wonderful). How did the Lages and Shattucks finally get along at the end? I'd admire Frank's practical nature, knowing just where to find eggs. Do you think he's old enough to have learned a little about keeping himself from falling out of the buggy? I wish it had a little higher sides but then I suppose it could be worse because it would be hard to get out of quickly. I don't believe Mary gets her love of cold water from me unless she's already grown up enough to go in it for a stunt, or old enough to realize that, though it feels unpleasant at the time, it can feel good afterwards. Every time you

---

96 My mother's sister-in-law, married to her brother Henry Hotchkiss.
97 Martha's Vineyard.

quote her in a letter now I'm surprised at how grown up she sounds. She must have changed a lot. It's too bad your father's picture doesn't show me with my mustache; I'm sure that would make up for all the differences in rank. That would show the lieutenant commander, even Henry!

I hope you aren't stuck with that billy goat, but maybe you can make a profit with him. The papers are warning that troops in Europe will have to go directly to the East when it ends here, instead of going home on the way. That's an awful thought, but I suppose it should be that way. They'd have a pretty hard time gathering them all up again after they'd let them all scatter to their homes. The idea, once home having finished a war, of going off to another one would be more than most people could stand. Besides the other way would obviously get it all finished much quicker and be only fair to those troops already out there. Maybe they'll keep us busy in Italy so long that we'll never get there. But it seems to me this outfit would be one of the obvious ones to send. I love you, and the idea is just plain horrible to me.

Note: I am planning to wash my hands and face today. I hope Dick Shattuck doesn't get drafted, it would seem so pointless to draft someone not perfectly well and with a family at this late date. I'm not sure what village that it is you speak of, because there were so many all over the hills and just a short distance apart, but it may be one taken while we were still in reserve, or at least behind where we watched a village being taken from a distance, and, where since then we've spent a great deal of time, where I complained of being too inactive. I'm glad the children liked the Easter cards, I thought they were pretty good ones and felt very curious as to what they would think of them. You mustn't keep on thinking your letters are selfish talking about your trials and that sort of thing, because they certainly are not. I like them just the way they are, telling how you feel and everything; I'd hate to have you change them. You're the only person in the world that I can really talk to, too. I know that you know what I mean when I say I love you and it makes me very glad. The pictures of you and Betsy haven't come yet and I don't see why not, but I'm not worried yet that anything has happened to them. I suppose if the garden isn't plowed it should be planted so as to crowd out the weeds. I'm glad the skeptics didn't keep you from trying it that way. Tell Joe I'll be glad to accept a ride home anytime, though of course a little red tape or something might interfere if the offer should come right now.

Today is a beautiful day and I'm sitting in the sun with no shirt and enjoying myself. The sun really does seem very bright in this country. There still isn't any news to tell, even if there weren't any censor. The mess behind this barn is terrific, it's rather as if I was sunning myself behind the goat stalls in Peterborough with a great many tin cans and papers added. I love you, I feel as if I'd been away a lifetime, I try not to think about how long it has been or will be. Just things that happened here a month or two ago seem like ages ago now. Time is bad enough now without it having to go and slow itself up so much. I keep thinking of how we used to lie in the sun together.

I love you.
Sydney

P. S. I'm afraid this is too short to hardly be a letter at all. I love you. I wish somebody would invent a way of communicating by distance that was less stilted than worn out words.

April 9

Dear Sydney,

The way I feel tonight, if it wasn't for you, I wouldn't care if I lived or died. I seem to have succumbed to the children's cold and it's one of those awful ones—sore throat, achy head and my legs feel like a dish cloth. However, if I can get to bed early I guess I'll feel better tomorrow. But now I know how the children felt! Sydney had one degree of temperature this morning, so I finally succeeded in keeping him in bed all day and he seems much better tonight—happy and cheerful and he ate all his lunch alone in his room and two eggs and a glass of milk (no, no dessert, that's right). Anyhow, I think he'll feel better tomorrow. Mary is mostly recovered and Frank is better. But Betsy has been pretty miserable today too. Her appetite especially, she wouldn't nurse at 10 a.m. nor at 6 p.m. However I got a little cereal into her both times. I will probably feel uncomfortable tomorrow morning but I am about to start weaning her soon anyhow. So I'll see how it goes. Betty and Allan both seem to have it too, and your Mother, I'm afraid. I feel as though we'd been responsible for that without a doubt, as it affected her first with loss of voice which is how Mary started. My voice is ok and I don't cough yet, anyhow. But my throat is sore and I certainly feel plain miserable. I want you more than ever when I feel bad.

Mother is in Tennessee.[98] I hope she escaped it all. She wrote me Friday and was fine then, so she may be all right. I have to write her

---

98 She grew up on a tobacco farm, "Wessyngton," north of Nashville.

tonight because I haven't since she left, so this will be short, as I can't do much writing I'm afraid! This afternoon I felt better than at lunch time so I planted 150 ft. of parsnips in my goat garden. It seemed like quite an effort but I'm thankful it's done! The Wilsons[99] are eager to share a garden this summer at the Dodge House. I will get it plowed and plant it! They have also offered to open the house for me and I think I'll let them! Leland will take down the sleep porch boards and put up the screens. So if they really meant it, it would help me a lot! I just wish it would happen that you'd get home during the summer and be able to come up there! Wouldn't it be wonderful?

But I must not let myself get too enthusiastic! I love you such a lot. It will be awful lonely without you, but I'll feel I'm doing something towards preserving our home! I have in the back of my mind the idea of making a few repairs if I can get anyone to do it, like whitening the ceilings or a few things to make it more cheerful. Probably won't be able to, but I may! I do hope the stove pipe and chimney are safe. Maybe I can get that repaired somehow, though we might have to move out. Still we'd have to be nearby in order to appraise the work. Well I'll see. Have you any ideas or suggestions?

This evening while the kids were drinking, I curried "Mitzi" and I must have taken out enough hair to stuff a sofa pillow! She's getting lighter as her old hair falls out. "Judy" really looks beautiful. I wonder if your mother will make any comments when she writes you? Mother has been riding a filly Uncle George raised who is not quite three, and she says she's as gentle as a kitten and not afraid of anything, threshing machines, tractors anything. She's half Tennessee walking horse and mother says perfectly beautiful. I think it's remarkable that mother hasn't been on a horse in three years since she was last there and then gets on a 2-year old colt and rides it, don't you? From both angles. I wouldn't think July could carry Mother's weight around yet. Though, she is a year younger. But Daddy rode this same one last year and [said] that she's gentle even for Mother. I am so glad Mother had a chance to go to Wessyngton, because after all it's her old home full of childhood memories and, though she was transplanted early, she is more, shall we say "simpatico" with that way of life. So that's one thing my being here has enabled her to do. That and numerous trips to New York this winter, to the theatre, etc.

Your father just called up to see how little Sydney is. He called this

---

99 Leland Wilson and his wife were caretakers of my father's parents' summer place in Peterborough, New Hampshire. The two properties (ours and theirs), while a mile and a half apart, were contiguous.

morning too, and to invite me to supper tomorrow. I said that depended on how I felt tomorrow. I couldn't go out to supper feeling like the spineless fish I am now. Well, I'm optimistic! I love you. I wish you were here—four sick children and me too is slightly depressing, especially plus Betty and Allan. Daddy has invited one of his English collaborationists for the weekend! A Mr. Ascoli, who he knew in years gone by and who is now over here on some British commission to do with rubber, I guess.[100] I am nervous, as Daddy wants everything just so and no Mother! I love you an awful lot and most stop now and write Mother. But you come first always! I love you. No mention of your Division for several days. I wonder.

I love you,
Mary

P. S. Gabriel Heatter just said they've launched the largest aerial assault in Italy since Cassino,[101] and he implies it's the beginning of something! I'm worried sick, but God will take care of you. I know he will!

༒

April 10

Dear Mary,

Last night I got your letter postmarked March 30th and a letter from Mary Fyffe. I got yours postmarked April 2nd first. I hope "Gay" gives more than three quarts. She should to live up to her family reputation.

Well, the radio said today that the 8th Army started to attack last night, I could hear their artillery faintly in the distance. It was just one continuous roar. I'm not ashamed to admit that the more of the fighting that other people do instead of me the better I like it. I'm still in the same place doing nothing but sleep or sit in the sun or at the telephone. Last night I was on the phone from 4 to 6 a.m., and when I finished it was sunrise almost, with a great many birds singing, a beautiful morning; so peaceful and quiet, and yet in the distance I could hear a terrific artillery barrage going on and see flashes. And now I have some idea what that sort of thing is like, and it made a strange contrast with so spring-like a spring morning. But all that the birds were thinking about was that it was spring. I guess this is the worst time of year of all to be separated. I hope you really will have arranged it so that it won't be too much work for you in Peterborough. It seems like a pretty

---

100 Frank D. Ascoli (1883–1958) was director of rubber for the British Ministry of Supply during the war.
101 The Battle of Monte Cassino, north of Naples, was fought between January and May 1944.

lonely place. Would Anna Mary be staying there at night? I love you an awful lot, I don't want you to be working too hard, but I want you to do what you want most.

I love you,
Sydney

April 11

Dear Sydney,

Well, if it isn't one thing, it's another! Tonight, I was early through everything, to have a nice long evening to write you. I got back from the barn before 7 and found Frank crying. He said his ear hurt. He'd mentioned it earlier this afternoon but then seemed to forget. Yesterday Jean's mother sent me the name of some wonderful ear drops the doctor had given her for Jean's little girl, and she said they relieved the pain considerably. So, instead of fooling around, I went straight to Madison on a special trip—gas or no gas—and got them. As soon as I put them in he was relieved and went to sleep instantly. Thank goodness I did, and not waited to 2 or 3 this morning. All that took time and I didn't finish supper until 8.

Well, I have a good hour anyhow, but must go to bed early as it was nearly 12 last night and getting up at 6 makes me short-tempered by the end of the day. I prevailed on Sydney to stay in bed this morning. He had a temperature of 101 last night but none this morning. It was precautionary, and I hope it worked. He had none this afternoon, so, as it was warm and sunny, he came out with us. He seems much better, coughs some but not much. I'm disappointed in Frank's ear, but I hope it will be okay tomorrow. Mary is quite recovered and Betsy much better. So, I think we're at last getting somewhere.

It's been easier for me not having Mother here, as she inclines to worry and would probably have stayed with Sydney more and made him more restless when alone. As it was, he was very, very good—no one to use his voice on and [he] took it for granted, when we were out, [that] he'd be alone, except for an occasional glimpse of Betty who, of course, was in the house, but not in his room. So, I'm really glad it's been this way; though I wish it hadn't been when your parents were here. I saw them this morning to say goodbye to. Mary and Frank and I went over. They left before noon. Your mother said she thought Mary was awfully pretty. I'm glad, because I think she is the prettiest little girl I have ever seen!

"Robert" has a sore foot. I can see nothing, but it hurts him to walk. "Little Mary" kid this evening was all bloated and seemed happy and loving. But she looked as though she'd just drunk a quart of milk and wanted no supper. They were in, and alone, all morning, as it was misting, and we were in Guilford.

The children play with them all the time—mostly Mary had them in the pony cart, giving them a ride. She pulls it around, with the two kids and Sydney and Frank. She certainly is strong! But I can't imagine what the kid got. Well, I think she'll be alright tomorrow—I hope so. Everything else is well. My own cold, much better.

Yesterday I never wrote you all the doings. The first thing that impressed me was "Mitzi." When I went to the barn at 6:30 I let the kids out to feed them. As their milk cooled off, "Little Sydney" was investigating. He discovered "Mitzi" and of course tried to suckle her. Before I quite realized what was happening, I heard the most peculiar cry and looked and there was poor "Mitzi" being bitten by him in the right place, and she was so good! Never even raised a foot, and he'd hurt her, so she squealed. I really think she's extraordinary. Of course, I grabbed him immediately. They have sharp little teeth now. I know!

I wish you'd seen Frank later on. I got a large wooden pail for "Mitzi" to drink out of—8 or 10 quarts, at least. It was down in the paddock. I asked him if he wanted to get it for me. He said yes and off he went. He tipped out the water that was in it and started the long trek home—the pail almost as big as he. I watched out the window now and then. It took him over ten minutes. He'd carry it a few feet, then put it down, rest, and start again. Finally, I heard a little voice: "Here it is, Mama." I looked out, and sure enough there he was! I never thought he'd really do it, but he is very determined. Then "Mopsa" got under the woodshed, after a skunk or rabbit or woodchuck, and got stuck! I had to tear up a lot of stuff and dig her out. She was flattened out on her side, just her nose out. She was very patient. Today I've heard of a registered Setter champion stock that I can breed her to, if and when we want to. I'm awfully tempted. So many people have asked for puppies already. But they would arrive, I think, just as we left for Peterborough. She's not in heat yet but should be soon. She's overdue, and I think it only takes two months, which would probably mean June. So, I may wait, but I'm tempted. What would you think?

The daffodils are at their height, and I saw the first violets in the field today, near the goat garden. I put a bag of lime up there this afternoon for the sake of the mangels, and I never saw the grass so green. Arthur's pastures are like something from an illustration. The lilac buds are bursting and the apple buds too. The magnolia trees in New Haven were out in all their glory last week and one here in Madison is opening. The dogwood is about to burst forth too and I saw a beautiful peach tree up by Anna's.

We do have such fun in the pony cart. So far, no governess cart[102] can I find. They are as rare as governesses! But I've answered an ad in last Sunday's paper, and I should hear tomorrow. Also, I saw advertised a one-horse trailer and have inquired about that. I think a two-horse one would be better, but a one-horse one would be great, wouldn't it? When we finally go home we could make two trips, if necessary and we could take "Mitzi" this summer.

Yesterday, I went to find out about a brood hen to hatch some ducklings, but no one was home. I want to go again tomorrow. We got four duck eggs today—four out of five ducks, not bad—and I do want to raise some. We've ordered 50 baby chicks for April 21. Alec says we can put them in his brooder with his that he's getting the same day. I think that's the simplest. Well, that about takes care of the livestock gossip.

Now to answer your letters. I wish you could say the things that just come to your mind. Those are the things I will never catch up on, I know, but you do write wonderful letters! And you are awful good to me the way you have been writing, and at least I can say anything that comes to my mind, so I don't think you'll feel I'm much of a stranger to you. I hope not. That's why I like to write every day. I have so much to say that I could never say it in letters further apart! And then there'd be things I couldn't say for lack of time and finger power, and then I never would refer to them as it is now. It's like covering a blackboard during the day and erasing it, item by item at night. So, there literally isn't a thing I do or think that I don't tell you in the evening, and I like it this way. I wish you could too, but I understand and, anyhow, your letters are wonderful. And, as I've said before, you are so reassuring, that you're still the same old you. You really give me the best description and account of what you can talk about that I've ever read—you and brother Joe are in a class by yourselves! I wonder if you realize how much more vivid your letters have gotten since the first. They always were good, but now they're really what I call exceptional writing. I love them, and I love you.

Is the house you spoke of made of stone, or what? How many are you

---

102 A governess cart is a small, two-wheeled, horse-drawn cart that would seat four on two, inward-facing benches, suitable to "be driven by a lady."

in it? You said it was really small. We'll have to grow all kinds of fruit trees, won't we and flowering shrubs. We'll have a lot of fun again, one of these days! I can more or less visualize the hillside farms, I think, because a Lilliputian variety of the same thing in the "hill towns."[103] How about pigs? I remember a lot of pigs, especially black and white ones.

All I think about is home, too, and how wonderful it will be! Perhaps you will pick up a smattering of "hep cat, jive talk"—if not Italian! The jazz echoing from the mountains must give a weird unreality to the whole setup. Americans have always been famous for their aptitude in bringing their environment with them, haven't they? Rather like a turtle, they're certainly ostentatious about it compared to the English, but I wonder if fundamentally and individually they aren't more adaptable. Of course, not in hordes such as you're in, but in isolated examples. I'm sorry for all the mess and dirt they bring and leave, but thankful for your sake that you have the cans and matches to scatter. Someday these things will return to the earth again and be forgotten. Perhaps the fields and hillsides will even benefit from extra fertilization! But it must be pretty unattractive now—gay festoons of toilet paper! I wish you could tear up the foul parts right now!

The radio and papers are full of the all-out 8th Army drive and the 5th Army drive for Spezia.[104] I wonder where you are in this now. Gabriel Heatter is just beginning. I may hear something. It makes me feel awfully good to think you fell asleep and dreamt about me when you were in such a predicament. Your account is very vivid and dramatic and makes me shudder for you and in the face of Almighty God who was always watching over you that night. I love you an awful, awful lot and my love may have been part of your armor. It must have been, or you wouldn't have dreamed about me just then. I feel fortified and reassured since you told me that.

Now you must have my letter that told you you're to get the *Reader's Digest* for two years. I found Stu was to have it three more anyhow. So you don't have to go to the Pacific just for that! I do hope you get to Rome eventually. You may have figured it wrong and get there sooner than you think. I hope so. Pat's messages, to the effect of how often she thinks of you, etc., etc., I haven't censored or deleted! I agree with you about horse training and people. I think it's always been a mistake to refer to "breaking" a horse—except for actually getting on "Judy" or driving her. She's completely accustomed to being harnessed, and now I lead her to and from the pasture—make her

---

103 My mother spent her first year out of school in Italy at a finishing school in Rome, during 1929–1930.
104 Spezia is a coastal city on the Ligurian Sea, west of where the 10th Mountain Division was.

walk with me. So, I think she's coming alright, I'm not so much afraid of its hurting her physically—to ride her—as I am of her doing something drastic the very first time, and me alone, perhaps caught off balance or something, or her rearing over something and me not able to chastise her sufficiently that very first time. Then it would be harder the next time. I think if it is done right the first time there'll be less and less trouble. I want someone at her head with the training bridle. I have to catch her if she starts to rear. She must realize that us humans can also exert brute force if necessary, I think, under the circumstances.

I hope you don't learn too much Italian. *Dio mio* (Oh, my God) and *Mama mia* (Oh, my Mother) are just two suggestions. I found Italian terribly easy to guess at, too. It is basically very simple to read and understand and eventually pronounce.

I love you,
Mary

April 11

Dear Mary,

Well, the pictures of you and Betsy finally came last night. I think she looks quite different from the other children, maybe a little like Frank. She looks like the same family alright, but it seems so queer to have my own child look like a stranger to me. I suppose I had unconsciously visualized her all the time as another little Mary, that being the only kind of daughter I was used to, and now I'm surprised to find that this is a whole new individual, a person that I don't even know, even if she has a vaguely familiar look. I hope to God that I will get a chance to know her before too long. Anyway I think the pictures are awfully good of both of you, but I've never seen a picture of you that perfectly satisfied me, maybe because they just make me wish all the more for the real thing.

I love you an awful lot. I'm still in the same place doing the same thing which is nothing and which leaves nothing to write about. I'm afraid my last few letters have been very unsatisfactory. I haven't got the rest of my pictures with me now and I can't wait till I get some of them to put in with these because I could always carry this with me. It's warm and sunny again today, like midsummer. I dreamt a lot about you last night in a delightfully improper way. I stayed in bed, only there isn't any bed, a long time this morning hoping I could go back to sleep and dream some more, but I couldn't. I love you an awful lot. I wish I could tell you how really much I love you.

Sydney

April 12

Dear Mary,

I'm sorry that I've finally had to resort to this kind of dehydrated letter, but the regular paper has momentarily run out. My news is still none at all and I haven't had a letter now for several days. I washed my face today and received a can of beer that I'm now preparing to drink. Otherwise I've done nothing but watch the grass grow, under my feet, too, it seems, and generally have been observing nature going ahead as usual, seemingly oblivious of armies and such. I love you.

It seems as if the spring must significantly be more beautiful than usual; though as I write this, a cold old breeze that March forgot almost ripped the paper out of my hands. There are all these stray dogs, which have joined up with us now with an allotment of sexes forming the usual triangle.

Perhaps I should only write to you when I've just washed; it is so much more proper and nicer that way. I don't feel ashamed. Now I've started on the beer and feel better already. I hope the children get a little more chance to learn how to swim before you go to Peterborough, it's too good an opportunity to pass up. Of course I don't suppose Betsy would get very far this summer, but Mary might. What about "Mitzi" when you go to Peterborough?

I love you.
Sydney

APRIL 14, 1945—MAY 2, 1945

Unbeknownst to the men of the 10th Mountain Division, the final push they were about to begin would last nineteen days, would involve very heavy casualties (including their costliest day, April 14), and would keep the men under almost constant shelling and machine gun fire as they made their way through ever-present minefields. It would be April 30 before my father could again write to my mother.

Operation Craftsman (the Spring Offensive) took the mountain troops out of the Apennines, across the Po Valley and River and into the southern Alps near Lake Garda, where the Germans would surrender on May 2, 1945.

The initial objective of the 1st Battalion was the small mountain village of Torri Jussi and Hill 903. The day was brutal. Lt. Colonel Ross Wilson, writing years later in his *History of the 1st Battalion of the 87th Mountain Infantry*, described the day: "The trail from the rear assembly area to the front was strewn with dead and dying men and mules . . . artillery bursts were falling like rain." For the division, the fourteenth of April would be the worst day of the war in terms of casualties. By the end of the day, 553 men of the 10th Division were dead, wounded, or listed as missing in action. Among the wounded in the 86th Regiment was a young replacement lieutenant, Robert Dole (future US senator and presidential candidate), and among the dead was Lt. William Callahan of the 85th Regiment, now memorialized by a tunnel connecting Boston proper to East Boston. Also killed that day was a nineteen-year-old private, John McGrath, from East Norwalk, Connecticut, the only member of the 10th Mountain Division to be awarded the Congressional Medal of Honor. It was also on that day that Felix Church, C Company's runner to the 2nd Squad of the 2nd Platoon, was badly wounded at the foot of Monte della Spe. My father took on his responsibilities.

These men saw horrors beyond imagination, which explains the reluctance of many to talk of their experiences. Because of my father's age he was, it seems, better able to handle the situation, at least emotionally, than many of his younger comrades. At any rate, in a letter dated March 10, he wrote, "I find that the kind of material they use for horror pictures in the Press doesn't affect me very much. I seem to have developed a strangely impersonal atti-

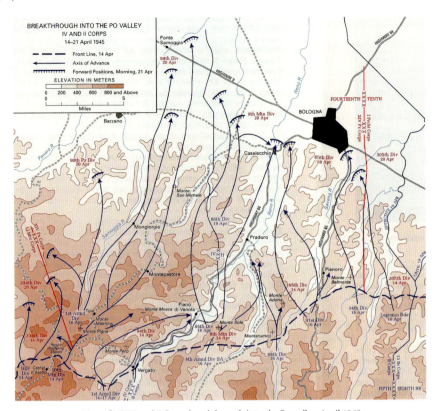

Map of US IV and II Corps breakthrough into the Po valley, April 1945

Men in Company F, 86th Mountain Regiment, 10th Mountain Division, advance after air and artillery preparation in big "push" on Bologna, Italy. 14 April 1945

tude. Ruined houses with the former occupants picking over the remains is the sight that affects me the most."

On April 20, the 10th Mountain Division descended into the Po Valley. The march across the valley was completed quickly. Villagers from liberated towns welcomed the victorious soldiers of the 10th, as the Germans beat a hasty retreat to the north side of the Po River. The 1st Battalion of the 87th Regiment became the first Allied unit to reach the south bank, which they did on the evening of the twenty-second. The next day, the 1st Battalion had the "honor" of being the first Allied unit to cross the Po. Companies A and B were the first to cross. C Company provided support. A few minutes before H-Hour, a German barrage opened on the American soldiers on the south bank. PFC Chester Vest was fatally shot, and so became the second member of my father's original squad to be killed. Bob DeWick told me the story of Vest's death. Bob said he had been standing next to Chester Vest and had just moved forward. When he turned around, he saw that Vest had been hit. Bob said, "Don't worry, a medic will be here soon." Vest replied, "I won't be needing a medic." He died a few minutes later.

Of the crossing itself, my father writes on April 30: "We made the bridgehead across the Po River which was without doubt the most exciting boat ride I ever took, and I hope I never take another like it." Resistance across the Po crumbled and the Germans fled toward the southern Alps. The 10th Mountain Division was moving rapidly at this time, once covering twenty-five miles in a single day. The final battles were in the region of Lake Garda, but death continued to stalk the 87th Regiment. On April 28 at Spiazzi, site of the 1st Battalion's final battle, Staff Sergeant Harold Creger of the 3rd Platoon, C Company, was killed, and ten men wounded when a mined house blew up. It was also at Spiazzi that my father's friend, Bob DeWick, earned his Bronze Star for heroism.

༄

The last two letters in this section were written during the two days prior to the end of the war in Italy. On May 1, word was received that Hitler was dead, and, given the general tone of these two letters, my father must have known that the war in Europe would soon be over. On May 2, 1945, the German army in Italy surrendered unconditionally to Allied forces. The conflict in the Far East, however, still loomed.

April 17

Dear Sydney,

According to the newspapers and the radio, things are getting very active on your front. I hope you may be able to write us after, some if really just a time, and let us know if you are all right.

The *Wellesley Townsman* has a quotation from the European edition of the March 16th issue of *Yank* with an account of the victory of March 10th.

I should like very much to subscribe to the *Yank* and am told that to get it I must have someone in the army subscribe to it for me. Will you please do so when you get a chance?

I notice there is a boy named Roger Iverson of Wellesley Hills in the 10th Mountain Division. Mary telephones from East River last evening to say she'd had two letters from you, dated April 6 and 7.

Your mother and I are back from a visit to Jane, during which I wrote you. Your mother got rather used up from the heat and the traveling. Dr. Lee told her the other day that her heart is all right again.

It is quite remarkable how quickly the country took President Roosevelt's death, and the change to a new president. Of course everybody is much interested to hear what Truman is going to be like, and the general impression is favorable—that he is a quiet, modest, and hard-working man. If anything a little to the "right of centre," who will cooperate with Congress—in other words just about what we want at this time.

We haven't heard from Dick yet and I hope to before long.

Much Love from Father

P. S. Your letter of Apl. 8 was brought into the room while I was finishing this

༄

April 20

Dear Sydney,

Just received your letter of Feb. 20th. So far I have observed many occasions when Mrs. Wilson's ingenuity would be of much aid. As for the news bureau, probably it was underneath as a blotter instead—although cannot recall the whole situation very vividly.

This is not so bad nor nothing what I thought it would be like. I am very well and even gaining weight—even though having had some exciting times since leaving Hawaii.

Not having heard from me for a month, father writes on April 3 all well, wondering why I haven't written. I thought the invasion here on April 1st had been pretty well publicized.[105] It is the largest force yet to operate in the Pacific. Now only 300 miles from Shanghai and 350 miles from Honshu Island.

All well. Good luck,
Dick

☙

Okinawa, Japan
Monday, April 23

Dear Sydney,

Things are going pretty much my way over here. All seems to be in good shape and the generals and admirals agree with me. Understand that you are doing very well too. The Army issues us shortwave radios; we have one in our tent to listen and laugh at the Japanese propaganda and to hear news from the United Sates as to how we are getting along. Reports are coming in all the time on the brilliant successes of the troops in Italy. As General MacArthur would say "Well Done"!

The Japs here on the Island must be getting pretty worried by now. I don't see how they can last much longer.

Take good care of things and get them cleared up over there. Germany can't last much longer.

Good Luck,
Dick

☙

April 26

Dear Sydney,

The news from Italy seems almost too good to be true! It will certainly be a lasting satisfaction to all of you to realize that you've made so large a contribution to winning the war against Germany.

We have had three letters from Dick within a week but all without date or place mentioned. So we have no idea where he may be.

Mary tells us that you recently had a chance to apply for officer's

---

105 His brother is writing from Okinawa where he, as an artillery officer, had landed on April 2.

training—there seems to me to be a doggone good reason for doing so, but of course the important one is that with your intelligence and education you could be more useful as an officer than as a private. The last *Science* newsletter says a survey shows, and is confirmed by company commanders on the basis of actual performance in the field, that "The worst combat officer is likely to have attended only high school or grammar school." The fact that you've been through the mill as a private would, I'm sure, help you with the men, as well as the fact that you don't like to give orders—neither do I! Being Americans and not Germans,[106] I think most of them would prefer your type as an officer.

A large gray cat has decided to come and live with us. The other night Mary[107] woke up with a strange sensation, and found it was the cat walking across her stomach! It had climbed up the vine on the front of the house, and got in through the window. The five dogs are frightened almost to death.

Your mother has been pretty miserable with a bad cold, her voice almost gone, and pretty steady headache for the last couple of weeks.

A V-mail letter has just been brought in from Dick.[108] It is dated April 11, and reads as follows: "I hope that everything is well, and that you haven't been wondering too much about what had happened since you last heard from me. I am now a long way from Hawaii, having already been in the Marshalls and Saipan and we are now fighting the Japs in Okinawa, having been unloaded from an L. S. M.[109] a while ago—You probably have read about the island here and are just as well informed, if not better, as to what is going on in this part of the world. We have quite a lot of news and they try to do their best in letting us know what is going on all the time—I have sent some other letters to you which were written quite a while ago—This may reach you just—the others were not numbered or dated. All well—will write some a long letter."

I notice that Dick has given a new post office number at the head of this letter—"A. P. O. 235" but go P. M., San Francisco, as before—and the 749th I. A. B. remains the same.

Much love from Father

ॐ

April 30

Dear Sydney,

My airmail paper is temporarily "fugit," so I must use this. But I guess I can do almost as well! Well, tonight we hear German resistance in Italy has

---

106 My father admired and loved his father, but had no interest in becoming an officer, principally because it would delay his return home.
107 This Mary refers to his daughter, my father's older sister.
108 My father's brother, five years younger.
109 Landing Ship Medium.

ceased. I hope it's true! This morning's paper at last said that the 10th division was north of Lake Garda, high in the Alps and the only ones meeting any resistance and that was "fairly strong." My heart sank at that and I prayed it was not an understatement. Now, I hope it is true all resistance has really ceased. I keep trying to figure out how soon I can dare to hope to hear from you! Possibly you can write soon now anyhow. If you couldn't before, I hope you were able to before this, but I can well understand if you couldn't. If I only knew you really were all right I'd rest easy tonight. Maybe I'll get a letter in another two weeks. I bet you are weary to put it mildly! Just traveling so fast, let alone fighting too! I wonder if you've fired your rifle yet, hope not. But after all that's why you have one I suppose.

Lowell Thomas,[110] the big quitter, never got up as far as the Alps, so he said. Mark[111] gave him the tip off as he was en route and he hurried back to Rome. We listened to him tonight hoping for first hand news, but no luck! I love you such an awful lot! It must be beautiful in the Alps! I wonder if it's cold and I wonder if you're cold and I wonder if you've used or needed skis. I can hardly wait to hear if it's true—no more shots are being fired on that front. I thank God with all my heart and I know that in His goodness He has spared you for us, but still I'd like it in your handwriting! The only day I had any real qualms about you was Sunday, April 22nd,[112] but I hope I was misinformed by our medium, the little spirit that floats between us!

Last night was the most beautiful moonrise I've seen in a long time. A blood red moon, a harvest moon, coming out of the water and leaving a bloody path in its wake. The water was still, and the reflection as in a mirror. It would have been wonderful lying out on the rocks with you, just looking at it and doing a few little private things too. My parsnips have begun to sprout. This really is an ideal spring here as well as where you were. It must be a good omen. This afternoon the children and I drove over to Clapboard Hill[113] to Alec's house to see our baby chicks and his. They are all fine. No casualties yet except that I'm told by those who know that our entire 50 are roosters! We won't starve for meat, but how about eggs? I could hardly tear the children away. They were simply fascinated. It was a most enthralling trip due to the weather. It threatened showers. Large black clouds and us in the pony cart but I said to Mary, "what would papa do?" She said, "he'd go, we won't get wet" so I said, "let's go" and we went and it only sprinkled once! So you were right. I always think in a situation what you'd do. I know it would be the more adventurous course. We follow it and it turns out right!

---

110 American broadcaster and traveler.
111 General Mark Clark, commander of the 5th Army.
112 That was the day before the Po River crossing.
113 The site of the Guilford water tower.

So you may be thousands of miles away, but still you influence all my important decisions and I have a nice comfortable feeling not having made the decision alone and I get more fun out of life!

The exhaust pipe on our car has parted company under the car, but Alex thinks he can fix it. You could if you were here, so I think he can. The trailer hasn't come yet. I expect it tomorrow or Wednesday and my hands have that clammy feeling until I get it. After all, $200 is a lot of money! But if it's really in good condition, why shouldn't we invest in it now? We couldn't get one at a moment's notice when you come home and maybe couldn't afford it as well either. Now I want a pony cart for Peterborough. There's a man in Pittsfield, N. H., that has several possibilities for $40. But I wish I could see them! I heard of them through the *Market Bulletin*. He's a horse dealer, advertises something every week. So I guess he's reputable, but I'm not sure. I do wish you were here to consult with about that!

"Little Sydney" kid loves to jump up on my back just the way "Beelzebub" used to do, and I find if I'm very careful I can gradually stand up with him on my shoulders! But children get down too and he jumps on them. But their backs are so small he just scrabbles around. Frank gets quite miffed when he slides off him! The kid loves to get up on "Mitzi," and so does "Mopsa." I just love to fool with the animals, just like Mary! One thing Frank said, before I forgot to tell you, that I think proves beautifully how he's never stymied. If he doesn't know a word he uses another. He had a piece of Mary's birthday cake and I saw it still on his plate so I asked him if he wasn't going to eat it. He said, "yes, I already ate the skin off it" (meaning the icing). He's never at a loss! I love you an awful, awful lot! Today was a big day in Betsy's small life. She stood up in her crib for the first time! I really think now she's standing up, it's time to wean her! I'm still nursing her three times a day but will cut it out now gradually, I think. She drinks out of a cup the fourth meal. So I think I've eliminated a bottle as well as a formula. She'll be nine mos. old Friday. I have a feeling I may get a letter that day! We'll see.

I love you an awful, awful lot!
Mary

P. S. I hope you weren't too busy to be able to think of Mary on her birthday, April 26th and forget our 7th anniversary on May 28th! But really we've only been married for 6 years physically. It is just too horrible, a whole year of our lives together gone.

April 30

Dear Mary,

This is the first letter I've been able to write for about three weeks and I'm afraid you must have been worried. During all that time I just got one letter, from Aunt Louisa in Wellesley. But last night and this morning I got seventeen letters and a package with fruitcake and maple sugar from your mother that was enjoyed by all, with the accent on the last word. The letters were dated all the way from March 27th to April 20th. So now, for once, it's hard to answer because there are so many instead of so few.

I love you. That was a terribly long time without letters; I'm getting mine now, but it'll be quite awhile before you get one. You've probably gathered from the papers that we've been pretty busy and I don't know just how much I can write about it. We made the bridgehead across the Po River, which was without doubt the most exciting boat ride I ever took, and I hope I never take another like it. I've shaved twice in the last month and haven't really washed yet. I'm enclosing a cartoon from the *Boston Herald* of all things. I got it from DeWick. I thought you might think it funny because of the name; very likely you've seen it already.

We stayed in one big farm house in the Po valley where they had every kind of domesticated beast. I was walking in the hall upstairs, which was rather dark, and hearing an odd noise I examined a long row of bushel baskets along one side: each one had a great big turkey sitting on eggs. Later on, in the hills again, I started seeing goats, all Toggenburgs, with enormous udders. I've seen some wonderful captured German horses. An anachronistic note—the people here mostly cook in open fireplaces, but they often have an electric light set up in the chimney so that they can see into the pot. I'm staying in a house now where the people talk some French and I wandered around the town this afternoon and met an old lady who talked French and took me to see her garden and was very nice. It's a great relief to find some natives I can actually talk to instead of just feeling like a deaf and dumb person. Also, the old lady was a lady, which was a pleasant change I found.

We've been going pretty fast, fighting a battle one evening and waking up the next morning ten miles behind the front lines. The units were leapfrogging each other. We marched through towns with the populace hailing us as liberators, shaking our hands, throwing flowers at us, and supplying us with food and wine and shouting bravo. At times it really got pretty embarrassing. I suppose your cold must be all gone now, I wish it hadn't got into your sinuses again. It's very late now, but I think I'll be able to write more tomorrow. I love you an awful lot. I hope at least it'll never again be that long without letters.

I love you.
Sydney

May 1

Dear Mary,

I've been trying to start this letter for a long time but there are people all around, and our not too willing landlord has been trying to talk to me in French mixed with Italian about his various adventures with Germans, and all the time the radio is going full blast, and I can't hear what he says and it's all been very harassing. Now, of course, it's late at night again, eleven, and I never know when I'll get another chance to sleep. Just this moment the German radio announced that Hitler is dead.

Well, the Italians came back at that news, of course, and talked until midnight; after that I went to bed to get up again and get sick, and was just going back to sleep when a German truck convoy rolled into town looking for a place to surrender and now it is morning again. Last night's experience was extraordinary, but I don't believe I'm allowed to say any more about it, if that much.[114]

The Italian last night was talking about slugs, he didn't know the word in French but finally explained it to me by drawing a picture of a snail and then crossing out the shell which I thought was pretty clever. He says they come into the house through the sink drain unless you keep the stopper in it. While he was talking and everybody was milling around making a noise as usual and the radio blaring, of course, his wife was sitting there nursing the baby, over a year old, and I couldn't help thinking how the pediatricians at home worry about the disturbing effect of even one extra person sitting quietly in the room.

There are a cherry tree and a fig tree right outside the door, and the cherries are ripe and rapidly disappearing. I wouldn't know if the figs were ripe or not but they don't look it. I wish I could tell you where I am now and describe the place, but someday I'll be able to do it. I suppose before too

---

114 I believe what he is referring to is that a German unit surrendered to him, even though he was a private, because he had some knowledge of the language, having studied German in school and college. He had told me the story.

many weeks have gone by, I'll know whether we'll be sent straight to the East or what. That's what worries me the most now. It's horrible to think of being sent even further away from you. I don't know if I'll be able to stand it. I love you. Poor Mary, with Julius and "Heidi" and "Mary kid."[115] I think over three quarts is pretty good for "Gay," the first time. I'd been doing a little wishful deducing about that 8 quarts grandma.

I love you.
Sydney

May 2

Dear Sydney,

I feel so cheered up now because of tonight's news. Unconditional surrender in Italy! What a moment for you! And all because you were there, I know! They took one look at that mustache and threw up their hands and pulled out their pocket handkerchiefs, I know! I long for word from you personally now and can hardly wait! Barbara Lawrence just called me from New York to congratulate me! I think it was the nicest thing honestly. She is a real friend. She said all she could think of when she heard the news was me! She really understands how worried I am but she told me not to worry anymore! Of course, I can't do that until I hear from you. But somehow its very reassuring to have one's friends standing by and know it! I wish I had more friends like her! Jimmy is in Florence and as I gather has been working with the partisans, so he's hopeful when that is straightened out he may get home! I wish it meant you'd get home too. But I doubt it. Yesterday's paper spoke of amphibious assaults by the 10th division. I wonder if you had a ride in a storm boat—ease your feet anyhow! But, it also said there was stiff opposition. But it's over now, I hope and I hope you'll get a good rest. Only I wish it would be here at home in bed with me! I shall continue unabated my prayers and pray that somehow something will take in our favor and we'll be reunited.

    Jane called up this afternoon and said your mother had had letters from Dick and he's on Okinawa and has been since April 2nd, the day after the initial landing. He said not to worry. He had 3 regular hot meals a day and a quiet rest every night! I don't know how true, but I suppose the heavy artillery is usually somewhat behind, isn't it? You know more than I do, that's certain. I know nothing! Anyhow they must be glad to at least know where he is. So they can follow his actions more definitely. This morning the children

---

115 The reference is to the fact that the two goats and Julius the handyman all died within a few days.

and I left at 9:30 for New Haven. They went to the Dunhams's while I went to the dentist. Mary was in heaven on Stephanie's tricycle! Stephanie was at school! Sydney just trudged along behind and Frank behind him dragging a coal shovel! Up and down they went, all moving. Lee was there and about six neighborhood children. On the way in, the dogwood was beautiful, and I saw a real Grant Wood scene—a house raising. It looked like a scene out of one of his pictures honestly. It was a small house and just as we went by they were putting up the ridgepole. There were several men, obviously neighbors and women and another man hoeing a bit of a garden and all in colorful clothes while the sides of the house were black tar paper. You would have loved it for its artisticness too, plowed earth around and the black sides of the house the framework above and two men lifting the ridgepole. I thought of you and wished you were with us!

In New Haven the trees are all leafed out and it looks like late spring! Lilacs in bloom, tulips going by even. "Mopsa" is in heat again, and if we don't have "Rollo" pups or "Paddle" pups I don't know why not! There's been a poodle here all day, one like Hollis's but so far "Mopsa" is immaculate. It's only because "Rollo" is a virgin, I guess, that he hasn't torn down the roof and the insides of the house too! "Robert" duck has really bitten a hole in his son's back! They forget so you'd think five ladies would satisfy two gentlemen wouldn't you? This afternoon I warmed up milk for "Sydney kid" and as I went to take it off the stove the handle of the pail was so hot I smelled my burnt flesh! I never had that happen before and now I can see the path of the handle seared across my fingers, like a path of dead grass where a mole has been. It doesn't hurt now though as I put some oil on it right away and my hands are very tough, of course! I have a mess of bills here to attend to but have balanced the checkbook with no trouble.

I got a letter from Anna Mary and one from Mrs. Adams. Anna Mary is all set to either join me here or in Wellesley for the trek! I wish it would be with you we were going! She says she should help her father round up the cows evenings and suggest she do it on "Jill." In Mrs. Adam's letter she says not to worry about that, that Anna Mary just wants an excuse to ride! Well, we'll see, perhaps we can all help him haying and at different, difficult times!

I see that Friday they are reopening the cable service to Italy. I wish it would be inaugurated by a message from you! That is the day I've pinned my hopes on for hearing from you by letter. I don't know why, but I hope I'm right in my intuition, I shall be very disappointed if it's not so! But underneath that I'll really understand. I hope you have been able to write today and maybe another ten days and I'll hear. Send me a cable on our anniversary, if you can, now they've opened the lines again. Well I cannot worry much about what's next until I hear you've come through this. I feel sure you're right but I want to know. Clap Mark and Harold[116] on the back for me and tell them you really did it with that mustache. You probably have a beard now by this time too! Lots and lots of love—I love you such an awful lot. I want you; you should come home.

I love you,
Mary

Okinawa, Wednesday, May 2

Dear Sydney,

Just received a letter from Father dated April 18th. He still apparently does not know where I am although I have been writing almost every day.

Another letter from Jane arrived this morning telling about mother's and father's visit there last month. Jane said that they both seemed very well. Especially mother being more energetic and stronger than for two or three years.

I think it is very unusual and you, no doubt, agree with me how well and energetic Father and Mother are, considering their age. Somehow I never seem to think they are getting older at all. Jane said that mother had weeded her strawberry bed and all around the house, while father was building stone steps. Guess they are in Wellesley now though Uncle Frank wrote that he was hoping they might come down to Virginia for a few days.

Manning Williams wrote from Hawaii hoping to meet us there. The letter took about a week to arrive.

The country on this Island is really pretty. The trees are of different variety, but from a distance lots of it resembles southern Connecticut in a way. There are, however some of those flat-top trees that you've seen pictures of and on Chinaware. These are very picturesque, also the small irrigated rice fields and Japanese huts although they are filthy when you get near them.

Jane says that you do not like getting V-mail. I don't very much either—although I'll admit to have taken advantage of it. It isn't always convenient to sit down and write a letter, "long fashion" when a lot of V-mail forms are sitting around and urged to be used.

---

116 General Mark Clark and General Sir Harold Alexander. Alexander, with rank of Field Marshall was in command of all military forces in the Mediterranean Theater. He was later elevated to the peerage and became governor general of Canada.

Arnold has been writing about once a week too. Sometimes I think he feels a little lonely and left out of everything, for I don't believe they have yet made many very good friends out there.

It's raining here again, but not very hard.

Thurs. p.m. (May 3rd)

Rain interrupted this letter for a brief period (24 hours). The Radio news is coming in continuously more and more encouraging. The last rumors being that most organized resistance in northern Italy has ceased. Hitler dead, Goebbels and Himmler dead and that Mussolini was shot a few days ago. What momentous news! These will be days long remembered in History. Whatever the case may actually be at the moment, it seems pretty definite that your job has been almost completed. You really did well taking care of the Huns! I fully hope that you will not have to come over here. As you were always very optimistic. I feel the same way now too. The battle on this Island isn't over yet, but looking at the picture as a whole it doesn't seem as though the Japanese could face the world very long.

Will write again soon, until then—

Best of Luck,
Dick

MAY 3, 1945–JULY 27, 1945

The next batch of letters, written between May 3 and July 27, is the longest collection in this book. They are humorous and revealing. The war, for my father, was over—although he did not know it at the time. Fear of being sent to the Pacific was ever-present.

On May 7, the war in Europe ended, though V-E Day would be celebrated on May 8. While there was still the threat—very real—of being sent to the Pacific for the expected invasion of Japan, there was relief and pride that he had survived his initiation to battle. He felt lucky and confident. The first few letters express a sense of camaraderie for those with whom he had fought, but that sense of fraternity soon deteriorated into impatience and intolerance, driven by his growing frustration with the rigidities of army life, coupled with the irregularities of mail delivery. When he was feeling particularly sorry for himself, he would lash out at his comrades, at times venomously. On May 20, he was attempting to write a letter when he was interrupted. "You'd think a man with the brains of an earthworm would see I wanted to be left alone so I could write. But then in my foxholes I often had long conversations with earthworms that understood the fundamentals of life much better than any of my companions." On other occasions (for example, after receiving a letter from my mother, or after having visited Florence, Venice, or some such place) he would become more magnanimous, and, in fact, could wax quite eloquent; on May 24 he writes, "The mountains are stronger than a magnet, beckon like a siren, are elusive in mists and then so clear you can almost touch them. . . . The mountains stand back to let in the day, at sunrise and sunset, and bring sparkling showers to make it fresh and clean."

It was during this time that his interest in art began to reemerge. He met local artists and commented on them and their drawings. He took up drawing again. He decorated the walls of a bar the GIs built in the village of Plezzo. And he visited the cities of Florence, where he saw the Bronze Doors, and Venice, where he saw the Bridge of Sighs and the Doge's palace. He often visited these places accompanied by his friend, Bob DeWick, who recalled my father's deep interest and knowledge.

Along Lake Garda

Road on Mt. Mangart and the mountains north of Caporetto and Plezzo

Most of the letters in this section were written from the village of Plezzo (then in disputed territory but occupied by the Allies, and now in northwestern Slovenia), nestled along the Isonzo River. The village, surrounded by the Alps, is about forty miles north and east of Udine, Italy, and about twenty miles south of the Austrian border. It is a beautiful area, and my father's letters express his awe and admiration. When the war in Italy ended, his regiment was on the eastern shore of Lake Garda. By the eighth of May they moved further north, but a week later they were back in the Po River Valley. On the twentieth of May, they moved north to Plezzo where they remained until the middle of July when they began their withdrawal to Naples for shipment back to the United States. On August 2, they filed up the gangplank of the troop ship USS *Mt. Vernon* (in peacetime, the SS *Washington*) for the voyage back to Newport News, Virginia.

The threat that he might have to go to the Pacific hung over my father like the sword of Damocles. The invasion of Japan was not expected to begin until the fall of 1945, and conventional wisdom suggested that it would take at least a year. (It had taken eleven months from the Normandy invasions to the German surrender, with Allied soldiers already in place in southern Europe.) Unlike the landing in Normandy, the invasion of Japan would begin with fighting the enemy on his home soil, and there was no question that the Japanese would defend themselves tenaciously. No one yet knew that the United States possessed a bomb capable of destroying entire cities and bringing Japan to its knees.

My father and his comrades were aboard the USS *Mt. Vernon* heading home when they first heard the news of atomic bombs dropped on Hiroshima (August 6) and on Nagasaki (August 9). On August 11, they docked at Newport News. Four days later, on August 15 (the day it was announced that Japan would surrender unconditionally), my father reached home. I remember that day: meeting my father at the railroad station in Nashua, New Hampshire, amidst the glorious sounds of celebration—horns honking, lights flashing. The world war that had consumed the United States for three years, eight months, and one week was over. My father was safe, and life could be expected to return to normal.

May 3

Dear Mary,

I've been thinking today about how nice you would look in that bathing suit you mentioned some time ago. I suppose it's been too cold to use it yet and it sounds like a very cold bathing suit.

Well they say the war is over in Italy, but haven't yet mentioned lifting any censorship restrictions. We've been resting ourselves for several days, but it's over a month since we've had a bath and that's beginning to interest me more than anything else. There didn't seem to be any particular celebrating or rejoicing at the news that the German armies throughout Italy and part of Austria had surrendered. Everyone wondered if it was literally all of them, and everyone seemed to breathe a little more easily and that was all.

I got a note from Mother today with a book on conversational Italian which is considerably advanced for me, as I have no Italian conversation at all as yet, and I hope I won't be here till I reach that stage, but also hope to be able to use it if I have to stay here much longer. I was able to go for a little walk today and enjoyed myself. I discovered that when you walk without a pack or rifle you practically feel as if you were floating through the air. All I can think about now is whether I might possibly be able to go home pretty soon. We did most of the work in these last advances, as we broke the hole through into the Po Valley and made the bridgehead across the river, moving alone at one time 40 miles ahead of the rest. I think all that has been published and can be said. I wonder if that will affect going home. Nothing else interests me but going home. I'm going to feel awfully impatient now till I find out whether I can go home eventually or whether I'll be sent East; that last would be awful!

No war trophies can be sent weighing over 70 lbs., so I guess I won't try to get you one of those beautiful German horses.

I love you,
Sydney

May 3

Dear Sydney,

The news from Europe seems almost too good to be true! The fall of Berlin, the deaths of Hitler and Mussolini and the surrender of 1,000,000 Germans in Italy all seem to indicate that the war in Europe must be practically over. Do let us hear from you as soon as possible. Your last letter to me was dated April 8th and to Mary, I think April 9.

Uncle Frank, Mary and Jane, Mother and I all had letters from Dick yesterday, dated April 20. He writes: "Our unit took part in the invasion of Okinawa Island and is now active in destroying the remnants of the Japanese garrison forces. If you hear much artillery here, remember that is our part of it. While I'm writing this, shells are flying over my head in the right direction. I'm now sitting behind our four howitzers, and ready to fire them at any minute when the order comes down by telephone. I hear a lot of Japanese propaganda by radio. Most of it is [so] ridiculous that it's even annoying to listen to. I have seen already many Japanese civilians and find that those living on the island here are very ignorant in lots of ways. They live in very primitive style in nothing much more than grass huts."

Much love from Father

P. S. Since I wrote this we've heard Gabriel Heatter say that tomorrow at 9:00 a.m. Truman will give the official Proclamation. So I guess tomorrow is to be V-E Day.

May 4

Dear Mary,

I'm waiting for mail right now; someone went to get it. Well it came and I got two letters postmarked the 25th and 26th. Did you mean that you'd bought the trailer or that you were about to do so? It certainly would be nice to have one. I really haven't much idea how much a trailer should cost anyway, and we'd certainly have plenty of use for it. We could use it for other things besides horses.

There's no more news about me. The only important change in my life since I last wrote is that instead of sleeping on the landing at the top of the stairs, where everyone stepped on me going by or to the bathroom (one of the few I've seen in Italy, and now has to be flushed with a pail), I slept last night under the kitchen table that offers considerable protection from people wandering around in the dark. The only trouble is that I find the tile floor downstairs harder than the wooden one upstairs.

Probably it's in retrospection that my hair brushing skill seems so gentle to Mary; as I remember she didn't always like it. I always did like brushing girls' hair and horses' tails!

It was rainy again today and raw, and I never even thought of swimming. I don't remember seeing that *Yank* you mention. The May 4th *Yank* also has an article about us when we started the last push, just a short thing with a few pictures, one or two of which are scenes I remember. I didn't know there was any difference between ponies' feet and horses', but I've heard blacksmiths complain that it was a lot more trouble shoeing them and that they didn't like doing it. I wonder whether if you found some old iron tires on a broken wagon or something the blacksmith couldn't cut them to fit. I don't know if they'd do that or not or whether it would spoil it for rubber tires later.

We are terribly crowded in this house; so that those two bits of floor space I mentioned are literally the only spots where I can sleep. It's pretty rough on the Italian couple with two little children trying to keep house at the same time. The youngest is rather a nervous-seeming child though plump and rosy-cheeked, and the woman told me tonight that he wakes up about every two hours during the night and that she has to take him up and nurse him to quiet him; he's walking and learning to talk. I asked why she didn't just leave him, and she said it would wake the whole neighborhood, etc. It's the same way about other things. I felt like giving a brief lecture on bringing up children. I'm glad you got rid of the billy goat so easily and happily. The radio now says the troops in north Germany and Holland and Denmark surrendered. There's practically nothing left. I wish I could go home. I love you an awful lot, and think I should be with you and the children now.

I love you.
Sydney

༄

May 5

Dear Mary,

I wrote you this morning dating the letter the fourth. I think for several days I've been one day behind. I got a big package from your mother this evening and this is some of the writing paper. The maple sugar is already all gone. I said that no one not from New England could have any because they didn't appreciate or understand maple sugar, but they all said they understood it very well and helped themselves with many thanks.

You notice how much more neatly I can write on this good block of paper; I really appreciate it very much. I got the Belmont *Alumni Bulletin* today. There was an article on the death of Theodore Clement of Peterborough; it's the first time I ever realized he went to the same school I did. I'm glad Mary has such a good idea for the looks of things; she even showed that some a long time ago didn't she. In fact, I think she's a very remarkable person. I'm glad they all had such a good time on her birthday. I just got the letter talking about it. You say B. Anne is bossy, I'm not surprised. Tell her I used to know her mother very well when she was a little girl. I think the pictures of the children and the kids are wonderful, but they all look so different, Mary the least, I guess, even if she did age a little on her birthday, and Frank the most.

We did walk in one day at least 25 miles of that 50-mile advance and a good part of it after dark, and we were pretty well worn out before it started, not having had much sleep for a long time, etc. Most of that day there was no opposition, and I remember wondering toward the end of that night how we would ever be able to fight if we ran into some Germans, whereupon in about five minutes we did. Luckily it wasn't too stiff, and afterwards I slept a few hours in a room so crowded the only spot I could find was the top of a chest of drawers about 3 feet wide and 2 long. I slept beautifully. We did go by Verona, but were not the ones to enter it, and I never even saw it. Then we were riding in trucks and waiting and letting others pass us. We had one more fight when we captured a small mountain village and that's all.

I love you.
Sydney

May 5

Dear Mary,

I'm in the same place still doing nothing. I see no reason why I can't tell you where I am, but have not been given permission to do so. It's one of the lakes in the foothills of the Alps and very beautiful, but I don't feel in the least happy. I think so much now about going home, as it all seems finished here, that I don't believe anything will please me again till I am home. I'm sick of calling ignorant adolescents "sir" and, in general, deferring to people whom I generally like but respect very little. During combat things are generally rather informal, and I'm afraid that now we'll probably go back to the old mumbo jumbo, and I will mind it much more than I did before. In the whole drive that we last made I don't feel that I personally performed any useful act whatsoever; I mean I know I didn't. I believe that the Germans have been beaten mainly because in the last few years they wore themselves out in their acts of aggression.

This afternoon I'm going to take a shower which will be a momentous occasion, although having been able to do superficial washing the last few days and having got pretty used to being dirty (or my own stink, to put it plainly) I don't feel as excited about the shower as I should. I don't know anything about our future at all; no one has said anything.

Yesterday, I saw the first red setter I've seen in Italy; he looked like "Mopsa" and was the most timid dog I've ever seen and very hungry. Somebody had obviously treated him pretty badly. He cruised up and down the chow line awhile and went away with a pretty good meal in his belly and I felt better. Now, it's all over I feel that I've got to get home. I can't stand being away any longer. I feel as if none of the children would recognize me. I know lots of people have been away a lot longer, but what difference does that make. If I have a sore thumb the knowledge that someone else has lost a leg doesn't ease the pain. In fact, I think I worry less and less about other people's legs.

I love you.
Sydney

May 6

Dear Mary,

I didn't get any letters today. I've moved out of the crowded house, and now the four runners live in style in one of the nicest rooms of what was in peacetime a good hotel—a big sunny room with a balcony overlooking beautiful blue water. It has electric lights and a beautiful enamel sink and big mirrors but unfortunately the mirrors are the only conveniences that still work. However the sink drain works and there's lots of water in the lake. Today was beautiful and sunny, and as I sat on my balcony and smoked a big cigar by courtesy of Bob DeWick and looked at the soft sky and blue water and yellow roses beneath, I felt considerably more cheerful than yesterday. At least I haven't yet heard that I won't go home. I guess the chances are very small but until I know I can still hope.

The crowds of former German slave laborers still go down the road and seem more numerous than ever. It's just an endless procession all day long. Mostly they have been on foot, but recently there have been truck loads too, both GI and captured German trucks and cars of all kinds. Some went in an enormous Italian bus they had picked up from the Germans somewhere. The Germans took over all the Italians vehicles, I guess. I wish I was going home now too. I love you. I saw that red setter again today and a puppy that another soldier had, but that wanted to follow me instead. I hope it didn't hurt his feelings, but it pleased me very much.

I love you,
Sydney

May 7

Dear Sydney,

Can it be true this really is V-E Day? I wonder—we've listened to the radio most of the day and it seems to be true all but for the official proclamation. Can Stalin be stalling or what is it? Anyhow I wish it was all on the dotted line. There has been little demonstration here in fact, none that I've seen so far. Only Betty has declared she's going out with the bus driver and his wife and get drunk! And what may I ask have any of them done to deserve it? Nothing! No, as far as I've seen the news such as has come in has been received in a sober fashion and naturally enough. It means the end of one war. The start of another, little chance of seeing our husbands, sons and brothers and only more sorrow for those who have lost theirs, only the people unconnected with the suffering and separation are in any mood to celebrate!

I spent the morning, after we'd heard the first reports, washing out the barn and drains, a thoroughly engrossing job! This afternoon the children and I went up to the Pierces'. We took "Sydney kid" and it was most entertaining! One of the children tied him to the leg of the tea table. You can imagine the results! Nothing broke however. Then he jumped on little Margot's back and that caused tears. He caught her by surprise. Otherwise it was a pleasant afternoon! They really have a nice place but it looks like money-folk farming. However, it gave me a twinge of nostalgia to see Henry cleaning out the pig pen in blue denims and his shirt off. Just the way you used to work around our place. They have a "staff" consisting of a couple and their six-year-old son and a mother-in-law! The man helps on the farm and the mother indoors. Goodness knows what Grandma does! They also have a 3-month-old baby of their own and you never saw such a "cluck" as Mildred Pierce! She's very nice but seems very confused and why shouldn't she with all that underfoot. But I would like to have you see their place. He is an artist too. He paints, or used to, until his farm took up most of his time. He's not well really, something to do with his lungs and that's why he's doing what he's doing. But it all made me a little more homesick, if possible. A family happily united, no worries and anxieties and separations such as we have.

Well we still have dog trouble. We took "Peter" Lage home this afternoon and he was back again tonight! He and "Rollo" have just had a fight while "Mopsa," the Princess in the tower, sits in the guest room and barks! This time has been fraught with complications! Before we were comparatively worry free—Charlotte and Mr. Pope are due to arrive any minute to get "Peter." I hope they won't stay long! But I'll just go to bed anyhow. I love you an awful lot. I wonder where you are now and what you are doing and when I can get a letter! It's been two weeks now since I heard and that's a long time, much too long, with all that's going on! I wish you could send me a cable!

Today, when Mary was taking her rest I discovered she'd gotten into Betsy's baby food and eaten two jars of prunes, 1 1/2 jars of apple sauce, 1/2 jar of peas, and a jar of vegetable with lamb! All this after her own dinner! Then, at the Pierces' she drank 4 cups of "tea"—small cups—and ate, I don't know how many cookies and came home and ate her usual supper! I'd kept the jars upstairs, so Betty wouldn't give them to Allan and now I find they've gone much, much faster!

I do wish I could feel you would be sent home before too long. That I could just see you and touch you again and kiss you again and feel you all over to be sure it was you and finally to go to sleep once more with my head on your shoulder. I love you such an awful lot I don't see how I can stand this much longer and I wonder what's next, but I wish I could just see you again before the next phase. Aunt Anne wrote mother a letter today and told her to tell me, if I hadn't already heard it, the joke about the two strawberries, it seems one said to the other "If we hadn't stayed in that bed so long we'd never be in this jam." I think it's awful funny but I don't think there's anything personal about it do you? Personally I'd like to get out of this jam and into that bed again! I think I'll write that to her!

The children are fine and so full of life. They were hitting on high when we got back from the Pierces'. Betsy is just wonderful. I wish you could see her. She has an engaging smile and her mouth turns way up at each corner. She's much like Frank in her ability to get mad and practically hold her breath. But not as much yet as he does. But she gets over it just as quickly too as he does. Mary gets perfectly furious too. But she screams and jumps up and down and beats her hands in frustration. Sydney doesn't seem to have much real temper and he's gotten almost entirely over his sit-down strikes. He's found they don't pay.

I love you such an awful lot and hate to have them growing up without you here to see and help them. I wish you could come home.

I love you,

Mary

May 7

Dear Sydney,

The war is going the way you thought it would. We are longing so much to hear you are safe.

We have heard from Dick from Okinawa, in a V-mail dated April 20. He wrote then to Mary F. and Jane and Uncle Frank. So, several V-mails came about the same time. He was fighting the Japs when he wrote, sitting by the telephone and waiting for the orders for him to fire his battery.

It's so hard to believe when all is so peaceful here. But we miss you—if you were in Peterborough, it wouldn't seem so lonely here—and Dick all the time.

Willard was back today for 24 hours and leaves for more training and a cruise to last until August. We have let Mary's house and now are arranging about a garage for her. The lease calls for a one-car garage. Where to place it has been difficult. It's to go north of the house, across the driveway. Sargent Cheever[117] is at Okinawa too. He wrote that he had just landed with 30 tons of D. T. D.[118] Are those the right initials for the new insect powder? Now, I am beginning to think cousin Harry said 300 tons. Zeke is out there on some island, too. Also, Howard and Parkman Shaw and young Manning Williams.[119]

I saw in the paper that Lydia Evans was engaged to a Canadian and was to be married soon. I heard through a doctor of Arnold today—all well in Denver and Arnold working mostly on the study of children's hearts and

---

117 A cousin.
118 She is referring to DDT, which was used during the second half of the war to control malaria and typhus.
119 In this paragraph, she writes of mostly family members—nephews and cousins.

how they grow and develop. He has about 150 children to watch. The other doctors there watch the children for other things. The whole thing is to study, in every way, the physical and mental development.

We are having a long spring. Trees and bushes are growing slowly now. They jumped out in March, so all April has been like the first two weeks of May. We have had days and days of lovely spring colors and lilacs and flowering shrubs, lasting and lasting.

Joe,[120] Mary thinks, must be far enough from home to be in the fighting zone by now. She heard from him a few weeks ago and is looking for a letter soon. It's almost time, she says.

"George," finally, seems to have given up rolling in the manure. He's so intelligent, perhaps he really understood when we complained.

Tomorrow, Sunday, we are having Mary's tenants to lunch. There are two couples and one child. But one of the wives is in the hospital, so only the two men and one wife are coming. This sounds pretty dull. I'm afraid I'm sleepy. It's 11 p.m.

Love,
Mother

May 8

Dear Sydney,

We have had more letters from Dick. The last one dated Apr. 26. He is fighting in Okinawa with the heavy artillery—I enclose a picture from the Sunday *Herald*.

We have been working hard all day digging dandelions and then cleaning the barn. Have burnt an enormous amt. of rubbish and oily rags. Was hard work. Father began to feel faint and I had to finish alone.

This note is really just to send my love. It's late and I should be in bed. I have been hoping you would have a chance to try for officer's training—giving orders is disagreeable work but one should do one's best even if things are disagreeable—you would make a good officer so you ought to try for it. To win both wars and for your children too.

Lots and lots of love,
Mother

---

120 Joe Fyffe, my father's brother-in-law, married to his older sister Mary.

May 9

Dear Mary,

I didn't write yesterday or the day before as we were moving. As far as I know there's no relaxation of the censorship; so I suppose I can't tell you about where we are, though I don't see why not. I now live in the greatest luxury, in a house in the style of a Swiss chalet with all modern conveniences, only three of us living in this particular house. The woman who owns it appears to be quite well off; she calls it her weekend cottage.

We hear all kinds of rumors as to what is to become of us now, but have been told absolutely nothing. The uncertainty is getting on my nerves. I haven't had any letters for several days though I got a copy of *Life* today. I did finally go in swimming before I left the last place and it felt wonderful. I wish I was starting home tonight; I wish they would decide that I was much too old and decrepit to be of any use anymore. I'm older than almost all the others, but I doubt if they'll think me too old. Maybe if I grew a long white beard it would help, but I'm afraid there isn't time. As we keep moving the scenery naturally gets better and better. I hope we keep on moving this way, but would be glad to stay in this spot for awhile. There's a very impressive view of the Alps right from my window, and nice country close by as well, green fields and pretty good-sized mountains. There still seem to be very few domestic animals anywhere. I don't know whether that's the Germans' fault or not. I'll be living a different sort of life now, more like the army in the States; we have to worry about being dressed right and saluting and all that sort of thing that I now haven't done for a long time. I love you. I'm going to stop this right now because it may go a little quicker.

Sydney

May 10

Dear Sydney,

This is V-Day for me and no mistake. I got your letter written May 1st this morning! You will never know how that made me feel honestly! To know you were alive and apparently uninjured was like a gift straight from God and so it is! Minnie Dole told daddy, who did not tell me until now, that the division had been, as he put it, practically decimated in crossing the Po, so you can imagine how we all feel here at home! Betsy's husband's brother, who had his leg shot off, wrote back and said in his words that "they'd been all shot to pieces," but she also did not tell me until now! So I, for one, am most humble and grateful and know more than ever that God is on our side! I called up your mother right away and she was as thankful as I am! From your letter I gathered you weren't in the snow belt and am dying of curiosity to know where you were with cherry trees and fig trees in fruit! I was a little worried about your getting up to be sick. But I suppose you were completely exhausted, and the rations and life you'd been leading. Anyhow while it worried me some, just to know you were alive was all that really mattered! I know you were tired, the tone of your letter told me that. I wonder if you haven't written before that I haven't gotten yet. You spoke of Mary-kid so I knew you'd gotten mail fairly recently. Though you didn't mention mail. I wish you could come home for good now. You've had a pretty bloody share. Perhaps at least you'll get a furlough eventually anyhow. I hope and pray it will be so! I love you such an awful, awful lot!

Tonight they announced the demobilization plan point system,[121] which you, of course know too. I don't see why they don't count any child beyond no. 3. It's not fair! The men with 5 and 6 and 7 children should come home that much sooner, I think. I can't count up more than 64 points for you, out of the 85. So that's not so good, of course if you've received four decorations that would make 84! You might suggest it to them! Well, for tonight just the knowledge that you were safe after the surrender in Italy is enough for me! Of course I still don't know if you were among those who went into Austria and if so, if you met any opposition there, but certainly the worst must have been over! I feel now I may get letters more often again. I just cannot bear to think of you going straight out to the last and I scan the papers daily for any inkling. Today's spoke of some troops in Italy having already been shipped out. I hope and pray that was not you! I don't believe it was but I'm never certain of anything. How I long for all the details of these last few weeks though I imagine they are not pretty. My heart goes out to you and I wish I could in some way make it easier for you. But I feel hog tied and can only pray and pray fervently!

To celebrate your letter I took the children to Madison this afternoon and treated them to ice-cream cones, they were thrilled honestly! As to myself, I just said an extra prayer of thanksgiving! Now we are expecting callers, Jean's sister, Helen and her husband who is just back from 8 months in the Pacific, the Philippines mainly I think. It should be interesting and espe-

---

121   The point system was known as the Adjusted Service Rating score: For enlisted men, one point for each month in the service; one additional point for each month overseas; five points for combat decoration or Purple Heart, and twelve points for each dependent under age eighteen, up to three children. By the time he left Italy, in early August, he would have had sixty-four points.

cially because everyone says he is optimistic. He's a Lieutenant in the Navy, in command of the gun crew on a liberty ship, I think. I love you an awful, awful lot! I hope they don't stay too long, but I don't think they will as she has a 2 mos. old baby she nurses and I guess she'll have to be home at 10:00. I loved the story of the Italian woman. I'm nearly as bad. Betsy is over 9 mos., and still not weaned. Also I thought she was very clever! I never would have thought of that!

I love you an awful, awful lot,
Mary

P. S. I noticed this letter came "free" in just one week. But I'm sending you a few airmail stamps anyhow. It's a wicked stormy night and has been very cold all day—here come the gusts!

May 10

Dear Sydney

It certainly was a relief to hear Mary telephone from East River this morning that she had a letter from you. The last was dated about a month ago. What an experience you must have had! We here followed it day by day in the newspapers and on the radio, and find not only the 10th Mtn. Div. but the 87th mentioned, as if you were at or near the head of the invasion. And now I'm wondering what will happen next! If you go to the Pacific, I hope it will be by way of the U. S. A.

Dick is in the thick of it at Okinawa, and it goes on week after week! He writes in good spirits, but the rain and mud must be pretty bad, in addition to being continually in action.

I think Joe must be in that part of the world, but we don't know just where. Mary is starting for the village.

Much love from Father

May 11

Dear Mary,

I haven't had any letters now for several days and am beginning to get rather unhappy about it. The *Stars and Stripes* today says that censorship restrictions have been lifted, but we have not been told yet, so I still can't tell you where I am. I probably can pretty soon. However I suppose you know approximately; so it wouldn't make very exciting news anyway. The paper also announced the way the point system would work and I figure the most I could get would be sixty-one out of the eighty-five necessary for a discharge; so I guess there's no use my thinking about that now. I just hope, not too optimistically, that I won't go to China or somewhere.

I met a painter this afternoon who had a little pointed beard and looked just like a painter. He knew a few words of French and German and we carried on a very halting and fantastically multilingual conversation. He took me in and showed me some of his paintings, one of which I thought was really very good, a little in the style of Dexter Dawes[122] (do you remember him?). But he complained that it was not as he really wanted it because he could no longer buy the colors he wanted. He lent me a wonderful book of reproductions of DaVinci that I've been looking at this evening. It's extraordinary how much pleasure it gave me meeting somebody like that for a change, even though I really couldn't talk to him at all. Just to know there still are people in the world interested in things like that, in the real stuff, not even the half-baked kind. I believe there are quite a few other artists living around here, probably all landscape painters. People walk around dressed in funny clothes looking just like the summer people in Peterborough, and not at all like Italians I saw before and further south. I love you. I should have plenty of time to write the next few days, I hope.

Sydney

P. S. The lady of the house where I live is young, blonde, and attractive, and is fond of painting and skiing. However, you needn't be jealous as she's engaged to a bald-headed doctor, who wears glasses and has a bushy black beard and is always around.

⌇

May 11

Dear Sydney,

Today I got two more letters from you and your mother called up and said they had had one written May 4th. My latest was May 3rd, this afternoon.

I got your first of April 30th. I think it's funny, the one sent "free" got here first! Daddy sends you his love and to tell you we all had a grand old

---

122 Dexter B. Dawes (1872–1951) lived in Old Lyme, Connecticut.

rejoicing over hearing from you! You said you got 17 letters from March 27th to April 20th, you must have missed out on a few, as there should have been at least 20 or 21 during that period. Maybe you've got them by now. How wide was the Po at the point you took your boat ride? Just approximately. I wonder you must have had a nice stubble at the end there or more likely a bush. I hope you have been able to get clean at last! We hadn't seen the cartoon and daddy and I laugh every time we look at it. We're going to send it to Joe. He'll love it! I was awfully interested in the German horses, what did the Germans use them for? In other words are they heavy horses or light? I remember at the horse show in Rome, and here in N. Y. too, the German army team had the most magnificent horses I've ever seen. Enormous powerful animals I was told it was because the army horse show team was [more] heavily endowed than any other countries. But as riders they weren't in a class with either the French or Italian. Tell me more about them, if you can't bring one home! Can't you send home a nice big-uddered Toggenburg? I gather you must be or have been there, near Lake Garda yes? No?

 I am dying to know what's in the cards for you now. I hope it won't be the East, or if it must be, I hope you'll go via the U. S. A. I just feel I can't stand this much longer honestly. I hope you've had a good rest now, before they start you on the extensive Athletic maneuvers they talk about in the papers now. I was interested in the lack of rejoicing and celebrating. I guess everyone was just too tired to care. As I said over here it was much the same—people do realize it's not over yet. It must have been wonderful to take a walk without rifle or pack. I love you such a lot. I want you to come home, I can't stand it much longer either. Maybe you will eventually. But I can't get 85 points to your credit, can you? I wish you'd let me know what it does actually come to as I guess by the time you get this you'll have filled out your cards. If only Betsy could add on another 12. I don't see why not. Where you said you moved alone 40 miles ahead of the rest. How many of you did you mean? Your whole regiment or division or what? I am hungry for all the details you can spare. But, your letters are wonderfully written and give a vivid description of what you can tell. I guess now you can tell more, don't you?

 Please let me know everything you and about past, present and future, won't you? I wonder if you are or were near Mussolini's villa. I saw that some of the 10th division was. I also wonder what's happened to you since May 4th. If you moved into the Brenner Pass and on to Austria. Someday

I will know, but now I wish I knew just where you were tonight. I saw in today's paper that 21 Americans were killed in an explosion. German timebombs at a command post in the Brenner Pass. I won't feel easy until I know that wasn't you. Although my hopes are pinned on your still being south of there. But, as that happened after your last letter, I won't rest easy again now until I hear. You said you lived at the C. P. most of the time, the law of averages is in our favor but it's discouraging—just as I felt I could really relax, to have spotted this in a little box in the paper is bad news! I do hope now you can write every day or so again and be sure to tell me all you possibly can. I saw by one of your envelopes that Anderson, Ozzie Day's friend, is still around censoring. What were your losses anyhow? All I know is they were very high, decimated at the Po crossing, as Minnie[123] told Daddy. He was very serious about it when he heard I hadn't heard from you. It must have been horrible, and I do hope for your share you'll be allowed to come home. I suppose if you get home too soon it will mean the Pacific. I live in dread you may go straight out. A few will, I gather, but I pin my hopes on the fact that most of the combat troops will go this way. I just wish they wouldn't send you out at all!

The children are all fine. Just as mischievous as ever! I got a letter from Ruth today. She says Pat is home, full of tales including the Ardennes. He's in the hospital with his shoulder again and may get a medical discharge. She said she'd just seen Arnold and Margaret.[124] Apparently they are expecting another baby. But I don't know when, do you? I love you an awful, awful lot. I want you!

I love you,
Mary

॰૩૦

May 12

Dear Mary,

I got three letters last night, yours of May 2nd, and ones from mother and father saying Dick was seeing action on Okinawa. I'm glad the trailer came and I don't think you'd better worry about whether you paid the right price etc. We wanted a trailer and now we've got one. I wish I could see it; it sounds good to me. Where I am now the cherry trees are just beginning to blossom and where I was a few days ago, and just a few miles away, we were eating cherries off a tree outside the house. I've never had such a mixed-up

---

123 C. Minot "Minnie" Dole (1899–1976) was married to my mother's first cousin, Jane Trowbridge Ely, and was the founder of the National Ski Patrol. He was not related to Senator Bob Dole.
124 My father's youngest brother and his wife.

spring; we were always going back and forth from one season to another. I've been seeing apple blossoms in all stages for the last two months, but have almost always missed them when they were at their best.

Mother apologized for her letter saying that Father often wrote his in pencil first and was so much more careful. I'm afraid that that's what makes Mother's letters so much better and more real than Father's, but I'm afraid if I told them it would hurt Father's feelings. I know just how he feels, as I'm not too different. He appreciates that a good sentence is a work of art, skillfully constructed, and, although he wants to be natural, he can't make himself put anything on paper without thinking of such things. I suppose it's too late now to hope to see Joe in Italy. I suppose everyone will be shifted around, and I am wondering about John Farlow. I'm afraid one of us will be moved before we ever have a chance to meet. They had sort of a battalion party this afternoon which consisted of a few formal speeches in the very hot sun and then G. I. and Italian music and a little to eat. The idea was for us and the Italians to all mingle and be sociable, etc., and to celebrate the end of the war here, which we hadn't done yet. Attendance at the formal speeches was compulsory, but afterwards a good proportion of the soldiers put on bored expressions and left. I stayed and wandered around watching the people. There were a tremendous lot of remarkably good-looking children all dressed up in their best clothes and carrying flowers and enjoying themselves immensely. I haven't seen a group of children that averaged so good looking since I went to England. They don't look in the least Italian; their parents look pretty good too and seem fairly well off, and were no doubt fascists once. But personally I don't care if they were; they are obviously more like my own kind of people than anybody I've seen heretofore.

I had another stumbling French conversation with a middle-aged man that lasted interminably so I thought I would never get away. It was mostly about literature and philosophy and such little trivialities. The real reason I wanted to get away was that the conversation finally got too learned and too deep for me. I began to get embarrassed. As I had hazarded a few opinions on such subjects, he immediately credited me with a great deal more knowledge than I possess. He started off on American writers, as for some strange reason all Europeans do, by asking about Poe. We then worked our way through the list to Sinclair Lewis, William Faulkner and Steinbeck. I asked him what sort of a picture he had gained of the United Scares from *Sanctuary* and *Babbit*, and he said he had sufficiently developed a critical sense to understand how such books should be taken. After a discussion of social conditions at home and in Europe, during which I could feel myself slipping fast, we passed on to modern French authors, most of whom I had never heard of, and then to Irish authors that I didn't know any better. By this time I was as if at the bottom of a well and could see but the tiniest rays of light. He ended up, of course, with references to French, and then I had a chance to ask him a few questions about Italy. He politely said that Italy had lost her best friend when Roosevelt died. He said he thought Italy had no future, that it would be just like one of the Balkan countries and no more. We talked a lot more but I've told you enough to bore you already. The interesting thing about it all was that he had a really detached point of view about everything, while all the ordinary people are so fanatically for or against everything, and make no attempt to reason, and even seem proud of the fact that they don't see two sides to a question.

    I think on the whole that my ignorance of good French served in good stead to conceal my ignorance of the subjects, and that he still believes that the American soldier is well informed. Seeing all those children naturally made me more homesick than ever and except for this one man I talked to nobody, I just stood around and watched. These children are light-haired and tow-headed and look much more like our own than those further south. In fact, I was continually being reminded of one or another of ours. I can't help feeling a little bit worried about you so remotely situated in Peterborough; promise that you'll have someone else with you practically all the time, won't you? I think getting the ceilings done is a good idea if it doesn't inconvenience you.

I love you.
Sydney

※

May 14

Dear Sydney,

Today I got your letters of the 4th and 6th and I think maybe tomorrow I'll get one of the 5th, because in the 6th you referred to seeing the red setter again and that was the first I heard of it at all. Also you said you felt more cheerful than you had the day before. I didn't get a discouraged sounding letter. I am so glad you moved into a room, large and only for you. I don't suppose you had a bed however, or did you? I live in hopes these days too that you might possibly get home. It would be just too wonderful. It sounded awful crowded in that house, maybe you should have given a brief lecture on child raising! I wish you'd send back a good Toggenburg, however, if you can't send a German horse! I'm dizzy for more news about them! I wrote Minnie last night and asked him what he could tell me about your past and future. I hope he can give me some clue. Also, I asked him if he could get hold of one of those May 4th *Yanks*[125] you mentioned. I told Mary what you said about brushing her hair and she is still adamant that you do it better than I do! She can hardly wait to have you tackle "Mitzi's" tail! Her tail hits the floor and laps over!

Your balcony overlooking the lake sounds wonderful and I was so happy to hear you were a little more comfortable. I gather you didn't have to go on into Austria. Though maybe I'll find you did later. I gather you were probably on Lake Garda or one like it. Fairly close to the Swiss border as you spoke of the natives speaking some French. I love you such an awful lot. I want you terribly! Today's paper said that the infantry men or some of them with the 5th Army think the point system doesn't go far enough! They think more points are due for the combat infantryman's medal for a month in the front lines as riflemen, and twice as many for combat medals as for non-combat medals. I heartily agree and hope they get somewhere! I wonder what you know tonight. I feel I can hardly wait. Oh if only I'd hear you were coming home even if it wouldn't be for several months. I haven't seen you now for 9 months and it's almost too much! It is a relief to be getting letters again, and to know you are all right. Honestly you will never know what those weeks were like to me, though imagine it wasn't much compared to what they were to you! I'm going to call your mother tonight and tell her I've had these letters.

This afternoon, it being Charlotte's birthday, the children and I picked her 3 bunches of pansies and decked out "Mitzi" in gala style. Narcissus in her tail and forelock and behind each ear. They got all dressed up and we felt very festive. Of course when we got there it was a little flat! Bill was there feeling very grumpy. Charlotte was asleep after a large lunch and cocktails and it would have been disappointing except that Charlotte's cousin, Jerry Russell Pitkin, was there and she is very friendly, though younger than Joe.

Bill got upish and said that "Mitzi" was ruining his grass, pulling it up by the roots etc. etc. She wasn't at all. Finally I said, "Yes, you should put a

---

125 The reference is to the army weekly magazine, *Yank*.

ring in your barn." He looked very surprised and said "Why?" I said, "So I can tie her up when I come over." He then said in a not too friendly way, "Oh, but then you won't come too often!" That really hurt my feelings a little, because he didn't say it in a friendly way at all. I can imagine saying it myself to be funny, but he meant it! The trouble is, he's pompous and gets worried over so many children running around, though his were still in bed. It's not comfortable to go there when he's around. I really feel unwanted and would have gone home immediately except that Jerry was there, and also it made me mad, so I decided I'd stay to irritate him! I tied "Mitzi" where she was all right and the children were very good, but he was clucking around! He woke Charlotte at 4 and she looked and felt awful. I talked to her a few minutes and then came home, and we'd gone to so much trouble, but the children loved it! Frank's bouquet, you can imagine, but Mary's and Sydney's looked nice. Bill never even noticed "Mitzi." Charlotte gave us some birthday cake anyhow to take home, and so they had it for supper with candles lit. Bill is more unpleasant than ever and honestly I feel a little sorry for Charlotte because she knows how he is and I think it worries her a little as after all I'm one of her really old friends and he has no excuse to be so rude. If I wasn't fond of her I'd never go there when he's around. But I don't want to hurt her feelings because I think she's helpless and does feel it some. Well he's a squirt and I don't give a damn. I'm going to continue to go over whenever I feel like it for the children to play with his. They like each other anyhow. He didn't say more than two words to me all afternoon. Never stopped what he was doing to be even a little polite! To ask about you or Henry or Stu or Joe. It fed me up, but I can be just as rude as he, so it doesn't worry me much, except for Charlotte, but it burns Mother up!

I think I forgot to tell you that the other day going to the Chalkers with "Mitzi" we met Rudy the truck man. Do you remember him? He saw us coming so he stood in the middle of the road with his arms outstretched. "Mitzi" stopped then he looked her all over and said to the children, where did you get that woodchuck! I had to laugh. He really is funny and all the children in Madison just love him! This morning I consulted Harris about the trailer hitch and he told me a blacksmith would have to put a brace onto the bumper and fasten it to that. So tomorrow I'm going to try and get started on it. Now we have the trailer I want it so it can be hooked up. It may take some time and I want it all set to use. I think the tinker shop in Guilford can do it but I'll telephone first and make a date.

I love you. Janie is now talking to mother. She has had a letter from Joe. I'll leave a little room to report what he says if they ever finish gabbing! Well, they finished and apparently Joe is not coming home for at least several months. They are doing some sort of intensive training. I suppose training others. It's a great disappointment to Janie as she really thought he might even now be en route. I love you an awful awful lot and all I want now is to have you come back to us.

I love you,
Mary

༃

Sunday, May 15

Dear Mary,

I got three letters from you today, dated the 30th and the 3rd and 4th. Now we are back down in the Po Valley, but where we can still see the mountains. We are camped in a field outside a big farm and have sadly trampled their clover. We weren't among those that crossed Lake Garda. We did our last fighting two or three days before it was over in Italy. We captured a little summer resort town named Scozzi,[126] or something, to the east of Lake Garda and then went to a town about halfway up the lake where we stayed for some time. I wrote you several letters from there. Then we went up beyond the lake into the mountains, but not nearly far enough to suit me, though it was a beautiful spot. It was called Serrada[127] but I doubt you could find a map that showed it. It was about as far above as it was away from Rovereto, you might find that it's just above the lake. Now we're a few miles south of it but I don't know the name of the nearest town.

Just before we left Serrada I was invited, by the artist who lent me the books, to attend an exhibition of another artist, his cousin. It was the kind where you all sit comfortably in chairs and the artist shows you his pictures one at a time. I never went to one like that before. I was supposed to be on duty as runner in the C. P., and thought I'd take a quick look at the pictures, but they ushered me to a seat near the front and once it started I didn't dare leave as I didn't trust my linguistic power to make a satisfactory explanation. However, no harm came of it, and I enjoyed the exhibition and also the people who looked just like the polite and well-groomed friends and relatives one might see at such an exhibition at home. There were several children in the audience who seemed just as interested as the grown-ups. The pictures

---

126 He is referring to Spiazzi, a resort village on Lake Garda, in the province of Verona.
127 He is referring to the village of Serrada, in the province of Trentino, about twenty miles east of Rovereto.

were all landscapes of the place and the surrounding country and were professionally done, but I thought the lone tree, or whatever it might be, was often placed too nicely in the middle etc. There were also a good many of different studies of the same spots, but there were some snow scenes that made me want to grab a pair of skis and jump right through the frame. I was sorry to leave that town.

That morning, it being Sunday, I'd walked way up on a hill by myself, which really seemed wonderful. My companions are nice but sometimes I get awfully sick of them. I thought I would run back, about two miles I guessed, to see if I was as young as I used to be. I either wasn't or else, more likely of course, I'm out of practice as my legs were so stiff I could hardly walk the next day and I can't walk straight and gracefully yet. The army gives you no chance to keep in good physical shape. Now they are playing baseball, but I'm no good at baseball so it doesn't do me any good and anyway I always thought it too inactive to be fun. Most of the fun seems to be in the talking and shouting which is hardly up my alley.

I got your clipping, but I should be extremely surprised if you saw anything about me in the *Peterborough Transcript*. This farm where we are now fascinates me, but apparently just looks dirty to the rest. It has an enormous courtyard lined with shed roofs on two-story stone pillars. It's so big with so many buildings around it that it looks like a fair-sized village and has quite a few families living in it with countless children of all sizes and descriptions, and all stages of good-natured dirtiness, running everywhere and playing in the irrigation ditches and working too. Children about Frank's age and size driving enormous gallivanting cows this way and that and carrying around those bushel baskets which now have chickens in them instead of eggs. They have horses, a colt, a pony, sheep, goats, pigs, also enormous hens, geese, ducks, turkeys, guinea hens, guinea pigs, rabbits and silkworms. As far as I can make out they are completely self-sufficient.

I should think the best way to protect "Mopsa" would be to shut up everybody and everything and then let "Rollo" loose. I don't think your letters have been bad lately, I guess you've finally heard from me now; I hope so. It's been terribly hot here, but this afternoon I took a bath in the irrigation ditch and felt good, also we've been allowed to keep our shirts off most of the time, which is pretty unusual in the army, I think. They said if anybody questioned it we were having organized sunbathing. They say the only thing we can't write is place or rumors about future moves. But I don't know anything anyway. I guess Dick is probably seeing a lot worse than I did. I didn't think there was room for artillery to be too far away.

I love you.
Sydney

May 16

Dear Mary,

I got your letter postmarked May 5th today and one of April 23rd from Dick in Okinawa. He sounded quite cheerful. The censorship is resumed, which is disappointing. Tonight we were issued some champagne that was captured from the Germans and the evening was enjoyed by all. Many had never tasted it before, and I was amused by some of the things they said about it. It was really very good too and was stamped 'reserved for the Wehrmacht' in French and German. At first it seemed awful to drink champagne right out of the bottle and lukewarm at that with none of the fixings, and nor the right company. But after I'd finished it seemed pretty good just the same.

I probably have John Farlow's last address somewhere but I can't find it, and if you should happen to have it or get an even later one from Cathy I wish you'd send it to me. I suppose very likely with all the recent developments he has been moved anyway. The heat here is terrific and this afternoon again I was lucky enough to be able to spend most of the time in the irrigation ditch, only this time before getting in I had to wait while a gargantuan sow and then a pair of oxen finished their ablutions. You can see that the water is not of the first water. In spite of the refreshing bath and the champagne, I don't really feel any too cheerful. I've no idea when I'll see you again and it's awful. But I suppose the whole works will have to be over before too long. But your news about Ombo rather confirms my opinion. Be sure and tell me just when you are moving to Peterborough so I can write you there right away. If you get started on repairs I wonder if the bottom pane of the bay window doesn't need some. It was getting rotten. I hope the barn and red shed haven't got a lot worse; the latter had a broken rafter in the roof under the apple tree. Mary must have a wonderful sense of color and of beauty too. I'm very proud of her.

I love you.
Sydney

May 16

Dear Sydney,

I have another cold! A miserable affair and the children have a touch of it, too; only they must be healthier than I am, for I have it worse. I know it came from Daddy. He had an awful one a week ago, and you know him! His colds are never the kind that he can give to anyone. Well, it's at its worst today, I hope. My nose is plugged, and my breath comes in short pants!

Well, early this morning I found an enormous four-leaf clover! And then, at the post office, there were two letters from you, written on the 5th. I was expecting one, but I was overjoyed at two. You see, I have yours of the 6th already, two days ago. You referred to a red setter in a way that I knew you'd written about him before. You thought you'd dated the letter May 4th, but they were both dated May 5th.

Gosh, how I wish I could hear you would get home! I can't stand it any longer, either, this separation and all the best and most fruitful years of our lives!

Did you have to fire your rifle yet? And, also, did you really come through without so much as a single scratch? Except for your "close shave," which makes me break out in a cold sweat to even think about!

I'm glad you got Mother's package. Did you ever get the first one with writing paper in it? You mentioned her paper and it made me realize I don't know if you got mine. I forget what else it had. I sent another off last week with mostly maple sugar, but I wish I could get it in really practical form. Also, has the lemon extract ever arrived? I wish I'd kept a record of when and what we sent and how many. I can't remember at all! I'm glad *everyone* enjoys the maple sugar. I hope you did too. There was practically no sap this year. It was too warm in March.

How are your feet and how were they during all that marching? It must be a nightmare to look back on, isn't it? I guess you didn't roll off the chest of drawers because there was nowhere to fall. At least, that's how I visualize it. I wonder how you'll take to a nice double bed, or will I have to take the blanket down under the kitchen table with you?

Captain Chipman was here for supper and now he and Mother have gone to the movies à deux! I told her I hoped she wouldn't spend the night in the car! Lizzie is here, but I must take her home soon. Betty is off today and tomorrow, to make up for not going last Thursday. Anna appeared today, sent by God to us, I told her, as Mother and I were doing the cooking. She's sold her house and moved into New Haven to her sisters'. But now she is rested and looks almost fatter than she did and is anxious to come out on the bus once a week. I hope she will, as cleaning 5 rooms and the sleeping porch is a bother to me! We occupy as many rooms as a small house. Because, besides the rooms we use 2 bathrooms, and by "we" I mean me and the children, so no one else is responsible for the carnage, but yours truly! It's all superficial what I do, but I do have to do something!

This afternoon we went for a short "Mitzi" drive, up Stony Lane. We haven't been there for several weeks and it looks like mid-summer! Wild azaleas, wild geraniums, buttercups and something that looks like a form of daisy aster, with large green leaves. I honestly get a great kick out of it and to my delight the children love it as much as I do! Mary was describing to me how hurried they were once; she said, "We ran and ran and were all in a 'rash!'" I know she doesn't know what a rash is.

Coming home, we saw a bunny sitting motionless in the Garvin's driveway. As soon as they got out of the cart at the barn, Mary took her shoes off—the others had their shoes off—and then they tip-toed all the way back to the Garvin's corner to try to catch a rabbit! I wish you'd seen them. You'd have died laughing! Of course, the bunny scampered off and Mary said next time she was going to take along a carrot! After that, they rode "Mitzi" a little and she bucked Mary off! She just gave the others little bounces, but Mary went sailing! Of course, she cried out she wasn't hurt and got right on again and rode some more, though she wouldn't trot that time! I honestly think Frank will be best of all. He really grips with his knees and his toes out. So far, he has no idea what the reins are for. He gets furious with me if I hold onto "Mitzi," but sometimes I have to, naturally, as he doesn't even pretend to steer her.

All the blueberry bushes around here—and there are loads on the place I never knew were here—are all heavy with flowers. If I'm here when they're ripe, I'm going to be sure to see if I can't find some berries. There are a lot of wild strawberry flowers too.

I love you an awful lot. Gosh, I wish that Congressman, or whatever he is, can get away with his proposition of cutting army expenditures by having them discharge all men with more than three children![128] It would be a real economic measure and most satisfactory to me. Wouldn't it be just too good to be true?

---

128 The bill, if there ever was such a bill, never passed. Despite being almost thirty-five when the war in Europe ended, having four children, having served in two combat campaigns—the Apennines and the Po Valley—and having been awarded a Bronze Star, my father did not have enough points for discharge.

I'm going to call Janet Shattuck tonight, just for conversational reasons. I haven't talked to her for about a month. The New Haven horse show is this weekend, but I don't think we'll go. It's sort of complicated, but you never can tell. I may weaken! Mary is looking forward to riding "Mitzi" in the Sargent Camp horse show—if they have one—and she talks of it all the time! I know you will love "Mitzi." She is so full of personality. I wonder what her coat will ever look like. The winter hair is still there, though I brush and brush. "Judy" just glistens! She's certainly strong and healthy. I never saw such a lovely coat, and I hardly ever brush her, as she's out in the pasture all day. But she looks as though she were polished daily. I wish "Mitzi's" would shine, but maybe ponies' coats never have the same gloss. I'd love to breed her this summer. Maybe I will, now we have a trailer and I can find a pony stallion within a reasonable radius.

My ambition is to someday breed "Judy" to an Arabian. They have one in Durham, haven't they? In 4 or 5 years we could probably make that trip alright?

I love you. I must take Lizzie home now.

I love you an awful lot,
Mary

May 20

Dear Mary,

Since I last wrote we moved to another area, by means of a ten-and-a-half-hour truck ride. The censorship is still on again; so I guess I can't give you any hint as to where I am. I figure that all together I have 69 points, with 85 necessary to get out of the army so there isn't much hope. I had just found a nice quiet place to sit down and write a letter when, as always happens, someone came and joined me and started up a long conversation and insisted on showing me a big bunch of postcards he'd collected. You'd think a man with the brains of an earthworm would see I wanted to be left alone so I could write. But then in my foxholes I often had long conversations with earthworms that understood the fundamentals of life much better than any of my companions. This over-friendly fellow left me so shaking with rage that I still can't control the pen properly. Another trouble with my companions is that, if or whenever I have a conversation with one of them, I always know just what he will say for the next fifteen minutes, or if it's any kind of a discussion I know all that he has to say on the subject, his arguments and opinions, before he says them with the result that I'm bored before I even start. Also I've had a cold the last few days which makes my mood even worse. By this time almost everyone in the company has been awarded a Bronze Star either for some partly fictitious heroic deed, or, if imaginations ran out in that line, for meritorious service, and I got one I think in the second manner, otherwise I would only have 64 points, not that it makes much difference.

The last letter I got from you, which came the day before yesterday, was postmarked the ninth. Betty's "husband's" wife's brother is either a liar or naturally very inaccurate, we never even came very close to Bologna. It was as you had thought, and I think the nearest we came to it was about eight miles as we went by. I never heard of him and feel no great urge to meet him. Of course most of these men don't seem to have any idea where they are most of the time anyway. It's not entirely their fault; the higher ups have a little of the attitude of the Catholic Church in the middle ages and for somewhat the same reasons. At least that's the way it appears from the worm's eye view. I got a package but I guess I already told you about that. It was some time ago and was eaten some time ago.

The trailer won't interfere with opening and shutting the back doors on the car will it? I don't suppose so. I couldn't possibly give you any hints as to my future anyway, because I know absolutely nothing. I keep being hopeful that my age or my family or something may get me home, but as yet there is absolutely no indication that it will and the point system certainly won't help me. I'm living in a pup tent again as at the last place, but this time of year it's almost pleasanter than a house. I love you an awful lot. Do you remember when we went to Boston to see Henry and Mary?[129] I remember coming back on the bus thinking it was the last thing we would do together for a very long time. It was awful, there was a moment there when, perhaps because we were having such a good time, I realized the whole truth of the horror that was coming.

I love you.
Sydney

May 21

Dear Mary,

Yesterday I got your letter written on the ninth. It certainly would be exciting if "Mitzi" was going to have a colt, but I don't see how it could be

---
129 Her brother, Henry, and his wife.

without anyone knowing about it when you bought her. People did always think "Wenny" was pregnant.

We've moved again now and are living in buildings with running water, a great luxury. And they say that after awhile we will have cots to sleep on. More and more I feel as if being in the army was probably exactly like being in jail. Except for the one pass to Florence I haven't had a pass since I met Dick and Arnold in Austin last November—no chance to go off independently by myself or get away from the ignorant bunch of morons that I have to live with. The trouble is that that's really not much of an exaggeration. They are nice cheerful companions and all that and better than the average, but the aggregate gray matter of the whole company wouldn't set fire to a match, and yet I would certainly hate to be transferred to any other outfit. It isn't so much that they have no minds at all as it is that they never learned how to use them; also, while we are always surrounded by many interesting things, natural and artificial, both concrete and abstract, they never take any interest in anything. There's nothing more contemptible than a lack of curiosity, it shows a lack of appreciation of the gift of life itself and therefore is an insult to God.

Right now we are in a place with a courtyard surrounded by a wall and although we are doing nothing in particular and have very little to occupy us, we are not allowed to go outside, and the surrounding country is unusually interesting and different from any spot we've visited before. Sometimes I have a horrible feeling: suppose somebody could read my thoughts; there would be moments when I certainly would lose what little popularity I may have because I haven't really got a very high opinion of anybody, though I like everybody of course, and also condemn things that many of them consider highly important or even sacred. I suppose most people get fed up once in awhile and feel as I do, maybe about me. But though no man can honestly say he's more intelligent than another, an accusation of ignorance is something fairly cut and dry. So at least I'm half right, I know. Sometimes I think the army is fast making me stupid too; maybe it's just that the others have mostly been in longer. If someone deliberately tried to invent a stultifying machine they could do no better than the army. I'm certain it never did anybody any good. If you ever hear anybody say anything like that you can just tell them they are a liar. It makes men stupid and lazy and in the most sinister sort of way. There is absolutely no way whatsoever in which it builds up a man's character. It does exactly the opposite. It discourages self-respect, initiative, imagination, a courageous view of life, everything, and for God's sake don't ever believe anyone who tells you differently. What's happened to the German nation now is a perfect example of that sort of thing. The more military a nation is the more certain it is to destroy itself; it's been that way all through history.

 I guess this letter is getting pretty boring, but it seems to me that the thoughts I've often thought before have now been proved correct. And anyway I feel generally fed up now and see so many stupid things going on all around me that I feel I have to let off a little more steam than is practical in any other way. I looked over the village tonight that is next to here. I wasn't able to talk to any of the natives as their language is most peculiar—that is the people, but I found a goat and a dog and could talk easily to both of them and they were very friendly. I love you an awful lot. I don't believe there's any use about thinking about getting home for a long, long time, and if I did get home to stay or on furlough I doubt if I'd be able to let you know about it ahead of time. It's all terribly discouraging and futile. I got another letter from Dick in Okinawa today. He said it was not as bad or much like what he expected, but I doubt if it's very nice, even in the artillery. I wish we would stay in one place for a little while then mail might come a little more regularly though I suppose it really comes through pretty well. I'm getting awfully sleepy. I love you. I wish I were sleeping now with my arms around you.

I love you.
Sydney

May 22

Dear Mary,

No mail today and no news to speak of or write of. I did nothing all morning and slept all afternoon. It was dark and rainy outside but cleared off beautifully this evening making the sur rounding mountain tops look deceptively close and filling me with longing to climb them, alone. I spent part of this evening talking to a boy named Stanton in Headquarters Company.[130] He's the younger brother of a friend of Dick's and is rather an intellectual, and I guess he thinks that in me he has found someone with whom he can discourse in the high plane to which he is accustomed. He showed me letters he writes home full of drawings, which reminds me of when, a long time ago, I used to write that way, but for some odd reason and also because of the censor I

---

130 PFC Henry B. Stanton of New York City.

don't feel like doing it anymore. I wish I did. I guess the army has ground all imagination out of me.

Tonight I don't feel quite so irritated at the world in general as last night, though I don't credit the world with having done anything to make me feel better. I'm writing in a nice big room, but it's full of people, has a radio blaring as usual, clouds of tobacco smoke, a spot where someone was sick on the floor, and stinks awfully of dirty clothes. Unfortunately it's a bit cool this evening and all the windows are shut. I thought sure we'd get mail today so I felt pretty disappointed. We seem to be living a more deadening life now than ever, but I think it will probably get a little better. Stanton told me an amusing story. In a letter he wrote he'd drawn a caricature self-portrait; he'd drawn his hair rather long and wild and the suspicious censors had decided it was really supposed to be a map and he almost got court-martialed. He doesn't draw too well anyway, which I suppose made it look all the more suspicious.

I love you an awful lot. I want to touch you and put my arms around you and go on from there and feel that you are still real. I want you to look at me the way you used to and to feel full of fire. Now I might just as well be dead, there's nothing live about this life. I never was really happy until I was with you and I've been terribly unhappy ever since I left you. I love the way you write about the children, don't ever stop.

Goodnight, I love you.
Sydney

May 23

Dear Mary,

I love you an awful lot. I frankly don't see any sense in my being over here instead of at home with you. I got a letter from you last night just after I had mailed mine and five more today and also letters from Uncle Frank and Arnold and mother and Mary. So today was definitely a good day. I wish I could expect that many tomorrow and every day. The orange paint must have been really something; are you sure they won't still be slightly tinted when I get home? I'm sorry it's so discouraging trying to be sociable with Charlotte these days, because I had been thinking how nice it was that you had a friend living so close by. We aren't supposed to talk about casualties so I can't tell you all about that sort of thing, but I guess you've got a pretty good idea anyway. The German horses were both saddlehorses and heavy draft horses that they had used moving artillery and wagons. They used a lot of them and a lot of horses were killed. We were on the wrong side of Lake Garda to see where Mussolini had been living; another regiment, the 86th, crossed to that side, and they went on a lot further north than we did. The dog problems sound terrific; I hope at least it has made "Mopsa" and "Rollo" learn to like each other a little better. I have practically no news at all that I can tell you. I guess it's going to be very hard on our patience from now on, and if I do go anywhere I won't know until I go. Arnold and Margaret's baby, he said, is expected in October. He said they decided that one didn't seem to make much of a family. It's funny to think he will probably have two children before I've even seen the first one.

Sydney's having no temper and being so outgoing with everybody doesn't sound at all the way I was. That's a great improvement on me; I hope to God he never will get shy. I think sometimes shyness comes from liking people, though, instead of the other way around. It's too bad Joe no longer thinks he'll get home soon. I wonder what he is doing. I suppose carrying supplies or something.

I love you.
Sydney

May 24

Dear Mary,

I wish I could come home to you. I got a letter from Dick tonight and one from John Farlow, none from you. I suppose I got so many yesterday I shouldn't expect any today, but a mail call and nothing from you is always sort of a letdown. Dick wrote a pretty long letter this time, but without saying anything about himself or what he was doing. He said the island was very pretty and reminded him vaguely, in its general effect, of Connecticut. John's letter was mostly directions how to get to his hotel in Rome, but I don't now see any hope of getting there. Just because we've been fighting doesn't seem to be considered a reason why we should get any breaks now, and I guess that anyway traveling around Italy is still not too convenient. John says he has 72 points which is three more than me. Though he's been in the army 6 months longer than I have, I selfishly feel, since I was in combat while he lived in Rome in a hotel and never saw it, that I should have as many points as he has. I'm not in a mood to be big about things and I think we both ought to be home with our children.

The mountains around here are slowly driving me mad—they almost look magical—I look at them all day and am watching them out of the window now. They are stronger than any magnet, beckon like a siren, are elusive in mists and then so clear you can almost touch them; the sunset turns the snow patches to gold and makes them crystal clear again, but this time aloof and too sacred to think of climbing. I'm conscious of them drawing me even when I'm asleep, and then in the morning they are cold and virginal. They could be the setting for all fanciful tales, all fairy stories, stories of heroic deeds or the word of God. The valley is small and level and very green, and, when you think of the valley, you think of the mountains as protecting it in a kindly circle. The outside world is too coarse to be allowed inside. The mountains stand back to let in the day, at sunrise and sunset, and bring sparkling showers to make it fresh and clean. So far there hasn't been any opportunity or anything said about mountain climbing. Our area of activity has been very limited, in a spot where any restraint is like torture, where you feel excited all the time, and that if you don't, in a moment, go soaring off into the sky like an eagle you'll burst. But we crawl around our area like a bunch of ants and pay no more attention to the mountains than they would. This afternoon I played tag football and had a pretty good time. It's more up my alley than baseball.

I love you an awful lot. There's no more news than before, nothing to tell you. We are comfortable now with good food and are treated well in the sense that you might say a herd of cattle, each in her stanchion, was well cared for.

I love you.
Sydney

༃

May 25

Dear Mary,

I got two copies of *Life* today but no letters. I feel lonely this evening; I find I don't talk a great deal with the others now. I was more sociable when we were in combat. Now that we've stopped fighting we no longer have so much in common, and our differences in interests and tastes have become more obvious. I played a little bit of tag football again today. I really enjoy that. When we were in a huddle before a play I happened to look around at the faces of the boys I was with and it suddenly came over me how very young they looked, just little boys. I could almost be their father and I burst out laughing. It seemed more as if I was playing with Sydney on the beach than anything else. After so many years of reasonably mature and dignified life it often seems funny to find myself cavorting around with eighteen-year-olds and even vainly trying to share their mental attitude.

I love you, I hope I get a letter tomorrow. A letter's the only thing that makes a day seem worthwhile. I keep thinking, even at the same time that I feel lonely, that I'll go mad if I don't get a little privacy. I've mentioned that once in awhile in discussions with the others, and as far as I can make out none of the others ever feel any need to be by themselves. I guess it's a difference partly in bringing up. Solitary meditation is hardly the kind of thing that interests them. Sometimes I think their minds are very superficial and other times I think they are just healthy extroverts. This isn't telling you any news about me, but there isn't any. I live in a large building on a sort of courtyard on the edge of a town about the size of Hancock or perhaps a little smaller. I practically never go outside the yard and have to get a pass to do so on my own and then only in the evening. I may not wander about the countryside. I sleep on a tile floor, we get regular meals and there is a place to take a shower, but I have no clean clothes and cannot wash them as I have to wear them. It's more like normal life in a United States barracks than anything I've seen here so far. The best thing about it is the shower. It's so long since I've slept in a bed that I really don't miss it anymore. It's the lack of company in the bed that I miss. That first night at home will seem pretty terrific.

The houses in this village are white or cream colored and covered with climbing roses. They are very neat and clean looking. I haven't been inside any of them. It is no longer considered correct to just walk into any house you feel like and take possession or even just to use the stove or something. The little boys around here pick up old hand grenades and such and have great sport throwing them in their backyards. It won't take much a few years from now to provoke them into throwing a hand grenade at someone that incurs their displeasure. They are nice looking children too, they might be those at the "frolic." I don't see any hope for peace in this part of the world for a long time. The people don't understand any of the principles on which peace is built. I believe the Anglo-Saxon, on civilization, is the only one that has sufficiently developed socially to keep the peace. It's a matter of individuals not social systems, and a recognition of individual rights is the key to cooperative endeavor. I'm afraid my letters are turning into pompous and unoriginal essays. But I guess that's me too.

I love you,
Sydney

May 26

Dear Mary,

Well, the day after tomorrow is our wedding anniversary, the second with us apart, and I hope to God we are together on the next one. I got your letter today postmarked the eighteenth and one from mother postmarked the seventh. Yours always comes fastest, but not usually that much faster. Well this afternoon we finally did go just a little bit of a ways up the mountainside and several of us have asked permission to go tomorrow as it's Sunday. I saw goats really way up on the cliffs the way they are in pictures. They looked vaguely like Saanens.[131] They say we can now say where we are; we are living in what was formerly the barracks of the Alpine troops in a place called Plezzo, about five miles from Jugoslavia and twenty from Austria.[132] The local people seem to speak mostly Slavic, but also Italian and German. We have on our bulletin board a long list of useful words and phrases first in English and then in Slavic. But I haven't learned any of them yet.

I hope Sonnichsen gets home as soon as possible and gets discharged. Did he say where he was? Those pictures of prisoners in Germany had made me pretty worried about anyone who was one of them. The Asa Messer I'm descended from was born in Haverill, Massachusetts, or thereabouts, and so I believe was his father before him.[133] However I've seen the name Messer from there all the way to New London, New Hampshire. It's fairly common in that section and I guess is no doubt the same family. Asa Messer was chosen, according to the old New England custom, as the least fitted for hard work on the farm and the most studiously inclined, so the family decided he should be educated. When he was president of Brown, Sydney Williams, a student there, married his daughter. The family has in Wellesley Asa's grandfather's will in which he leaves all of his house except one room to his son. He left the extra room to his daughter. I'll bet the family have no idea where that will is. It was dated seventeen something or other. The house was really in Methuen, next to Haverhill.

I don't like the idea of those boils on Mary's leg. I shouldn't think they'd

---

131 A Swiss breed of domestic goat.
132 Plezzo, now known as Bovec, is located in northwestern Slovenia.
133 Asa Messer was born in Methuen, Massachusetts. He became president of Brown University in Providence

need many vitamin pills. What's Dick Shattuck working at in Saybrook? I'm glad Alec hasn't been biting off potato plants. I'm pretty sure even the goats wouldn't eat them.

This letter became interrupted as we started doing stunts etc. I said I could do more push-ups than anyone else, and I did, but they weren't very good at push-ups. I was also the only one who could turn a handspring; so I'm not really getting very old. I doubt if you could find this place on a map but at least now you know about where I am. I got a letter from Mother with a whole long list of people who were in Okinawa or somewhere in the Pacific. Seems to me that with so many of my friends and relatives taking charge of matters out there the war will be over pretty quickly. I'd hate to be a Jap right now. I hate to think of you going back from that gas stove to that anachronistic contraption in the Dodge house, though I wish I was enjoying some of its products right now. The Italian open fires of twigs or charcoal seem more convenient, but that old stove would be a beautiful sight to me now. But I don't want you to have too much work and you'll certainly have your hands full.

I love you.
Sydney

May 28

Dear Mary,

It's our wedding anniversary and not a very good one, is it? I love you. I got a letter yesterday postmarked the nineteenth. You asked about the combat infantryman's badge. We all got those last February and I guess at the time, as I took it sort of as a matter of course as everyone got one, I never even bothered to mention it. Well I never did climb any mountain Sunday as I had hoped because I had to go on guard duty instead, and I've just about given up hope of ever being able to see or do anything I want in this country.

The grass around here is full of bright green lizards eight or ten inches long, I'm sure the children would be fascinated by them. Anyway, I am. They brought us a lot of GI paperbound books, and I'm reading *The Education of Henry Adams*. I'd always planned to read it but never did and I find it very interesting; probably partly just because it's about Boston. This afternoon I had a chance to go off by myself for a little while and I tried to draw, but without much success. I wonder if I'll ever get back into it. I'm getting older, and I should be drawing all the time and infinitely better than I do.

One trouble is that ever since I started considering myself a professional artist I became much more self-conscious about my drawings, which is a very bad thing. Tell Frank that the buttercup is beautiful. I tried it out and find, as I always suspected, that I'm exceptionally fond of butter, just like "Mopsa."

I like damp weather just as Mary does, as you know. I feel very sorry for those people who think the only good kind of weather is sunny weather. After all in this civilized age most people live in houses that don't leak very much, and don't have to be wet every time it rains. Besides, if I were home with you now, I could think of plenty to do on a dewy day. I don't see how I'm going to stand waiting for it. I'd do a lot better than I did seven years ago. In fact I've had that sort of thing on my mind very much today, almost driving me crazy.

I certainly do remember how understanding Mary always was. I always thought it was extraordinary. I'm living in a tent tonight, it's part of the guard duty, which is over tomorrow. There are several of us taking turns standing guard on the road and there is practically nothing to do. It just gives me all the more time to wish I were home and think about you in a way that's not purely spiritual. I love you and I want you in every imaginable way, but at the moment mostly in a fiery physical sort of way. Most of the company was taken today to see Venice. A four-hour truck ride each way and I suppose they were herded around the town like a bunch of sheep. Imagine seeing it that way and not even staying overnight. But I'd rather go that way than not at all and hope I get a chance, though it would probably make me so irritated I wouldn't enjoy a minute of it.

I'm beginning to realize what tremendous advantages I had when I was a civilian with a great deal more money than most, not to mention a few other things. There are stonewalls around here that look very much like those in New England.

I love you.
Sydney

May 29

Dear Mary,

I am never satisfied. Just as soon as I've finished reading one of your letters I am as impatient as ever for the next one. Today I got one postmarked the 17th which antedated yesterday's, and said how you had caught cold which you referred to in the other. I hope you've forgotten all about the cold by now. I suppose you will be swimming by the time you get this, and maybe you have been already. Even though we are fairly high up in the mountains the season here is ahead of at home. Corn is already way up and so are other things. I think I'll be able to start right off again in a great big double bed when I get home. I don't think we'll have to sleep on the floor first. That is if I can wait until we get into bed.

I wonder if the children have been able to catch a bunny with a carrot yet. When we all get home I'm sure I'll be able to arrange some way, through DeWick, to get one of the horses bred. I guess I told you that the stable he was connected with had bought quite a few of the Brown's Arabians and that they had raised some Arabian colts. I think also that he of all these people is the one that I'll be the most likely to see after we come back, unless Harley Cass lives in Peterborough. For the last two or three days Harley has been reading *Lively Lady*,[134] and he has been so deep in it that it's no longer possible to talk to him; you might as well talk to a brick wall.

There are a lot of goats around here. I haven't seen many close to, but some that I have seen look very much like "Becky"; though none of those around here are Toggenburgs. This morning I had goat milk on my cereal. To purchase dairy products is strictly against army regulations because of disease, but I boiled the milk mainly to answer any criticism that might be forthcoming rather than because I was afraid of Malta fever.[135] Naturally milk is one of the things we never have, so it was quite a treat even boiled. The goats really do climb the rocks and no doubt about it. You look up and see a bunch of them grazing on the luxuriant foliage of a place just like the face of East Rock, only higher. I'm now wondering if I'll get a chance to go to Venice the way the rest of the company did yesterday. I guess from all accounts it was a pretty terrible way to go, but a lot better than not at all. I'd probably be able to see it at least somewhat by myself; as all most of them do is just make the rounds of the bars and whorehouses. While we were on that road guard job, we had great fun negotiating with some children for eggs. They'd trade them for candy and such, and were smart as could be in making bargains. Fresh eggs are another great luxury after powdered ones that we have regularly. Today we finally got some clean clothes and now I really feel respectable. I still haven't climbed any mountains yet. The houses here are not at all Italian in style. They have steep, fairy story roofs with enormous overhangs that sometimes come all the way down to the ground. The

---

134 A novel by Kenneth Roberts, published in 1931.
135 Also known as Mediterranean Fever or brucellosis, a bacterial infection that can come from unpasteurized milk.

animals often live on the ground floor, and then there is an outside staircase with blood red roses on its side and sheltered by the overhanging roof, and the main house starts on the second floor. They look very clean and neat and very attractive. Any little bit of woodwork that shows is painted some bright color. Besides the roses there are flowers around and about and more in pots on the windowsills. The language, to me, sounds like a quick series of mild explosions, but nevertheless not unpleasant. It sounds completely impossible to ever learn. I still know nothing about what will happen to us.

I love you.
Sydney

May 30

Dear Mary,

I got your box today with the cookies and things. I've already eaten half the cookies and they are very good, also your letter written Sunday. We had a pretty easy day today I guess partly because we get up early tomorrow and will be out all night, I suppose bush crackling. It was very hot again today. They give us salt tablets, or pills, to eat with our meals. Right now we are having a downpour with thunder and lightning. The company street has become a river in about 2 seconds. The ground is clay and hardens up like cement and the water doesn't seem to soak in at all. I wish all this water could have fallen on your garden when you needed it. I hope it wasn't too discouraging having to plant the parsnips over again. In spite of its raining outside it still feels too hot in the hut. Do you remember how at home sometimes when it was like this we stripped and went out in the rain, that's just what I'd like to do now.

Today was mostly physical training and lectures—the lectures being much the most uncomfortable. This evening we got through rather early, and had time to take a shower etc. before supper. So there was lots of time after supper with nothing to do compared to usual. It should be pleasant, but instead it seems very unsatisfactory. It's in your free time that you really realize you're in the army, when you notice how many things you can't do. Tonight I feel lazy and restless at the same time. The heat bothers me this evening more than it has anytime. The shower has stopped, but it hasn't got any cooler. You mustn't get too hopeful about going to Denver, or at least I mustn't, because it would be too disappointing if it didn't work out. On the map the camp looks at least sixty miles from Denver in a straight line and

I don't know if I ever will know how long I'll be there.[136] But it certainly would be wonderful if you could come. Anyway none of it will be definite until it happens. I wish I was with you this minute instead of all this talk about the distant future, at least, though, something will turn up. It certainly would be wonderful if you came out with the children. Army life would seem pretty different.

I love you an awful lot.
Sydney

May 30

Dear Mary,

Your letter that came tonight was postmarked the 24th. That's the quickest yet. I also got a letter from Aunt Louisa. My relatives are very good about writing, but sometimes I wish some of my friends would write. John Farlow is the only one that's written me since I've been overseas, but my friends who were never numerous seem to be dropping out of sight anyway and I haven't made any real new ones, just acquaintances. I suppose it's as much my fault as anybody's that I've lost contact so completely, but I feel badly about it now. However, I suppose now we've all branched off in such different directions that not much can be done about it. But again that should make it all the more interesting to talk to them. John seems to be the most faithful friend, and yet his interests are the least akin to mine of any of them.

There's no more news of myself, nothing at all happens from day to day. The most important thing as far as I'm concerned is that I can take a shower, often really hot, almost every day, and finally I begin to feel reasonably clean. I never think very much about my future, because if I do I get too discouraged. I'm sorry Minnie couldn't tell you anything, but I didn't expect that he could. I find that my life at present does not interest me in the slightest, though if I were in the same spot under different conditions I'd find it exceedingly interesting. Aunt Louisa says that Mother, though she has been going to the church in South Natick for fifty years (it's really nearer 70), still thinks all the rest of congregation, about twenty, look just alike and she can't tell them apart, but that she can recognize a horse or dog a mile away. The funny thing is that instead of laughing with Aunt Louisa I can see just why Mother thinks the other people at church look just alike, though of different ages and sexes. I never knew any of them apart.

---

136 The reference is to Camp Carson, about ninety miles south of Denver, in Colorado Springs.

As you know Mother's family's favorite sport is laughing at each other.

I like the cartoon about the censor, I gather he has never cut anything out of my letters. I'm glad Mary thinks there are at least some people still alive who can remember when you were little. Mother would like that story. She always maintained that I once asked if she could remember the cavemen, though I remember it differently. Anyway I guess she's often told you about that. I'm glad you don't have dinner with Mr. Pope every night. I couldn't stand that sort of thing and I don't see how anyone with ordinary feelings could.

I'm beginning to get discouraged with my mustache, it's too bristly and prefers to grow every which way instead of in the directions I want it to. I've developed a very impressive gesture; every now and then I take a poem, I mean comb, out of my pocket and comb it, much as did Dickens with his beard, which disgusted the Americans and no doubt amused him greatly. However I'm beginning to run out of jokes I can make about it and think I'll cut it off pretty soon. I had hoped to carry it to Rome as I'm sure it would horrify John Farlow. But I hardly hope to get there anymore.

I love you.
Sydney

May 31

Dear Mary,

I got two letters from you tonight postmarked the 22nd and 23rd, the two before yesterday's letter. I went out and walked around the town this evening and really enjoyed myself. There was a baseball game going on inside so there were not too many people around town, which is really remarkably attractive. It's a little bigger than I thought with lots of little alleys full of flowers and greenery and all clean and fresh. I wish I could get to know and talk to the people. If I only knew German a little better I could get along; as all the older people seem to know it. Most of them speak three languages and you'd think with that many I should find some way of conversing with them. I'm afraid part of the trouble is that I'm a little shy about trying. The same trouble I might have anywhere. I spent quite a bit of time this evening walking around with an English soldier who seemed fairly congenial, at least he seemed to enjoy walking around on the footpaths in the countryside outside of town in a little more ambitious fashion than the GIs want to do. Most of them seem to take no interest in anything like that.

The bulletin board announces that there will be a ski tournament Sunday. I don't know where, I haven't seen anything but small traces of snow around here. I'm very excited about it. I'm not good enough to enter a tournament, but it might mean there'd be an opportunity to do some skiing. We never did any, but some other parts of the division did a little fighting on them, and I guess we would have if the winter hadn't turned unusually mild when we first went to the front. When we attacked Belvedere the snow was melting and patchy but there were lots of old ski tracks from patrols who had been out a few days before. When we got to Lake Garda other parts of the division had just gone up into the Alps and I believe got some skiing. It seemed that we always missed it, but maybe missing the combat skiing was just as well. I like the picture of the setter and the rabbits; her expression is awfully good. I should think the white roof on the Garvins' house would make it quite a bit cooler.

I haven't got the letter yet explaining what happened to Sydney's ear. What were you doing, cutting his hair? I guess it wasn't very serious. I didn't know Sydney was so good on his feet. I guess he's grown up quite a bit. I hope he likes and learns every kind of sport and then does not become just a sportsman. I wish I hadn't missed all those nine months when you were nursing Betsy. I love to watch you. It's absolutely impossible for me to imagine her standing up now. I suppose she's certain to be walking by the time I get home. But then it seems as if I'd been away so awfully long that I'd expect anything. I love you and it's all terrible. A woman in the village this evening pointed at my magnificent mustache and wanted to know if I were Russian. Harley Cass has been showing me his snapshots; they seem to be mostly of himself. The company seems to have acquired a puppy about 6 inches long and four inches high with a nice fat tummy and very self-confident.

I love you.
Sydney

June 1

Dear Mary,

No letters today. I've sent three postcards to the children: one of Lake Garda and two of here. None of them are very good and are hardly of a kind to amuse the children. But they might give you a vague idea of this place. They've got pretty far down the alphabet now and the three K. P.s for tomorrow are Williams, Williams, and Williams. The other two are new and I just know them by name as I learned that much today. I think one used to be an auto salesman and the other a Virginia moonshiner. I'm just hoping I can get to see the ski meet Sunday. There should be some of the very best skiers, way above my class. I wish I could get a little skiing in too, but I doubt it. This afternoon we climbed a little on the rocks on a mountain side but it didn't amount to much and didn't in the least assuage my desire to get up the mountain. I'm still reading *Henry Adams* slowly and still like it. He somehow reminds me of Arnold. The mountain that shows in the card I sent Frank is the one I see outside my window, and while by no means the highest it is the most conspicuous hereabout. Ever since we got here there have been arguments about how long it would take to climb it but nobody has made any move to find out. I'd be glad to find out if they'd let me.

The other mountain on the card I sent Mary is right behind these buildings where we live and the one I was about to climb last Sunday. I was actually going out the door with my hand in my pocket when I was called back to go on guard. It was very disappointing and then the next day being still on guard I missed going to Venice and now I'm just hoping that K. P. won't interfere with going to the ski meet. I'll have to not write too much and go to bed early tonight as doing K. P. is the only time in the army when you ever really do any work, and naturally I'm no longer used to working. I forgot, also they rationed out a little liquor tonight and I didn't get any, so I feel that I've been unfortunate lately.

This place was the scene of quite a bit of fighting in the last war and the mountains, that are limestone and covered with snails, are full of caves natural and artificial that were used for gun emplacements and such. I'm glad the Germans didn't choose to use them this time.

I love you an awful lot. I think I'll have to go to bed without writing anymore. I'm afraid it's not a very good letter tonight. I'm getting tired of all this living with nothing but a bunch of children, I was talking today to one of the few others my age and he felt just the way I do. All this adolescent stuff begins to get on your nerves eventually. My age hasn't bothered me any physically but it does mentally. I feel all the time that I know too much and understand too much to get along easily with any of them. I have to pretend to be on a level with them. Henry Adams said in that book that General Grant once said perfectly seriously that Venice would be a very nice city if it were only drained, and these people are about that speed without even his practicality. Of course some of them may have been intelligent before they came in the army, but since then their minds have gradually atrophied. I think I shall have to go to bed.

I love you.
Sydney

June 2

Dear Mary,

This will have to be a short letter because after K. P. I took a shower which seems like such a wonderful luxury after which I've been listening to a friend named Simpson from the repl. dept.[137] who has been telling me over a bottle of Cognac about his friend Cecil "Cesspool" Smith, the pipe-less plumber and other things. And it's been difficult to start writing without offending him, besides which he is pretty amusing. We all were issued a bottle of captured liquor, a bottle of Cognac and a bottle of champagne for every two men. I haven't even opened mine and the man who drew it with me doesn't drink much if any. Old Simpson is still talking to me all the time and this writing is very difficult.

I don't know about the ski meet. They say there may not be any transportation for anybody in this company to go to it. I think I've had enough disappointments anyway and this morning someone stole my cup and the supply room has no more and I'm wondering how I'll drink my coffee. It's sad, isn't it? No mail again today, now it seems ages since I got any. I had no interesting adventures today, naturally, being on K. P. It consisted mostly in sweeping and mopping and washing kettles and dishing out the food to the company as they walk by with their mess kits. K. P.s have to do that again the next day. I think they issue us the liquor because they figure we haven't had much fun even though the fighting has been over for quite awhile and it is about the easiest and really about the only thing they can do to entertain us to improve our morale. They also sent a donut girl today who gave each man three donuts (excuse modern spelling). Imagine coming all the way to Italy to do that. This letter is short and bad, but, therefore, better short.

I love you,
Sydney

---

137 Replacement department.

June 3

Dear Mary,

No new letters today but one mailed the sixteenth, a week older than the last one I got. It's the letter telling about Henry, Stu and Joe and Betty's night in the car. Were they sleeping inside it or outside it? I went to the ski meet today and really had a wonderful time even though I wasn't able to do any skiing. The race really was one for experts and I would have looked foolish if I'd entered it. It's eight years since I really did any serious skiing or have been on a mountain slope like that one. I went with DeWick and Sgt. Bronson[138] who is another I've got to know pretty well, and besides watching the skiing we walked around and climbed up the mountain a bit. Great cliffs dropped into Austria and it was very impressive, or you might say breathtaking with climbing up and looking down. I thought at first I'd go mad if I didn't get on a pair of skis, but after I'd become resigned it was all right. Really, though, when I first got up there and saw all those people on skis I got so excited I thought I'd burst, and it was an ideal place for skiing. It was warm and about half were stripped to the waist and it seemed just like spring skiing in Tuckerman's ravine. I drank some of my champagne tonight and DeWick drank what was left. It was good, only it was warm which seemed too bad. I wish we were sitting in the kitchen drinking a little spot of sherry before supper.

I love you. I'm very sleepy and I'm sorry this is another short letter. This one also would have been longer if people didn't always start talking to me when I'm writing, any other time nobody bothers to talk to me. This time it was Harley Cass talking about Peterborough and the Clements where his mother and grandfather worked.

I love you.
Sydney

June 5

Dear Mary,

I got five letters last night, two from you and one each from mother and father and Dick. Dick's letter gave practically no news about himself except that I noticed on the envelope that he was now a First Lieutenant. All the rest of the letter was urging me to apply for OCS, which there is no opportunity

---

138 Staff Sergeant Verne D. Bronson of Tangent, Oregon.

to do even if I wanted to. I guess it was because quite awhile ago I mentioned in letters home that some men had been asked to apply. I wasn't anyway, and also those that did never went, as soon after we went into an attack and they are still here and the whole thing appears to be forgotten. Besides I suppose there is a very minute chance to get out now and if I did that there would certainly be none. Which is enough reason for me. Another thing is that if an opportunity to do it doesn't come soon I will be past the age limit.

One of your letters yesterday was postmarked the 26th and the other was an old one, when you slipped with the scissors. I'm glad you took the children to the horse show; it must have been quite an adventure. I just got two more letters from you. One saying that Dick had been wounded, at least that'll keep him in a safe place for a while. The letter I got yesterday was postmarked May 14th (written May 11th). His letter to the family must have come very fast. I had just been thinking he was probably much safer than I was being in the artillery and I still believe he was. I noticed his envelope said First Lieutenant. Nobody had ever mentioned that. They always seem to take their time about operating to remove shrapnel, I don't know why.

I guess we were thinking very much the same thoughts on the 28th. I'm glad you had a sort of celebration and that your mother and father were such a help. It sounds as if you would have "Judy" all trained by the time I get home, you know more about it than I do anyway. By the way, Okinawa is fifty or sixty miles long with a couple of RR lines. It's not just a little island. So Mary appreciates "Becky's" voice, I feel as if "Becky" ought to be told about it, but no doubt she understands a great deal anyway. Mary must really have a wonderful understanding of animals.

I wouldn't worry much about Betty's philandering. It didn't sound to me as if she was doing very much work to help you. I guess I'd better write Dick a letter tonight. I'm afraid that we all got in the habit of envying those that were wounded, and who, for a while at least, would no longer have to risk being killed. Their wounds hurt them for awhile and then they recuperate in luxury while we kept right on fighting. Except for those who lost legs and such it never occurred to us to feel sorry for them. However I can see now that being wounded could be pretty terrible even if it had no permanent effects. Yesterday we climbed up on the mountain but not high enough to suit me. We sat around for a long time when we could have been going further and then came back. Maybe I can go next Sunday.

There is so much talking going on in here it's making me frightfully irritated as it's so hard to write. It seems to be getting on my nerves much more than usual tonight. I'd like to strangle the bunch of them. We saw a lot of goats up on the mountain, I kept wondering whether our goats would have nerve enough to go in the places they did. I feel rather low tonight as every night. I love you. I guess I'll keep on feeling low every night till I get home.

I love you.
Sydney

June 6

Dear Mary,

Here is a picture that Bob DeWick took of me while we were on the front line on Mt. Castelana[139] just before jumping off on our last push when we broke into and crossed the Po Valley. The mound in the background is a dugout. I've forgotten who lived in it. It's too bad that the picture doesn't do justice to my mustache, which anyhow I had foolishly trimmed a short time before that, in an attempt to make it look villainous. I think you can just see one point sticking out on the right-hand side. I don't know how the branch got in the way. I got two letters from you tonight, postmarked the 28th and 30th. They put up a notice on the bulletin board tonight for all those to sign below who would like to go skiing Sunday and said boots and skis would be furnished. Now I'm really looking forward to Sunday and am just hoping that too many haven't signed up or that I won't have guard duty that day or something. I did a little rock climbing today which was fun.

I don't suppose that 3 1/2 quarts a day is wonderful for "Gay," but I think it's pretty good for the first freshening just the same and that she should be proud of herself even though of course she's not in your class at all. With "Becky" you'd at least have more than a quart apiece.

I didn't mean the beam really, just the woodwork in general under the bay window and over the bulkhead. It's a little rotten. You'll see what I mean if you look at it. I don't believe a carpenter would be very easy to get. I really am surprised and pleased that Mary could outrun Shawn, as I thought he was quite an athletic little boy. I'm pretty certain the children don't get their speed from me. I was always very slow in a sprint. People, who are really in no way qualified to know, keep telling me, too, that maybe I'll not go to the Pacific or get discharged or something because of my age and the children. And I have to be careful not to let them make me

---
139 Monte Della Castellana.

believe it; as of yet at least there is absolutely nothing indicative of such.

I'd like to hear where Walter O'Malley is. I guess I told you he must have been in Florence either when I was there or just before. I agree with you that it would be much better if no one else handled "Judy" while you are away this summer. I think you're doing wonderfully with her. I don't see why you should worry about what other people say as they know nothing whatever about it. I don't think, either, that she'll forget anything during the summer. I haven't heard anything yet from Mother and Father about Dick. I should have pretty soon. I love you an awful lot. Maybe we ought to go back to that field in Roxbury,[140] but I don't want to take the time to go any distance at first. Though we have electricity, the bulb is so small and high I still have to write by candlelight and I've written Mother and Jane and Arnold, too, tonight and can hardly even see now.

I love you.

Sydney

Plezzo, June 7

Dear Mary,

Tomorrow, they say, I will get a pass to Venice along with those that didn't go last time. So I'm not so unlucky after all, and if I can follow that by going skiing Sunday I'll be really lucky. Some kind of a USO show was shown to us tonight, which is the first thing of that sort we've had overseas. It was a small crowd but they used a microphone. I suppose someday it will reach a stage where if you go to see a play you'll see the actors handing the microphone back and forth around the set as they speak their parts. In the old days a girl sang to the audience; now the microphone gets all the attention and the whole show gets more and more impersonal. Besides, I think a good voice is ruined by a microphone though it helps some weak ones of course.

I don't know whether I come back late tomorrow night or what, or whether it will interfere with writing. I got a letter tonight postmarked the 31st, another that came in six days. I wish I could go home that quick right now. I'm getting very fed up. This afternoon I played baseball. I played once last summer and once each fourth of July, and then, back in 1923, I played several times, and in 1921 I was pitcher on a baseball team, believe it or not. This was not real baseball, but something like what I used to call three old caps back in 1918 when I played it with Mary and Father on the lawn. This

---

140 My parents spent the first night of their honeymoon in Roxbury, Connecticut.

afternoon I was surprised to find that I was having a very good time. I hadn't lost my 1918 form at all, though of course not quite up to my 1921 style. That was before all the people I was playing with today were born, so naturally there was no one else to remember my great days.

Your last letter is the one itemizing all the things that you did on Memorial Day. I know you are happier when you are busy, but that really sounds terrific. Please, I'll be really worried if you take on anymore everyday chores. I'm glad you will be seeing Jean again; will you see her before you go to Peterborough? I should think it would be better if you left "Sweetie" and "Mocha" behind and let the kids nurse them awhile, but could someone milk them if the kids died or something, if not they would be spoilt till next time at least. But I think it's more important for you to not have to worry about it and take care of them in Peterborough. I'm awfully glad you wrote Dick, I wrote him when I first heard about it from you but only a V-mail as I ran out of airmail stamps; also your letter last night was sent free. I've stamps coming tomorrow and I'll try to bum one for this letter. In this letter you speak as if you hadn't heard from me for a long time. I've written, except for one night, everyday but for the times when we've been moving and I don't think that's ever made me skip more than two days. I am picturing the children marching up and down after the parade; I guess they really appreciated it. The name of this place, Plezzo in Italian, is Flitscher in German and something else in Slavic depending on what map you have. My days are exactly the opposite of yours, empty.

I love you.
Sydney

☙

Plezzo, June 9

Dear Mary,

I mailed my last letter without a stamp so this one will probably get there first. Well I did go to Venice yesterday. We left here by truck at five in the morning and came back the same way at one-thirty last night. It made a pretty long day, but was certainly worthwhile, being a lot better than nothing. It turned out to be somewhat the same problem as in Florence. I went in very pleasant company again, but would have seen more of what I wanted to see if I'd been alone. However there wasn't time to do more than just look around. I saw the bronze horses, but, also, as in Florence, a great many things were still in storage for safety. I suppose very likely there were more gondolas and fewer powerboats than in peacetime with the gas shortage. We wandered around and looked at the cathedral and rode in several gondolas and had a few drinks here and there and had a rather quiet and very pleasant time. It was terribly hot, and we were still dressed in woolen clothes, while everyone else—soldiers and all—were dressed in cotton. I planned to get a photograph of my mustache—the rest of me wouldn't show much—but I didn't get around to it until too late. I was with DeWick and another boy, who I believe would have rather done something a little more gay but didn't know just how to branch off by himself. No letter came from you while I was gone and I still haven't heard from the family since Dick was hurt. I don't see why not. Today I'm barracks orderly, which means I have really nothing to do all day, just to see that the two rooms in the barracks occupied by headquarters platoon stay neat and tidy. The job is a sinecure much sought after, though personally I find it a little too inactive. However it's nice to get more time for reading and writing. I think the main purpose is just so the barracks won't be empty. This morning I was rather looking forward to being by myself, but several others stayed in too for one reason or another, and part of the morning everybody was in and now everybody is getting the afternoon off, and while most are outside so it's quiet it's still not quite what I hoped. If I'd been really alone I would have tried to do some drawing and also could have written you a really good letter. There still has appeared nothing to keep me from skiing tomorrow. I'm just waiting till they post tomorrow's guard list. I think, with nothing to judge by but Florence and Venice and small towns, that English gothic churches are much better looking than Italian ones. Maybe there isn't any gothic in Italy. I don't know much about such things. It seems to me as if there were just a very few really good things in Italy, and all the others were copies of them. Or perhaps it's that there were just a very few times when common Italian styles approached perfection or maybe achieved it.

 Bob DeWick, himself, I don't believe takes really much interest in such things. But he's willing to take a little time looking at them; as he's educated enough to see there is something to be got out of it and as his wife once took a course on "Art" in college and is apt to question him about it. He has the regulation tourist point of view which, sad to say, is still a lot better than the GI point of view in sightseeing, but I would like to just wander around in a foggy sort of way taking infinitely longer to see things and very likely not being able to tell anybody, even myself, afterwards what I'd seen, but I would be enjoying myself immensely and have been thinking the most exciting thoughts which would also evaporate immediately on completion. I like to think that just the same, the images and thoughts that seem to vanish so completely from my brain are perhaps distilled rather than evaporated, and from great volumes produce just a really precious little bit that becomes part of me.

    I thought the lack of any kind of vehicles on land in Venice as much of an attraction as the multitude of them in the water. No streets, but just walking places, are so extraordinarily peaceful. The Lido was off-limits anyway and we only saw a small part of the town; so I'd like very much to go back there someday. I expected to be a little more conscious than I was of the vanished grandeur of the ancient merchant princes. Very likely it was because I was too ignorant and didn't know where to look. I saw an unusually pretty girl of about Mary's age that I wished I could sculpt. At the GI restaurant I ate two dinners and then two suppers and was still hungry so I bought some walnuts and ate them too, but it didn't do any good. Recently I've had the most terrific appetite and if I can get enough to eat I'll probably get fat the way I did in basic training.

    Well, now today's mail has come and I didn't get any today either. I really wish I could hear some more about Dick. I guess he's alright but I'd like to know and I can't understand why the family haven't written. I feel sure if it was any sort of permanent injury he would have said so in that first letter, but I'd like it confirmed. Now I keep hearing talk of people being flown home for a discharge. Everybody still admires the pictures of the children and I have that one in composition glass up too, the one of all of us. Lots of the men here now, almost half, have never seen me without a mustache, and lots of the others didn't know me well before, and they are very much surprised and say they would never recognize me in that picture. They seem surprised, too, at how much younger I looked last summer. That makes me want to cut off the mustache. I was planning to write a lot more this evening, but there was so much talk it was impossible at first, and then, when it finally quieted down and people started going to bed, Bob DeWick came in to see me and talk and he just left and it's after 11 and I didn't get much sleep last night; so I think I'll have to go to bed.

I love you an awful lot.
Sydney

Sunday, Plezzo, June 10

Dear Mary,

I sent three more cards to the children, and two of them I'm afraid are almost identical with ones I sent before, but the third is I think rather amusing. I'm wondering what you think. Just as I thought, I got up this morning all excited with the prospect of a full day of skiing to be told that for some reason we couldn't have the equipment and couldn't go. Then later I found my name on the guard list for tonight so my day of rest does not find me in too good a mood. Mail is supposed to come sometime today, though Sunday, and I'm waiting for it impatiently and hope I get a letter finally about Dick and lots from you.

Since I wrote that I did my first turn of guard, and meanwhile letters came from Mother, Father, Mary, Jane and Uncle Frank, but none from you—none for quite a while. I wish the mailman would get on the ball or something. I'm getting unhappy. Mother and Father's letters were almost identical telling about Dick, and Mary Fyffe's, too, of course; so now at least I know all they do and I guess he's not too badly hurt. Uncle Frank talked about what a remarkable person you were to be taking off for Peterborough by yourself with such a car and trailer full of animals and children. My family all have great admiration for you. But please be awfully careful and don't do too much. I don't want to come back and find you all worn out, and as I don't know how far off that is you'd better be extra careful. I love you an awful lot.

Everybody seems rather proud of how little and how sober the celebrations at home were on V-E Day. Personally I don't see that a little celebrating would do any harm. There've often been times when I've thought people might relax a little more instead of a little less. I'm terribly sleepy now as I didn't sleep much last night or the night before, and I've two hours guard tonight and again at five-thirty in the morning. I love you an awful lot. I wish I was guarding the Dodge House and doing it asleep in bed with you, and our arms around each other. I don't know just what time to start writing to Peterborough but I guess I'll wait a few days longer, or at least until I hear from you again. I love you such an awful lot, and I feel I'll die if I don't see you soon.

Sydney

Plezzo, June 11

Dear Mary,

A *Peterborough Transcript* and a *Life* came today, but no letters. It's getting on to a week since I've heard from you though mail has been coming every day. I'm not worried or anything, but I don't understand and I'll be a lot happier when I get one. *Life* had a picture of a miniature governess cart which reminds me did you ever hear anything about Hollis's? I suppose it might be rather heavy and not much use in Wellesley, but I was wondering about it. Perhaps it wouldn't be any use anyway. Today I did nothing but guard duty, and thank God now it is finished for about another two weeks I think. I spent a couple of hours this afternoon reading the *Education of H. Adams*; I think it's the best book I've read for some time, though often I don't know enough history or other things to appreciate his allusions. Apparently he was a success because he wrote such a good book telling about his failure. One can't help wondering all the time what sort of a book he would have written if he'd been married with a family. He had the same detached attitude towards the world that I've noticed in Uncle Frank; though lots of people around home have it to a certain extent. I know of some men with high scores in points who are going home the day after tomorrow, by plane probably. You can imagine how the rest of us feel. Large groups of children collect around the kitchen after every meal to beg for leftovers. They carry away coffee grounds and everything. They are, of course, ragged and dirty but pleasant looking and cheerful, when they are not fighting over some choice scrap, and I always enjoy having them around. They are a glimpse of humanity at least. Also I've always been glad that they get at least that much extra food, some of them are pretty skinny. But the rule, fortunately usually disregarded, is that they are not to be allowed in. The guard on that post, the one I had, is supposed to keep them out. I let everyone in and I believe if an officer had come by and ordered me to keep them out, that I would have been so mad I would have refused point blank.

Everybody is sitting around now talking about, or rather rehashing, all our combat adventures; that's the main subject of conversation always. I hear remarkably different stories about the same incidents. The stories, too, naturally improve all the time. The only point on which there is no variation is that they all say they were scared to death all the time. However, it certainly is surprising how very differently certain days impressed different people.

That little black six-inch puppy I mentioned awhile ago is still around with the white one who's a little bigger. The other day the black one chased away the Slavic equivalent, I suppose, of a police dog. My *Life* that just came is the one with a whole collection of artist war correspondents' pictures. I've been watching the different men look through the magazine and I haven't seen one yet that stopped to look at them. Now is that the fault of the artists, or just that the average man is more interested in the documentary value of a photograph? But it should be possible to draw or paint a picture that would hold a man's attention for a second or two. I love you an awful lot. I hope there hasn't been something to keep you from writing. I'm still sleepy partly from the guard duty and partly perhaps from my wrestling with H. Adams. I spent part of this evening looking at pictures of DeWick's wife and children. They look very nice. I wish I could see mine in the real flesh.

I love you.
Sydney

Plezzo, June 12

Dear Mary,

Still another mail and no letter. I really am beginning to get a little worried and I don't understand it. I thought for sure I would get one tonight. There's not much to write about anymore. I never do or see anything interesting because the army won't let me. The weather has been sparklingly clear lately, making the mountain tops look very inviting, but I haven't yet and doubt now if I'll ever climb any of them. If I should get to climb one it would probably be on an organized hike and not much fun. This afternoon we played some tag football which was not taken too seriously and was very good fun. But when we came in and I was sure there would be some mail for me and then there wasn't, I felt terrible. I suppose it must be that the mail just got delayed somehow. But it never happened before like this. I feel sure that if something had happened someone else would have written, at least I hope they would.

They've been giving out passes a little more lately and I think that someday I might get a five-day pass to Rome. I think if they offered it now I wouldn't take it because that would be five more days without a letter, or if anything is wrong I mightn't be on hand to get a message about it. I can't seem to write very well tonight. I just wish I were with you and there wouldn't be any writing. If you go to Peterborough on the 21st, I ought to start pretty quickly sending them there, but I don't know for sure. I'm glad it's summer and you won't have to be using lamps much.

Mary, I love you so. Please always be careful of yourself. The longer I stay away from you the worse I get. I don't give a damn about anything anymore. I gave up trying to be a good soldier long ago. I just want to go home. You're ten times as capable as I am, but I still feel as if I ought to be home helping you with all the children and everything so you won't get tired, and so you can help me from getting discouraged and feeling as I do now. I guess it's always been more you helping me then my helping you. I think more than anything else I want to just see and touch you. I love you. I started to sign at the end of the last page forgetting this one. I have to write tonight to Dick at his hospital address. I should have last night. The papers report an agreement concerning the Trieste area in which Tito will let Alexander[141] hold it until the peace conference. I understand that I'm not supposed to discuss things of that sort, but I would like to very much. My own observations have been limited. I wish I could get a pass to go to Carrara and see the marble quarries. But I think it would be pretty hard to get there. I want to start being an artist again before it's too late altogether. Most successful artists were well established before they were my age and I've hardly even started. Do you think it will be too late? I'm serious; I'm really afraid. Yet I want to be an artist more than ever. I'm sorry this is such a gloomy letter.

I love you.
Sydney

❧

Plezzo, June 13

Dear Mary,

I finally got another letter, postmarked the second. I got one of that date from Jane some time ago. My last letter from you was the thirty-first. I think there's something the matter with the mail. Today has been a rainy day and we've done practically nothing. The rain was snow on top of the mountains and they look very impressive now. Seems to me somebody like Sonnichsen certainly ought to get out of the army instead of a furlough no matter how long it is. I don't believe anyway that he'll ever be sent out of the States again. Maybe Mary is right and you should get some fancy clothes to put on once in awhile. It's extraordinary to me how much the men I see care about clothes and their general personal appearance. They care more about clothes than I

---

141 General Sir Harold Alexander.

used to think even women cared. They also all use hair oil, which I think is disgusting. I'm talking about the GIs not the natives. However the German soldiers were worse and usually used perfume and had long hair, which they were continually combing, not at all like the rough looking cropped haired variety that is usually caricatured.

We now have pin-ups on the wall, which is the first time I've seen them since I've been in the army. They include, besides the usual thing, a picture of a bottle of whiskey and a big juicy steak. At the moment I'm eating peanuts, drinking beer and smoking a cigar all at once. We just got our PX rations which means we each pay a certain amount and get a supposedly corresponding amount of peanuts, cookies, soap, tobacco, and indigestible candy, etc. It's usually mostly candy if you could call it that, kinds that we used to hear advertised over the radio in Peterborough, and that I never would have thought of buying. The cigars are not good but passable and there are very few cookies. It all comes haphazardly in odd amounts and today the whole afternoon was most noisily spent dividing it up, and this evening in trying to trade what some didn't want for something else. The ration included a watch which they raffled off, and I won it and gave it away as I have one.

I remember thinking the White girl's work was good and better than her husband's. If you see people like that sometimes it might help to keep from forgetting about sculpture. We'll have to do an awful lot to make up for all this wasted time. I wish I could start now. I'm going to go right on working on the same things I was working on when I left, unless when I get home they look a lot worse than I expect or remember them. Sometimes I get awfully worried that you might look different when I get home, but I don't think so.

I love you.
Sydney

Plezzo, June 15

Dear Mary,

Yesterday afternoon I got a pass to Udine and I didn't get back till after midnight, and this afternoon I finally got a chance to climb a mountain and I didn't get back from that until eight tonight, then had a shower and supper, then DeWick came down to the room where I live to tell of his adventures in going to Austria today on a detail to get wood and to hear my adventures on the mountain. Now he's gone and I've just finished your letters mailed the fourth and fifth. I got one of the sixth and another one last night. So I guess I'm all up-to-date again and I'm sorry I complained about the lack of letters. In Udine I walked around the town and went to a Russian stage show for allied troops. I suppose it was meant to promote good will and it certainly did, as it was very good. When I got back into the barracks I was surprised to hear the Russian song which they had used to complete the program, coming from upstairs and found a boy of Russian extraction was making merry with some others for the benefit of a man who went home this morning because he had over 85 points. The Russian boy was playing a fiddle and doing it very well too. Anyway I didn't get much sleep last night and it's 10:30 tonight and the mountain climbing was the most strenuous thing I've done for a long time.

We went just as fast as we could the whole time and it was wonderful fun, but I'm pretty sleepy now and I'll have to tell you more about it tomorrow. The enclosed is a picture this same man who went home took during our last push, about a week after the other picture was taken, and I hadn't shaved in between and was not to for quite awhile yet. There is a disagreement as to who the medic is. I think it is who I think was far and away the most heroic man in the company, and a very pleasant and unassuming fellow. His name is Winbush.[142] The others in the background are all German prisoners that we'd captured shortly before. They seemed very pleased to have their pictures taken. I love you an awful lot. I've heard that we are now classed as occupation troops but it could be changed, if it's true, any time. A lot of Jugoslav troops have moved out of the town and the situation is easier as you probably read in the papers. We are right on the Isonzo River[143] which is the temporary boundary till the peace settlement decides where it is to be eventually fixed. They goose-stepped out crying 'Zivella Tito' (long live Tito) the only Slav word I know. It's too bad Bill Lage is getting so bad. I think you're doing wonderfully with "Judy."

I love you.
Sydney

˜

Plezzo, June 16

Dear Mary,

Lately I seem to be lucky, and today DeWick somehow wangled passes for us to go to Austria this afternoon to come back tomorrow night. I never thought I'd get passes enough to interfere with letter writing but I have the

---

142 PFC Robert Winbush, from Jackson, Tennessee, was in the Medical Detachment. In the *History of the 87th Mountain Infantry*, published in October 1945, the author Captain George F. Earle writes about how PFC Winbush, caught in shellfire at the foot of Monte della Spe, went ". . . running from casualty to casualty throughout the bombardment, took care of both these men. . . ."

143 Now called the Saco River. It flows for about eighty miles from the Julian Alps in northwestern Slovenia and through northeastern Italy to the Adriatic.

last few days. In last night's letter I forgot to enclose the picture I talked about, so here it is. The mountain we climbed yesterday is extraordinary in that it is all covered with caves and military installations of the last war, even way up in the most inaccessible places. We saw an old human skeleton lying in a hole, but went so fast we didn't have time to look at most of the things. Just six of us went, and, though an officer was leading us, we were able to cultivate the illusion of being civilian for the afternoon at least.

After what I've seen now, I can picture exactly Bill Lage talking to Allan Banister; we have a not too nice name for that sort of thing. What rank is Bill Lage now, Lt. Commander? I think Mary's names for "Becky's" kids are very good, particularly "Poison Ivy;" after all it sounds nice to a goat. But it's a little as if we called our children Lemon Pie, Banana Split and Fish Eyes in Glue. I hope you arrange the Peterborough expedition in every way so that it will be as easy as possible for yourself. I had another letter from John Farlow who's still in Rome and didn't mention any prospects of moving; also his job sounds like the kind that might keep him here. So maybe I might see him sometime. DeWick is here waiting for me to go.

I love you an awful, awful lot,
Sydney

June 17

Dear Mary,

No letters yesterday or today. We went to Austria all right and spent the night in a British camp at Klagenfurt.[144] It could be the other side of the world from Italy. The country and people look so different. It's infinitely more attractive than Italy. Good looking people, clean and nicely dressed; in fact, I kept thinking all the time that for an enemy we were supposed to have just beaten they should look much worse.

German soldiers were strutting around with very pretty girls admiring them, and the British soldiers were pretty irritated that they weren't allowed to talk to them, I mean the girls, naturally. Some parts of the country looked like New Hampshire and more of it like Vermont. We thumbed rides up there and then on the way back got a ride by a different road all the way down to Udine which is forty odd miles south of here and then back here so we really got to see a lot of country. The only trouble with the trip was that we got very little to eat. You can't go into any restaurants or such and anyway of course most of

---

144 Klagenfurt is the capital city of the southern Austrian province of Carinthia, located on the eastern shore of Lake Wörthersee.

them are closed. We subsisted on tea and buns from British canteens. I feel now that I've got around quite a bit recently, and that I shouldn't have complained so much about not being able to see anything and being bored.

We stopped and watched the people by a swimming pool today, and I wish I didn't feel so self-conscious about drawing because it would have been a wonderful place to draw. I didn't have anything to draw with but if I'd been doing it all along I would have.

I have an idea that tomorrow we are to go on a two-day hike, in which case I won't be able to write tomorrow night and there won't be a chance to get a letter till the day after tomorrow. I don't know whether to send this to East River or Wellesley or Peterborough. I feel worried about your trip to Peterborough. I hope Mrs. O'Malley or somebody can have the house all ready for you. Couldn't somebody even get food for you ahead of time? I think, though, I worry most about the automobile trip itself.

The other day I saw a girl walking along the road with a pack on her back, they almost always carry packs, and a young goat was riding in the pack. After spending the whole weekend riding in the backs of trucks, I find sitting down now none too easy. Also dust has been blown under great pressure into every crack and pore on my body. However you get a much better view from the back of an open truck than you ever could from a car. This trip wasn't like going to Florence or Venice and I was glad to have company. Where is Henry now, still in Egypt? I should think he might be moved. I want to know what the children think about Wellesley. I love you an awful lot. They've been having a movie and I hear a terrific racket showing it must be over, and peace in the barracks along with it.

I love you.
Sydney

§

Plezzo, June 19

Dear Mary,

When we got back from the overnight hike I found your letters of the eighth and ninth. You must have somehow overestimated my points. Those ten were already counted in when it made 69 and I'm afraid there's no way to make the number any bigger. I'm glad it takes eleven months to produce even a pony colt, as I suppose there's a possibility I might be home by then. You know beforehand that I don't think it's a silly idea. This morning, as we had slept on a mountainside and had nothing to do till noon, another man and I got up at 5:30 and started off at 6:00 to go and climb by ourselves. It seemed wonderful to me, and it was a clear windless day when we could rest comfortably up on top of things and see for miles. We went up onto snow fields that would have been perfect skiing if they hadn't been rather inaccessible, and we saw at a great distance some sort of animals that went bounding off up practically vertical slopes having seen us almost as soon. The other fellow said they were goats, and later I saw their tracks, which were more like deer and bigger than goats.

I slept last night on a soft bed of leaves that I spent quite a little time making. I find that sleeping outdoors in such a situation with peaceful surroundings is quite different from combat and nicer than a tile floor. I slept better than for months and woke up feeling miraculously fresh even at 5:30 in the morning. What with passes and mountain climbing the last week or so has been very pleasant; we are even getting better food to eat. It seems too good to last. Caporetto[145] is not as I thought, as yet at least, in Jugoslavia, though right next to it; also, it's not where headquarters is. It's the next town down the road from here and occupied by us. It's on our side of the river and Tito's men on the other side. I'm very glad your father's going to make the trip with you. Do you mean to Wellesley or Peterborough? I'm still not sure whether you are going to Wellesley or not or when to write to Peterborough. I feel that it's surer to write to East River. I don't think if you take "Sweetie" to Peterborough that you should ever try to come back with the kids. I should think you'd have to get rid of them somehow, but I'm afraid I don't know how. I don't think my letters are very vivid. I wish they were. I hope I can describe the things I do better when I get home. All my last letters have been short. But I love you an awful lot. The trouble is the atmosphere isn't good for writing usually till late at night when I'm pretty sleepy as I am now.

I love you.
Sydney

Plezzo, June 20

Dear Mary,

Today I got your letter of the twelfth and letters from mother and Jane and surprisingly enough a letter from Joe Fyffe's[146] Aunt Bess. She said she thought I might like to hear about my family, and how they seemed from

---
145 Caporetto, famous as the location of a battle during World War I in which 40,000 Italians died. It is now in Slovenia and called Kobarid. It is also where Ernest Hemingway wrote *A Farewell to Arms*.
146 His brother-in-law, married to his sister Mary.

somebody outside the family, and she wrote a very nice letter describing a visit she made. It never occurred to me that I might get a letter from her; even when I saw her name on the envelope, I assumed that Mary had perhaps written me a note while visiting at Miss Fyffe's house.

I'm not surprised that "Becky" had trouble with four; that's quite a lot, after all goats aren't supposed to have litters. The last time that I remember she had a very easy time. I'm sorry the strain was so hard on everybody else too, but after all it usually isn't that way. It's hardly time to start worrying about "Mitzi." The letter from Mother said something about my being so brave to get the Bronze Star. When I wrote about it I carefully explained, just so they wouldn't get any such silly idea, that I did not do anything brave, that everyone in the company, practically, got one, and that I haven't even got it yet, just that my name appeared in the list on the bulletin board in an announcement that it had been awarded. As a matter of fact it is awarded so freely and indiscriminately that no one attaches any importance to it whatsoever and it is generally considered pretty much a joke. It's like the rank PFC, there's hardly any longer any such thing as just plain private, anyone who joins this company automatically becomes a PFC; there are no privates. There is a like situation all the way up and down in ranks and awards. But occasionally someone is forgotten. Besides all that I think my Bronze Star is for meritorious service and not for bravery. I wisely kept as much as possible in the rear whenever I could. The Stars are given out at a formal ceremony, and, as so many are to get them, they can only give out a few at a time otherwise everyone would pass out from standing so long at attention. Mine was one of the last awarded and I don't know when I'll get it.[147]

I wouldn't have written so much about it if I hadn't been worried as everyone seems to have got a false impression; although I had been afraid of that and had tried to make it plain when I first mentioned it. I hope it's plain now. I have to go on guard again tomorrow evening and I'm not looking forward to it.

I love you an awful lot.
Sydney

Plezzo, June 21

Dear Mary,

Your letters mailed the seventh and eleventh came today. The letter was the one about the coming of the pony stallion. It must have been very exciting.

---

[147] I suspect my father was being modest. His Bronze Star was awarded for "meritorious service." In *Green Cognac: The Education of a Mountain Fighter*, William Putnam writes, about the 10th Mountain Division of which he was a part, that ". . . almost 300 were awarded the Bronze Star and nearly half received Purple Hearts." Putnam received a Silver Star, Bronze Star, and a Purple Heart. As a runner, my father was a moving target for German snipers.

I should think it would be a good idea to keep him another three weeks so as not to be disappointed. I've just finished my first two hours of guard and I go on again at eleventhirty tonight. This time my post is on the square in Plezzo and I can watch the people walking around which helps to pass the time. The only trouble is that a good bit of the time there is nobody in sight at all, and, except for a rare Jugoslav soldier's truck; the only traffic is GI vehicles. Women carry hay in from the fields in big bundles on their heads. One walked by leading a black sheep. A Jugoslav soldier that looked about fourteen years old was eating an ice cream cone (they have them all around here). Two boys went by on a horse and came back later driving it in a wagon; another man went by on horseback. A very small girl rushed down the street pursuing a still smaller boy. A group of girls looking quite well-dressed and clean walked by, and that's about all the activity there was in the village square for the two hours. It's a pleasant village, but you can see why the men think it a little boring though it's gay enough to suit me.

Your package came with the books and maple sugar and cookies. The cookies are all gone now but not forgotten, and the maple sugar would be too if there wasn't such a wonderful lot of it. At least the books aren't used up yet. I didn't see anything in the paper about lowering the minimum number of points, but everybody seems to assume that they will sometime not too far off. But they'd have to lower it quite a bit to do me much good. They give up passes to Trieste now. They just started doing it, and I will certainly scan the harbor, if it's not off-limits, for Joe's boat. I'll be interested to go there too just because it's been the subject of so much dispute. I'm going to go to bed now and sleep a couple of hours before going on guard at 11:30 because I go on again, the same as last time, at 5:30 a.m. You didn't say anything in your letter about the four-leaf clovers and the daisy that were enclosed. I'm going to send this to Wellesley just in case you might be there. It seems as if it must be too late to write you in East River. I love you an awful lot. I wish I were going home with you. I'm pretty sure I won't have to start getting used to a soft bed gradually.

I love you.
Sydney

P. S. I sent yesterday's letter to Wellesley and this to East River, as I'm not sure when you go. I'll write both places so you'll get some at least without delay.

☙

Plezzo, June 22

Dear Mary,

Tonight it's terribly hot. The first hot night we've had in these mountains. This afternoon shortly after I had come off guard they came into the room and said three people could go skiing and to be ready at three o'clock. The rest of the company was about half a mile away and playing baseball. I was sent down to get two others who were to go skiing with myself. Of course when we got back, and got ready and waited about half an hour and nothing happened we found that somebody had misunderstood somebody. It was meant to be that the names of those who wanted to ski on Sunday were supposed to be turned in by three o'clock. By the time we found that out it was way after three, but at least we got our names in for Sunday. They say the patch of snow they've been skiing on is getting very small, but I'm hoping it'll still be longer than the skis so I can slide a little.

Your letters of the thirteenth and fourteenth, I mean postmarked so, came today. I can imagine how shy Warren Sonnichsen must have been coming to see you. They ought not to keep him in the army any longer after all that. The last time I was on guard today was at noontime and I practically melted away. The post is on the sunny side of the street with the heat reflecting from buildings and sidewalk. I was facing the square house that shows in one of the postcards I sent the children, and all the time people were going in and coming out with both hands full of ice cream cones, (we aren't allowed them anyway) and taking them to the little park-like place nearby where they could sit on benches in the deep shade by a little fountain. However, I stood the torture bravely.

I wonder if you had been giving "Mocha" a little too much grain, whether that might account for her not seeming well. After all, I suppose that during all this time when she wasn't doing anything she needn't have had any at all unless the hay was bad. I gave her quite a little in Peterborough when I thought she was bred. I hope you can get rid of those kids quickly before the children get fond of them, but they probably have already. I guess we'll never be cold-blooded enough to be real farmers. But I don't see why it should affect our kind of farming too much. While I was on guard in the heat dressed all in wool, an English soldier came up and spoke to me; he was with a group of them and they had nothing at all on but shorts and shoes.

But at least they weren't carrying cool drinks in their hands. I had quite a talk, which is against the rules when on guard, and we admired the pictures of each other's children. Married soldiers spend a great deal of their time doing that.

I love you.
Sydney

⁂

Plezzo, June 23

Dear Mary,

No letters tonight. However I've been getting them pretty regularly lately so I shouldn't complain. We find now that when we put our names in for skiing Sunday, tomorrow, that it was as spectators, as they are having some kind of a meet. I'm not so sure I want to go now unless there's some chance I can get on some skis. Next week I'm going, I think—in the army you can never count on anything—to intelligence school. That means military intelligence; they are not so optimistic as to try and make me intelligent. Everything is called a school around here; so I don't know whether it will amount to anything or just what to expect, but it could be very interesting. Bob DeWick is going too.

Some ambitious fellows have built a fine-looking bar in the cellar and are hoping to get some kind of a ration of beer and liquor to dispense thereat. Somebody having heard that I was an artist wanted me to draw pictures on the wall. I got a piece of that coal and drew a beefy damsel in vaguely Demetrios's style and it was awful, but they seemed to be satisfied. Of course there were a number of guys standing around watching and the surface of the wall kept peeling off and making white where it was supposed to be black. I didn't feel in the mood to draw anyway and kept wishing I could get a cup of coffee or something to stimulate me. Altogether I think I went through more strain doing that, almost, than I did in combat. I felt worn out afterwards, but I did feel anxious to draw some more. I don't believe anybody else feels the way I do when drawing, and I'm sure it never occurred to the others that I was under such stress, just drawing a barroom picture. I'm looking forward though to drawing some more, but I think I'll make caricatures unless I'm feeling pretty good.

This morning about 49 others and myself, in front of the whole battalion, were formerly presented with the ribbons and citations that go with the Bronze Star. A major pinned on the ribbons, and as far as I know he didn't prick a single man, even accidentally. It appears to work out that everyone who went through all the fighting without missing any of it, and didn't get a Purple Heart, gets a Bronze Star. Though a few didn't. I think it's just a way of giving us a few more points. The citation was written by a couple of imaginative friends of mine.[148] I believe the war department sends a copy of it home. I was walking around town this evening and thinking again that it is an unusually attractive place. I wish you could see it. The only trouble with it is that it has these big barracks, so I suppose it will always be full of some kind of soldiers, and they will always complain that the place is completely dead.

I hope Anna Mary doesn't starve to death this summer. I don't believe Mrs. Adams is invariably boasting when she appears to be. I think some of the time she's just talking, but also, no doubt, she does take an only child's mother's point of view. All New England women feel a little sorry for themselves; it helps keep them contented.

They are going to give five day passes to Trieste; so if my turn ever comes around, and Joe is anywhere about, I might find him, though then of course I could only address him from a respectful difference. I wonder if he might meet Ombo. I wonder if you are in Wellesley now. It's prettiest, at least more flowers, earlier, but I always liked it best this time of year or even a little later, when weeds begin to get really tall, and the pond is black and sensual at night. I hope your father did or is going with you, and I want to know whether "George" remembers you. I know he will. What about "Mopsa"? I don't even know, but I suppose you are taking her. How much do you think the children remember about Wellesley? I wish they could know it well. I hope you are sure the water and everything is really ready in Peterborough before you go. You haven't said yet what you are going to do about the pump. If we only had electricity in already, it could be automatic. Everybody is supposed to study something or other now, and they posted a long list of courses, some correspondence and some not. They are mostly, of course, various trades such as plumbing, automobile mechanics, poultry raising, etc., but also there are some which are supposed to correspond to school and college courses. There isn't anything very suitable for me, and I rather doubt if anybody learns very much, but I still think it's a good idea. There are no courses on any of the obvious things to study in Italy.

I love you an awful lot.
Sydney

---

148 One friend, apparently, was PFC Joseph J. Ziminski of White Haven, Pennsylvania.

Plezzo, June 24

Dear Mary,

No mail today and I suppose those three sweet ladies[149] are against my ever getting a chance to ski. This morning I set off with full equipment with a lot of others in the truck and we followed other trucks. But after a ways I noticed that we began dropping behind and only went uphill with difficulty. It appears that the brakes were too tight and that the wheels would hardly turn. Can you imagine anything in the world more useless than a wheel that won't turn? They say that the invention of the wheel was the original great mechanical discovery of primitive man; so you can see how far back the situation carried us. However with the help of low speed the wheels would still turn perhaps even as well as the original wheel, so we continued slowly at the expense of the great quantities of gasoline necessary to furnish the extra power. Well, we dropped quickly from the sight of the other trucks and then naturally lost our way. Finally, after going 140 miles alternately at a snail's pace uphill and a terrifying pace downhill, we met the other trucks coming back. The skiing place was on Mt. Grossglockner, the highest mountain in Austria. It was only three miles ahead and we could see the whole mountain was covered with snow and it was only 2:30 in the afternoon, but the truck turned around and followed the others back. I was really disappointed. We got back at 7:30, having sat in that truck for twelve hours. Anyway I saw a lot of Austria and it was a beautiful trip all the way and I enjoyed all of it except for the last little bit when I began to wish I could get back onto solid ground.

Italy seems to be all fruit and gardens, and Austria is hay and grain and pasture, mostly livestock, and lots of lumber. There aren't any woods in Italy that I've seen. I saw big Saanen goats that looked good and cattle, and the most surprising quantities of horses, a great many with colts. There were both heavy horses and light and mostly good horses. Smooth green fields in the valley and velvety pastures on the hills and mountains that would make wonderful skiing in winter. I haven't been down to the improvised bar yet to see if they painted out the picture I drew yesterday. They really should, but I hope they didn't. There are lots of pretty children in Austria that look just about like our own at home, and I'm afraid I would probably notice the same thing if I went to Germany. Austria reminds me much more of home

---

149 The three fates of Greek mythology: Clotho, Lahkesis, and Atropos.

than does any place I've seen in Italy, so I got homesick today. I wonder each evening if you are on the way to Wellesley.

I love you an awful lot,
Sydney

***

Plezzo, June 25

Dear Mary,

This is the day you said you might go to Wellesley. All day I've been wondering if you did. I think I'll send this letter to Peterborough, but I don't know how long you'll be in Wellesley and I guess you couldn't tell beforehand. I got letters today from you and Father, both postmarked the fifteenth. Yours was the one with the clipping about the ski troopers in Norway which I thought was very interesting. I never heard the intelligence school mentioned at all today, so I don't know if I'm still to go to it or not. I went down to the bar this evening after working up enough courage to try to draw another picture, but I found the place locked up and deserted.

Last I heard Walter Bailey[150] was in Florida at an infantry replacement training camp. They might have thought he was too old to come back to the division. I understand that he wanted very much to come back. I should think if "Mocha" had only one kid it might not be enough to keep her milked out and might spoil her. We got our beer ration (we pay for it) tonight; so the place is quite noisy though this particular room is quiet. I don't see why the family hasn't heard again from Dick. He should have left the hospital by now and I don't know what his address would be. A letter to his old address would get to him eventually, but from what I've seen here it might take a very long time, and there, I should think, it might, with so many times greater distances, be much longer.

We still have the two puppies, one black and one white, in the camp. We also have now two Jugoslav boys of 14 or 15. They fought with Tito and for some reason don't want to stay with his troops, or their families who live here. I'm still hoping that someday I'll get a pass to Rome. Sometimes I get pretty worried thinking about you all alone up there in Peterborough. Is Anna Mary going to be there all the time or what? I should think she'd be wanting to go home or see her friends all the time and she probably should. Now I really wish there were more conveniences there, and that the barn was better and everything in better shape and easier to handle. I wish the barn

---
150 Another friend and classmate from school and college.

door were easier to open. Maybe you should get somebody to come and split up a supply of kindling. At least if that wood we put in just before we left is still there it ought to be pretty dry. I hope you won't see a lot of things that ought to be fixed, or taken care of, and get yourself tired out. You should put that padlock on the well. Do you remember I never got around to doing it? It wouldn't take Mr. Wilson a minute if he were over there sometime. I'll think of you sleeping in our bed.

I love you.
Sydney

P. S. I hope this letter doesn't get forwarded to East River and then back to Peterborough or something like that. I've tried to guess so they will go about right and you will at least get some of them without delay. It is greatly to my credit that I didn't on several occasions today commit gruesome murder.

෴

Plezzo, June 26

Dear Mary,

Believe it or not I spent the whole day drawing. They got permission for me to take the day off from training so I could go on drawing pictures in the bar, and, more important than that, this afternoon I felt as if I was really getting the feel of it back again. I've drawn four pictures on the walls and have one more to do, and one of the pictures I think was really all right.

I believe that the real reason for building this bar is to give us something to distract us, and keep some men occupied as a change from drilling and training. They've put an awful lot of work into it, and have made as good a bar as many real ones; it even has a rail. The whole thing consists of three rooms in the cellar: one with the bar and two with tables, and they've completely done over the walls and ceilings of all three rooms. They really worked hard, like civilians instead of soldiers. It's supposed to open tomorrow night and there's plenty of liquor for the opening, but after that I don't know where they'll get it, and of course after all that work no one knows when we might move out. The point of it all, as far as I'm concerned, is that all this time I've been afraid to draw unless I was alone, which naturally I never was, but now I've finally broken that, and it wasn't very easy. It was drawing under as much psychological difficulty as you can imagine and one of the hardest day's work I've ever done. I feel as if I'd accomplished a great triumph over myself. If there hadn't been two or three that encouraged me greatly I never would have been able to do it. It would never occur to anybody what a terrifically important occasion it was for me, just drawing what the soldiers call dirty pictures (though they aren't) on the walls of an improvised bar. Now if I can only make myself keep on drawing whenever there is occasion, regardless of the situation, maybe I can get back into the swing of it or even go ahead.

The main point is to never again let myself get so self-conscious about it. I don't think I will if I keep on doing it all the time. I'm going to try to do that, and I know I would if I only felt as brave all the time as I do this evening. Besides the self-conscious part, drawing even the simplest or most childish thing is for me an enormous emotional workout and I've no idea why, but for that reason too I sometimes don't dare draw. I'm afraid this is a terribly self-centered letter. I didn't get any mail today. I wonder if you did go to Wellesley yesterday.

I love you.
Sydney

June 28

Dear Mary,

I got your letters written on Friday, Saturday and Sunday the 17th today and one from mother saying Dick had just telephoned from California and expected to be sent east. So that's why he hadn't written. I'd just written him last night, and I suppose he'll get it in a few months. I wonder whether he's hurt more than we thought, or whether it's just that there isn't much hospital space in the Pacific and cases that will take any length of time have to be sent to the States. I'm rather worried about it but I guess I'll hear more pretty soon.

Last night was the grand opening of the bar, and I didn't write any letter. 190 gallons of beer were consumed by not more than 200 people. However it was very weak beer, and, while there was lots of noise that everyone cheerfully mistook for music, there were not very many really drunk. A few British soldiers and a sizable group of the local gentry attended, the latter adding a few resonant Slavic touches to the din. A good time was had by all, even though no one got hurt. My pictures were admired, but more attention was bestowed on the picture drawn by Sergeant Stone[151] (who owns a farm in Westmoreland, New Hampshire) of a male chasing a female each of their

---

151 Staff Sergeant Vernon A. Stone of Biddeford, Maine.

hips being constructed of the appropriate parts of an electric light plug and socket. Underneath was inscribed something about when the lights of the world go on again.

    I drew pictures yesterday and again this afternoon, and I hope I'll be allowed to draw some more. The training doesn't seem to be too rigorous, as I was allowed two days off to draw and another boy was given a day off because he wanted to practice the piano. Some others, for some time now, have done nothing but train for a boxing match, and we have a company baseball team which does nothing but practice baseball etc. One man from the company left for Brazil to represent something or other of the U. S. forces that are to welcome the Brazilian troops back home from Italy. It sounds silly, but maybe not. It's a long way to transport a man for a ceremony.

    The clipping about Bill Mauldin I like, because I didn't see the cartoons reproduced and because I like to read anything about him. But I find plenty of fault with the text. The pictures are definitely not exaggerated. It makes me sort of mad that Mr. Sheehan,[152] who undoubtedly was sitting in a comfortable chair, immaculately shaved and with his stomach making comfortable noises as it digested a good meal, has the nerve to say such things. In combat, soldiers that I saw looked just as dirty and unshaven most of the time and often a lot worse. If you go two or three weeks without shaving and sleep in holes and sweat and hit the ground or mud or dust or whatever happens to be under your feet when a shell comes over (sometimes it was manure), you don't end up looking like the beautifully groomed soldier you see mowing down the enemy in advertisements. Mr. Sheehan says they are not portraits. They are the only realistic portraits of GIs that I've ever seen of real soldiers that do their own fighting on foot. The captions are almost invariably things that have gone through my own mind at one time or another, and I've only been overseas a short time. All this must seem much more so to a soldier, by which I mean an infantryman, who's been doing that sort of thing for a couple of years. Another thing, Mr. Sheehan thinks they look about forty, perhaps they do to someone who's used to rosy-cheeked youths in white flannels, but most fellows lose that blush of youth when they get a three weeks beard and haven't slept in a bed for months and often haven't slept at all and have been scared as hell for long periods of time and maybe saw their best friend killed the day before yesterday. It's true that after they've washed up and got drunk and been to a rest camp etc. they become presentable, so that war correspondents can go and look at them, and they

---

152 He may be referring to Fred Sheehan, a colleague of Bill Mauldin's on the army's *Stars and Stripes*. Sheehan wrote a column called "Bulletin," while Mauldin drew his popular cartoons, "Up Front."

begin to look like little boys again, to me anyway and even more probably to Sheehan. I wonder when Sheehan saw soldiers shaving "under the direct fire of the enemy." I remember once in awhile someone would get an opportunity to shave, and that I thought it gave him a queer unnatural appearance as if he were part woman or something. I'd like very much to have that book of Mauldin cartoons. I think he's a damn good artist too.

I hope you can make some arrangements about the pump. I don't want you to spend all summer worrying about saving water and when someone can run the pump and the like, or to go down and struggle with it yourself. You're going to have much too much to do anyway. I'm glad you're joining the Blue Cross. I think that if nobody interferes with your training of "Judy" she will be perfectly trained. I wish one of your friends could come up to Peterborough and stay with you, and I wish that it might be possible to find in Dublin or somewhere some people who could be real friends and come to see you sometimes. I doubt if you got very soft among the luxuries of East River, but I wish there were more at home.

I love you an awful lot.
Sydney

Plezzo, June 29

Dear Mary,

I got one letter today, postmarked the nineteenth. I can't wait to hear how your trip to Wellesley came off. I suppose you are in Wellesley now. I haven't drawn any more pictures, but there's still lots of room on the walls and I hope I'll be asked to draw some more, but I doubt it. The beer is all gone at the moment and the bar is dispensing mixed drinks made from vodka, cognac, some kind of cocktail mixture that comes from Amsterdam, and GI fruit juices and ice. Considerable hell and noise was inspired by those last night, but by tonight the bar seems to have come of age, and it is a pleasant place to sit and talk. They tell me that I still am going to the intelligence school but I don't know when. I've been talking quite a bit about it, naturally, and I really don't think I'll get out of the army for a long time. There seem to be a great many people with 69 points or thereabouts, too many, perhaps, to let out one day all at once. My own guess is that we'll stay right where we are for some time to come.

Where is Henry now, is he still in Cairo? I should think he might be reassigned now with all the changes being made. There isn't much to write about tonight. I think mostly about what you are doing instead of me, so that I can't think of much to tell you about me. My mustache is still getting bigger and I'll have to get a picture of it for you,[153] it's too light-colored to show up well in a snapshot. Someone suggested that before I remove it I put so much wax on it that I can cut it off all in one piece and send it home like that to be hung up over the mantelpiece or something. I think it's a very good idea.

I don't see how Dick stood going two months without a letter, even if he hasn't got a wife. I hope when you get to Peterborough you'll write and tell me exactly how you're going to manage doing everything. I wish I'd finished putting up that goat fence. It would save a lot of trouble, and I wish I'd fixed a million other things so it would be easier for you now. I wish you had electricity and an electric pump. I wish we had got the cesspool cleaned out and fixed better. Will the Palmers be at home? I don't think you should hesitate to spend money if you want something done and think you can find someone to do it. I'm worried that there might be some part of the red shed that might fall on the children. It seems as if I must have done nothing at all when I was home. I can think of a million things that should have been done.

I love you.
Sydney

Plezzo, July 1

Dear Mary,

Today is Sunday and so far I haven't found anything interesting to do, and have done nothing. I had thought of climbing a mountain but the sky is pretty overcast and the mountain tops are hidden in the clouds. So I thought of trying to spend the day drawing but haven't yet, and am not in the mood. There is a boy named Morley[154] who lives in the same room who gets terribly on my nerves. He's a harmless and reasonably quiet sort of fellow but I can't stand him and will probably someday kill him. We have a big table in the room that we use for reading and writing letters and he is invariably sitting there when I want to read or write.

It's evening now, I wrote that this morning; except that I did try to draw some childish looking pictures I've done nothing all day. I haven't even had any exercise now for some time and I feel rather unhealthy. I went this evening to see a boy named Stanton, younger brother of a friend of Dick's. I was

---
153 I never saw a photograph of my father's mustache, if he had one taken.
154 PFC Berl M. Morley of Lake Forest, Illinois.

going to borrow some books from him. He was sitting there with a friend of his writing poetry of the most fanciful kind. They are both dangerously close to being affected in manner and talk about only the most intellectual subjects. Rather a contrast to the men I usually see who have been talking all afternoon about the most intimate details of their exploits last night with a couple of whores. There aren't very many between these extremes. Stanton and his friend, whose name is Kevin Andrews, both draw a little as well as write poetry and such. Stanton is almost a little effeminate seeming but really clever, he's not in the least like his brother, Dick's friend.

I didn't write any letter last night as I got involved at the bar, not as you might think in a drinking bout but just in a little sober drinking and conversation, and after I came upstairs again there was a great deal of uproar going on which was inspired by a little more serious drinking among some others so I decided it was hopeless to try and write and I just went to bed. Yesterday and today I got your letters of the 19th and 22nd. I think, with the help of my dictionary, that "congedato" means having just been given furlough. It's just about like the French "congé" or "congédié," or something.

I've been worrying about the swing etc. behind the house. I'm afraid the thing is probably no longer safe. If it isn't too bad Father might fix it. He used to like making things like that for us. He had a fancy system for binding the joints with string. It says in the paper that the 10th Division may be made occupation troops in the Trieste area and one rumor says we'll go back to the States next fall. They say we can now call up home from Rome. If I ever get there I'm going to try to do it. The idea almost scares me.

I love you.
Sydney

॰

Plezzo, July 2

Dear Mary,

I got your letter of the 21st tonight together with the dairy goat journal and a letter from Uncle Frank. I'm worried about the swing and stuff I made for the children. I'm afraid it's probably not strong anymore. I mentioned it in last night's letter, but I thought just in case the letters don't come in chronological order it would do no harm to mention it twice. The swing itself was in the studio when we left, if you can find anybody to fix it up again and make it safe.

I wonder if the leak in the studio skylight has got much worse, I guess it has. I suppose you are there now. It's almost time for the blueberries to be ripe. I wonder if Mr. Wilson left any of that hay that was in the barn. Today has been cold and rainy with a cold wind too this evening, almost colder than it gets in summer in Peterborough. But I guess it did get pretty cold sometimes. I wonder if the tennis court in Wellesley is usable this year, most likely not. I sort of wish you could have been there over the 4th and I hope at least that it was celebrated in the usual style. I'm afraid Hunnewell family parties would be rather hard for you without even me there.

There's another rumor going the rounds—that we'll go back to the States in September. In a way I think I'd prefer to stay here longer, till it was too late to go to the East, for me at least. We drew cards tonight as a few passes came up to Rome; I lost, of course, but I think by next time it ought to be my turn. The trouble is that the next ones might be to somewhere else and I want especially to see Rome. They are not what I call real passes as such things would be impossible, they are passes to go to "rest centers." They have them in Florence and Venice and several other places. I've never been to one but I've seen the one in Florence. They are just big camps with a lot of recreational features and no work to do. You just play, as little Mary would say. I don't know about further south but in the northern part of Italy that I've seen it would be impossible for a man to travel about on his own anyway. Nowadays there are no hotels or restaurants anymore for the tourists and the only transportation is army trucks. Probably, too, they don't dare let the soldiers run completely loose in a foreign country. There would probably be even less privacy at a "rest" center than here.

This same boy who irritates me so is sitting at the table now as usual. He's very conscientious about writing his wife everyday but goes out with women here all the time. He's always humming or singing with complete disregard for the tune—that's what irritates me most. And he's very childish even compared to the others. But he is very young. I haven't decided just how I will kill him. I may not even do it. I feel in a magnanimous mood tonight. What does "Mitzi" think of Peterborough? You'll write about every little detail, won't you?

I love you an awful lot.
Sydney

Plezzo, July 5

Dear Mary,

I didn't write last night or the night before—the night before because I went down to the bar and became involved in what you might euphemistically call singing and it was pretty late when I got back upstairs, and last night because, as it was a holiday, I got a pass and went to Udine and then suddenly felt very sick (I hadn't visited any bars) with a terrible headache when I was on the way back so that I went straight to bed feeling that I was about to die, but instead woke up this morning bursting with health and leaped out of bed in my usual vigorous way that you know so well. I've been for two mornings now to intelligence school. So far it has been mostly a study of maps with which I am fortunately more familiar than most people. The school is quite appropriately held in the local elementary school building and we sit squeezed up behind children's desks very much like the one I used to spill ink on almost thirty years ago. I think tomorrow I will bring an apple for the teacher and try to get up a good game of hopscotch at recess. I always did like hopscotch.

Yesterday it took us all morning to bum our way the forty odd miles to Udine, we had dinner in the GI restaurant, lined up for a movie for servicemen, saw that and lined up for supper and when that had been eaten we started back. It was a cold unpleasant sort of day and looked all the time as if it was just about to rain. I resolved again that the next time I went anywhere I would go by myself, but it's awfully hard to do. I like company most of the time.

No letters last night, but I got one postmarked the 21st the night before, they haven't been coming quite so fast lately. I guess I told you in a letter a few days ago that when I had said 69 points I had included everything, 5 for the Po Valley, 5 for the Apennines, and 5 for a Bronze Star. They don't seem to be going to add any more as each month goes by but to lower the minimum instead. I'm awfully sorry that you got the idea that I had more because this will be disappointing. It goes like this: 14 months in the army = 14, you get two points instead of one for each of those months you spent overseas so you add four more (not eight) that makes 18 plus 36 for children and fifteen for battle awards which all adds up to 69. Other people who were inducted about when I was are naturally very jealous of those 36 points and you can't blame them. There were quite a few who went home. The old ones get 12 points too for 6 months in the Aleutians, you know, and a good proportion of us now are replacements who were converted to the infantry after having non-combatant jobs overseas, some of them for three years. You see every time we lost a man, we got another one; we were never under strength more than just a day or two. I don't know but I believe our average number of points is fairly high.

I just got a letter back that I wrote Dick on May 3rd. Tonight I got your Saturday and Sunday letter postmarked the 25th and with all the pictures in it. I guess I wouldn't have recognized Betsy, and Frank looks awfully different. I thought you looked thin, maybe, or rather probably, you work too hard and don't eat enough. I'm afraid you won't eat enough when you get by yourself to Peterborough. Right now I'm doing practically nothing and eating an awful lot and am always hungry for more. I'm afraid when I come home there'll be too much difference between us. I'll be big and fat and you'll be little and skinny. The picture of Mary with Betsy and Frank on the porch is wonderful. All of them look so much more grown up that I was almost rather taken aback. It certainly is a wonderful thing to be able to get pictures to keep me posted. It would be terrible to come home and find them entirely different from when I left without having any idea how they were changing. They are getting more wonderful looking all the time but now when I come home I'll know them a little bit. They won't be just wonderful-looking strangers.

The room where I live shelters nine of us and now we all refer to each other as brother so and so and although it is really about as motley an assembly as you could imagine we get along pretty well. The one that irritates me so by his inane remarks is Brother Morley. Others are Brother Bennet, another runner who was always next to me during all our battles. Brother Simpson, a former stock broker is the wittiest and most urbane as well as the fattest. Brother Coates I've mentioned before, he went with me yesterday to Udine. Brother Yesnick is a very pleasant but half-witted boy of Ukrainian origin. Brother Wulf is a tough looking Catholic German Jew. Brother Womer has been in the army too long and doesn't give a damn for anything much. Brother Ziminski looks like a Mexican but says he's half Polish and half Spanish. He's a very nice fellow and wrote my Bronze Star citation. Coates and Bennet are the only two old 87th men. Ziminski and I came in at Camp Swift and the rest are replacements from rear echelon outfits. There are two or three living in other rooms that we include in this fraternity such as Brother Carlton. They are all headquarters platoon. DeWick, who's in the second platoon where I was before I became runner, lives on the floor above. You asked about him. I think he's 32, he has two children, used to be an insurance salesman in Portland, Maine, and round about New England. He came in the army when I did. He went to the University of Maine and his main interest in life is horses. He's small, getting bald, and has a long Yankee-farmerish chin, and smokes a pipe.[155]

 I hope very much that you saw Stu, it would be terrible as well as foolish to get away just before he got there. The children are more skillful than I was, I never could pin the tail on the donkey at children's parties and I was much shyer than they are. I remember seeing Eddy Lafarge with "Judy" last summer and I know just what you mean, but I wouldn't worry about what someone who knows that little says. I've got to go to bed. It's midnight.

I love you,
Sydney

July 6

Dear Mary,

I got two letters today from you, one just before you went to Wellesley and one just after you got there, and a letter from your mother postmarked the 29th with pictures of you driving "Judy" and a few taken with "Mitzi" on the beach. I suppose she sent them to you too. I wish you hadn't been so unhappy when you got to Wellesley. I'm terribly anxious now to get your next letter and find out whether you felt any more encouraged the next day.

 It really does seem too bad that you didn't see any more of Stu. I really worry about you so far away and alone in Peterborough even though I have great faith in your ability to look out for everything. What I'm afraid of is that you won't look out for yourself. I hope Anna Mary really is as much help as she should be. Please take care of yourself. There isn't anything much to say about me, nothing happened today and there aren't any good rumors or anything. I suppose our length of stay in these parts depends a good deal on what Tito does. Probably we, or somebody, will have to occupy this area for quite a long time, all the way from the Austrian border to Trieste. It'll be pretty complicated deciding which country will get what. I've heard of various Balkan problems all my life but I never expected to be so nearly involved in one. I guess our presence here irritated Tito quite a bit, and I don't think he would have minded a little trouble like that the British had in Greece

---

155 Berl Morley, Lake Forest, Illinois; Norman Bennett, Piedmont, California; Ralph Simpson, Brooklyn, New York; Clayton Coates, New York City, New York; Mike Yesnick, Cambridge, Pennsylvania; Henry Wulf, Fresno, California; Robert Womer, Oil City, Pennsylvania; Joseph Ziminski, White Haven, Pennsylvania; Thomas Carlton, Perry, Florida, and Bob DeWick, Topsham, Maine.

because of the sympathetic sentiments he could arouse, as did the Greek so-called communists.

My opinion of the average American soldier's mentality sinks lower and lower, not so much really stupid but just that he never thinks. They can be told things and shown things a million times and nothing ever sinks in. For instance, though the effects of so many years of war in Italy are hardly difficult to perceive what with ruined towns everywhere etc. and people fighting for the garbage from our kitchen, it simply does not sink in at all. Nothing does. I have no patience with them and never bother to discuss anything with them. And the few like Arnold's friend that have a little education seem to me as stupid as the rest, though it might be partly just immaturity. To my old-fashioned mind none of them have any morals about sex at all, which doesn't worry me, but it does worry me that they make it into something so cheap and ugly. My morals are mostly aesthetic, in conjunction I hope, with a certain amount of regard for other people. Tonight I see no hope for the world, they might as well give it up as a bad job and start collecting a few nebulae to use building another one. It might even be better to purchase a new site over in some other solar system.

I love you an awful lot. I hope you feel happier now than when you wrote that letter. I love you. "Judy" looks as if she'd worn a harness all her life in the pictures. She looks big and strong.

Sydney

July 7

Dear Mary,

This will be a short letter because I've foolishly sat talking over some drinks until it has got pretty late and I'm awfully sleepy. No letters tonight. This afternoon I drew a picture of one of the men who lives in this room and while it wasn't a very successful picture, I guess it was good for me to draw it both as practice and from a psychological point of view. I've got to do something of that sort. I was thinking of going to Trieste tomorrow, Sunday, and had asked for a pass, but I see that I'm to be on guard tomorrow afternoon instead. However, I may be able to get a pass sometime next week.

I played a game of chequers this evening or rather several and was badly beaten each time. Whenever I play chequers I begin to wonder if I have any brains at all. I'm always beaten. The picture I drew was of Brother Ziminiski who says now that he is part French, Spanish, Polish, Lithuanian and Indian. As you might suppose he's quite unusual looking, and very interesting to draw. I wish I had made a good picture. He's very dark and high cheekboned.

You ought to be somewhat settled in Peterborough by now. I've felt particularly discouraged this week, I feel as though I was wasting so much time and rapidly becoming middle aged or more middle aged. At the time of life when I should be most actively doing what I plan to do, I have been doing absolutely nothing. I guess everything will seem like a waste of time anyway until I get home. I wish I was the kind of artist that could make quick sketches on the battlefield and sell them to magazines.

I love you an awful lot,
Sydney

Plezzo, July 8

Dear Mary,

No letters tonight, and as I'm on guard again now this will be another short letter. I should be able to write a long one tomorrow. I had all day to write, but I didn't, as I thought I would have plenty of time this evening, but I didn't get the relief I expected. I got the second relief which comes right in the middle of the evening.

Today was another day that seemed completely wasted; it was a beautiful day too. I try to draw a little but not very successfully and really did nothing but mope around. I spent a long time cleaning my rifle but still not doing it very well. I got out all my pictures of you and the children and looked at them. You look much thinner in the recent pictures than in the older ones, I hope it isn't because you are getting yourself tired all the time. I've probably said that too many times already, but now that I can't see you I worry about you. The children certainly look healthy in all the pictures, and that makes me feel very happy. "Judy" looks enormous now. I can't believe it's the same horse. It looks as if you took care of everything but yourself. I love you an awful lot. I wish this nightmare would be over and I was home.

I love you.
Sydney

July 9

Dear Mary,

The only letter that came tonight was one from mother postmarked June 14th, almost a month in transit. I was on and off guard duty all day today and nothing happened to laugh at at all so there's no news of me for today. Three of us have got a pass to climb a mountain tomorrow. We are to be waked at five a.m. and tonight they issued the beer ration, and several who are going on pass to Rome get up to leave at one a.m.; so I don't think I'll get an awful lot of sleep tonight.

We have to say where we are going beforehand and I was the one who picked the route, and I don't believe the others, Coates and a man named Sickler,[156] realize quite how long a trip it will be. It's the same direction I went when I saw the chamois. I don't know what time we'll be back as we plan to go over the mountain to another road and then try to bum our way back and I don't know how much traffic there is there.

I find it much harder to write a letter when I haven't got one to answer. I wonder if the porcupines and all the other beasts of the forest moved back into the house while we were gone. Look by the rock on the right as you go into the goat pasture and see if there is any sign of a rosebush. I planted one in the fall before we left, also I think somewhere else behind the house too but I'm not sure where. I wonder if the cows ate up all the grapevines. Tell me whether the elm tree on the way to the barn still looks sick or what.

There are some goats around here the color of Guernsey cows; they look very strange. The people never seem to put their animals out to pasture as we do, except for dry goats and sheep that go up on the mountains. They cut grass and carry it green back to their barns. One of the most common sights is of women carrying enormous bundles of hay on their heads. Most of the people you see working in the fields are women. There are some old men too and children, even the smallest sizes. There are practically no young men. They are or what's left of them are, across the river with Tito. Except for a few that you see sauntering around the village in civilian clothes, they aren't supposed to be here without permission.

I drew some more today in my time off, drawing just the way I should not draw now, trying to make a finished picture. The result is naturally pretty amateurish. However, as it is a naked lady the men seem to find it interesting. I'm getting used to again, I hope, to drawing in public. That's the main thing first

---

156 Paton G. Sickler of Saguache, Colorado.

of all, but I don't think it would ever be possible to feel or draw the way I want to in the army. That sense of not being a free and independent individual seems to permeate all one's thoughts and emotions, you can never get away from it. I think it has a very bad effect on mind and character and it affects everybody.

I love you an awful lot.
Sydney

July 10

Dear Mary,

I got all the rest of the letters you wrote from Wellesley today together with ones from Mother and Father and Mary Fyffe. I'm glad you heard that old bullfrog; nobody else ever thought to mention him, and I haven't heard news of him for several years. He was probably expressing approval of the children after inspecting them from the bottom of the pond. Now I'm very excited to get a letter from Peterborough. The next one should be from there.

Well, we climbed the mountain today and had a very good time. We had breakfast at quarter past five and set out at a quarter to six. We went over the mountains and down the other side to another road and then bummed rides and got back to the company area in a couple of hours at about six tonight. Everyone thought it would take much longer including myself, as I didn't dare count on such good luck getting rides and thought we would have to do a good deal of walking on the road. I felt remarkably healthy the whole time and would have liked to go further and faster. I think I'm a pretty tough old man. It was not clear all the time, though usually sunny, and the mountain mists rolled back and forth like the curtain in a theatre exposing first one view and then another. There were millions of Alpine flowers growing bright colored on miniature plants, and the air was heavy with a sweet smell that suggested some sleepy garden and seemed odd in the crisp mountaintop air. I sniffed at every single different kind, I think, of flower trying to trace it and finally discovered it was a little blue flower which, not knowing what it really was, I decided to call a forget-me-not.

There were battles in the very tops of these mountains in the last war and we spent a good deal of time looking at fortified caves (it's soft rock), trenches and pieces of rusty shrapnel and such. Tomorrow I'm going to Trieste, but unfortunately with a whole group of men that I know pretty well so I won't be able to do just what I want to do. However the first thing that I will do will be to go down to scan the waterfront and see if Joe's boat might be there. I'll also keep an eye out for him in every bar or saloon, but of course he would be much more apt to be found in some swank officers' club having Cognac and cigars with a bunch of admirals. I wonder if he really is still in the neighborhood of Trieste. You haven't mentioned it for some time. I wonder what Anna Mary thought of Wellesley. I hope it didn't make her think we were millionaires instead of just simpleliving neighbors. I wonder if Stu will be able to come up and see you in Peterborough. I wish lots of people would go to visit you; particularly those who make themselves useful about the house. I'm glad you saw Dick; I want to hear his adventures.

I love you an awful lot.
Sydney

P. S. I wonder if this might get to you on your birthday or thereabouts. I hope you can somehow give yourself a party.

July 12

Dear Mary,

I got back from Trieste at one o'clock last night and found your letter of July 3rd. The first one I got from Peterborough. I wonder if you didn't write one the day before as you didn't say anything about the trip up. I thought I might get that one tonight but I didn't get any. I didn't see any LST's at Trieste, but there was an empty place with a sign "LST landing" where I suppose Joe had been. But I didn't recognize his footprints anywhere. Trieste is a pretty big place and it would be pretty hard to find someone there even if one had some idea how to begin. When we got there, I tried, in the general confusion of getting off the trucks, to slip off by myself, but Coates who had assumed all along that we were visiting the place together yelled to me so I went with him which was some advantage anyway as he'd been there before. We went down to the docks and rode around on the street cars and went in swimming outside town at the end of the car lines; the water was very warm and very dirty even though it was little ways from town but it felt wonderful. It was rather like swimming in south Boston or some such place, both the water and the company, though the latter amused me, lots of children and miscellaneous specimens of all ages and shapes.

I felt rather irritated a lot of the time because I would have rather been alone, but if I had been I wouldn't have known where to go swimming etc. We were told the trucks would leave at nine p.m. and I was irritated even more when Coates insisted on going back to the trucks at eight so as to be sure to get a seat (a sort of wooden bench runs along each side, but lots have to stand up as they fill the trucks full). So we got to the trucks a little after 8 and we did get seats but they didn't leave till almost 10:30 and we sat there all that time and 3 hours more on the way back. It was very cold and too dark to see anything of course which disappointed me as we came back a different way.

We were in Trieste almost five hours. There are practically no shops open. The only things that are open are the bars and whorehouses, and the former are almost all off-limits but the latter are heavily patronized. I was surprised how many new buildings the city had. It all looks perfectly calm and peaceful. I looked at the newsstands and I only saw one paper printed in what I suppose was Slavic. Everything appears to be Italian. Today I was put on special assignment to draw pictures for the officer's bar. The walls are not suitable to draw on so I spent a good part of the morning finding some big pieces of cardboard and the rest of the morning trying to think of something to draw. Guard duty, the mountain trip and going to Trieste, altogether has made me pretty sleepy today and I did not feel in the least inspired. I worked all afternoon and made one picture that wasn't much good and started another one. I don't know how long they expected me to take, but there isn't supposed to be much of any training this week. They decided to take one week and give a lot of passes instead of a few all the time. A good many are gone for the whole week but I wasn't that lucky.

Where do you keep "Mitzi," in the barn or in the pasture? I can't wait for the next letter with more details. I hope Anna Mary is with you most nights even if you do like the evenings to yourself sometimes. I'm glad she gets along so well. You never mentioned "George" when you were in Wellesley. Where was he?

I love you.
Sydney

༃

Plezzo, July 13

Dear Mary,

I got your first letter from Peterborough tonight, written before the other one. Which Wilsons greeted you at the door when you arrived? I'll bet the bottom of the chimney is full of soot and that's why the heater smoked

Leland out of the cellar. The place where it collects is way into the chimney where you don't notice it putting on a new stovepipe or such.

 I'm sorry you haven't got "George." I want to know about his meeting with "Mopsa." Mother probably thought that "George" would make things extra complicated for you before you got settled, but mother should have realized you wanted him anyway. I spent all day today again drawing a picture with charcoal and chalk and a colored pencil of a girl on skis. When I finished I didn't think it was too bad, but it was hardly art. But it looked more professional than my drawings usually do. I'm afraid I won't draw anymore as they have enough decoration. I wish they could find some job for me where I can draw all the time. I'm going to try now and draw at every opportunity. I think if I don't I'll never get anywhere when I get home. I want to know all the details, which room everyone sleeps in, everything, so I can visualize you all in the house. I think I should rebuild the el on the red shed when I come back. I love you an awful lot. I walked all around the back alleys of this town again tonight, and it really is fascinating; nobody seems to think so, but me. The houses are all tumbled together every which way. They are covered with vines with garden patches full of both flowers and vegetables stuck in all the odd corners and fruit trees here and there.

I love you,
Sydney

Plezzo, July 14

Dear Mary,

I got your letter of July 3rd tonight. As you've no doubt noticed our letters are censored again. Which is a fate worthy of note. You say Mary doesn't remember my working on the stone behind the house. I wonder if she remembers when we worked in the studio or on sculpture anywhere. I don't know why but I'm disappointed that she doesn't remember. How much does she remember? Of course, I hadn't worked at home for a year before I left.

 I guess Arthur must be alright or Miss Perry wouldn't still have him. All that seems like years and years ago. Does she still keep chickens? Who patronizes Pat's store? Between her and Mrs. Gunther we should certainly make some deals. I hope you've at least got a newspaper by now. I don't want you to be too much shut off from the world. What do you use now for a milking stand? Maybe there are so many things for the goats to eat now they won't do any damage if loose. You haven't told me yet how the horses really look.

Nothing of interest happened today. I wish a little more that was interesting would happen. Does "Jill" still seem foundered or stiff in the front legs. I hate to think how old "Nona" is probably beginning to look. How about "Wenny"? I feel that I hardly dare ask about her. Have you got enough wood? Maybe if I should come back to the states and get a furlough this summer I can cut some more, but I don't think I would do much work. I hope you light the heater once in awhile for your own comfort.

I'm awfully sleepy tonight though this time it's not very late and there's no excuse. It's been very hot today. I love you an awful lot. I get pretty discouraged lately in my associates; it seems like years and years since I talked to anyone of my own kind, though a few of these are not too different. I can drink with them, but I can't carry on a sober conversation. I get along very well with everybody, but talk to them very little and sometimes I am frankly disgusted by them. I wonder how Walter O'Malley got home so quick.

I love you.
Sydney

࿓

Plezzo, July 15

Dear Mary,

You've no doubt seen in the paper that we're coming home to be back in the middle of August and have three months training and then the Pacific. They put on censorship yesterday and said today at about quarter to one that we could send no more letters after one o'clock, so I hurriedly finished a letter I'd started to Mother and Father and thought I wouldn't be able to write to you again. Now they've taken off the censorship and said we could write again, and I hope they don't change their minds again before I finish the letter.

I knew I was coming home since the day before yesterday but didn't dare mention it. I don't think, unless things are changed, that it'll be worth your while writing many days after you get this as I suppose we'll leave early in August. The newspaper says we'll get twenty-one-day furloughs. I hoped it would be more. This was all announced suddenly when we had just about made up our minds that we would be occupation troops. The newspaper said we might be. Now everyone's elation at going home is a little tempered by the Pacific prospects, which unfortunately carries that capital P which does so much to the meaning. But it should be almost six months before we get there. Most would have much preferred to be occupation troops.

My main worry now is whether that three months training will be anywhere near home. I've felt very nervous and restless all day. You'll still be in Peterborough and I'm glad, and I'll be able to help you to move back to East River. I don't suppose there's any chance that Dick will still be there when I get there, but I hope he doesn't get well too quickly. You'd better start teaching Betsy to say Papa. Mary, I love you an awful lot and anything might happen between now and next winter. I don't know if, as we move around, I'll be able to write every day. I think we leave Plezzo the day after tomorrow.

I love you.
Sydney

P.S. This was written on my knee by the light (so called) of a most inefficient candle.

෴

Florence, July 19

Dear Mary,

We got here yesterday evening after a day and a half in box cars. It was very hot, but not nearly as hot as it is here which is terrific. I spent most of the trip down sitting with nothing on but a pair of trousers, on top of a boxcar. The train kept stopping every few minutes and I didn't think we'd ever get here. It was fun on top of the box car, but you can imagine how dirty I was when we finally got here. But it did seem like a novel way to travel in Italy, and was rather exciting when we went through tunnels some of which were long. It was cold, absolutely pitch black, with noise seeming to be the only thing left in a dead world. We are supposed to be ready to leave by the 23rd and most say that we'll sail on the second. We've been told nothing definite of course. They say that when we get home, which should be before the middle of August, that we'll be sent to camps near home and our furloughs will start from there. I'll probably be sent to Fort Devens. So you were right in thinking I'd be home this summer.

I got six letters from you tonight and one from Dick. You needn't worry that I won't like the way you've painted the house. I didn't know "Cricket"[157] was dead. I'm surprised Mother never wrote me. I'm afraid it might be like when I burnt up Father's tennis racquet. It made him think that he was getting too old to get another one. I wish they had bred her. I hope Mother does go to ride again on something. I'm glad Anna Mary is so congenial and Mrs.

---
157 My grandmother's horse.

Adams and the Wilsons have been so nice.

We are camped on a race track just outside town and I haven't been to town yet. There wasn't much opportunity today anyway and besides the heat is so perfectly awful that the idea of putting on woolen clothes and then trying to move at all is too much. Around the area we are allowed to go shirtless and in fatigue trousers. There's a swimming pool where I went swimming this evening and tennis courts that you have to sign up for several days in advance. Today we did nothing but sit around and were not at liberty to go anywhere. A pretty bad kind of day. Also the only clothes that I have are the ones I wore on the train and on top of it. I hope you do have me to yourself practically all the time when I get home. I liked the clipping from the paper about Billy Wilson in the pool.

I love you an awful lot. It's pretty exciting isn't it. I still have my mustache and in the swimming pool I heard some pretty facetious remarks about walruses. Shall I mail it to you when I cut it off? Even now at almost eleven p.m. I'm sweating so that my hand keeps getting the paper damp. I don't know if I'll know exactly when we sail soon enough to let you know in advance but I should be able to let you know when we land. You'll probably be ten days or more without a letter before that happens. If Joe's wedding should be at about that time I could go back to Peterborough with you. I hope you can go to it. Couldn't Forrest Wilson take care of the goats. The children should be able to milk them pretty soon. It's going to be worse than ever leaving home the next time. The intelligence school was hardly as impressive as its name might suggest. In the army they refer to any kind of instruction as a "school."

I feel as if I would burst. I love you.
Sydney

July 20

Dear Mary,

I didn't get any mail tonight and they say that army post office 345 will close tomorrow, so I'm wondering now if I'll get any more. I came into Florence this evening to see what I could see and haven't seen a great deal. Then I began to look for a cup of coffee and came into the rest camp where I'm writing this. It's always been a mystery to me who uses the rest camps. The cathedral and things like that all are closed in the evening, and as yet we can't get off in the daytime. I understand that more things are uncovered that were formerly not to be seen. All restaurants and bars in town are off-limits, and, while it doesn't really interfere much with my pleasure, it makes me mad not to be able to go anywhere I might feel like. I feel more and more irritated every day with the company I'm in and wish I had a few more congenial to talk to. That's the wrong word though because these are friendly enough, I mean some a little more intelligent. I saw Osborne Day today, I was feeling at rather a low point when he appeared and I flattered myself that he had sought me out; it made me feel much better. I'm afraid I wouldn't have recognized him at all if I'd just seen him walking by. He just got here and seems to be a little sorry that he's going back again so quick, seeing so little. I'm afraid I can't associate much with people like him. I think it's pretty lucky I'm going home now as my morale is pretty low, and otherwise I might start going around letting the air out of the tires on generals' Jeeps and things like that.

I love you an awful lot, and now I can think I'll be seeing you soon, thank God.

I love you.
Sydney

July 21

Dear Mary,

This is your birthday or at least I hope I haven't got the date mixed up. I hope you haven't changed overnight the way Mary thought she did. I love you, but anyway you won't be able to do much changing before I get home now. I mailed home today two pairs of German army skis and a package of ski bindings etc. I should get home long before they do. One pair is really not much good at all and the other not remarkable but at least in good condition. Yet it only cost me seventy cents and besides being usable I like the idea that they were taken from the German ski troops. They are the only souvenirs I've picked up.

Today has been hotter than ever. Sunday morning. It's hotter still now. We went to some movies last night, and went to a carnival where we walked around and watched, and back after dark. There are no lights in our tents. Now they are taking certain men out of the company and they will stay here. It's quite a letdown after they've been all set to go home. They haven't picked them all and I don't know on what basis they are chosen but I feel pretty sure I won't be one of them.

I got your letter of the 13th last night, I'm glad you spent the whole day doing nothing useful. The children must be learning to ride fast. The more children that come around our place the better I like it, but I don't want you to wear yourself out entertaining them. In case the skis should get home before I do they should be untied as now one pair, the poorer one, is bent the wrong way. I'll write more tonight.

For the last month or so we've done nothing and have been getting a lot more to eat. We are stripped to the waist most of the time and I noticed in the chow line yesterday that the cook was gazing with satisfaction at all the great pot bellies he had produced, mine too.

I love you.
Sydney

Florence, July 22

Dear Mary,

I spent the day wandering around the streets with two spells in the swimming pool. The shops were closed of course, and everywhere else that I tried to go was closed too but I had a pretty good time anyway. I was by myself most of the time which was a wonderful relief, and then towards evening when I'd wandered all I wanted to I met some men I knew and had a drink and supper with them. I got your letter of the ninth this evening. It's just as hot as ever, I used to think heat didn't affect me but it seems to now. Maybe I'm too fat. There certainly are some awfully bad statues in Florence, but I also keep seeing things off in odd corners that I like. You get the feeling that the Italians are a people extraordinarily lacking in imagination. Everything seems to be a copy of something else. But there are a lot of things I like just the same. It's beginning to get dark now.

I saw Osborne Day again today in the swimming pool and therefore felt a little less conscious of the difference in rank.[158] I've often thought of trying to find something to bring home to the children but have never been able to find anything. The toys are few and not remarkable, about what you could buy in Peterborough, and as for other things I just don't know enough about them, I mean nice things. Everybody tells me that with my age, the children etc. I'll never go to the Pacific. I wish I could believe them, but I don't, unless the war should be much shorter than I think. I wish Dick would still be there when I get home.

I'm getting myself tanned for you. Did I tell you that at the carnival where I was yesterday there were several "Dodgem" establishments[159] and

---

158 Osborne Day was an officer; my father an enlisted man, ". . . and never the twain shall meet."
159 "Dodgems" were small electric bumper cars, usually found at fairs and carnivals.

the cars were full of black bearded, turbaned Indians. They looked very dignified. Stanton has some friends of his family who live here, and I'm hoping to get a chance thereby to go to some private house. The nights here remind me of midsummer nights at Wellesley. I'm wondering now how I shall get from Devens to Peterborough. Where we are now is just plain an unadulterated hell; we have to sit all day long in our tents, except Sunday, with nothing to do and are not allowed to leave the area till 5. The tents are like ovens. We have the stupidest privates too. My opinion of the average American has reached a new low. I'm beginning to hate everybody. I've still had no opportunity and will probably leave Florence without the opportunity of seeing anything worthwhile. The people of Europe are undernourished and the army throws away tons of food three times a day. I've done nothing for so long I think I'll burst, though I'm a lazy person. I'm probably, through lack of good exercise, in the worst physical condition of my life. A good day's work would kill me. You used to sometimes complain that I was too cynical. I certainly will not please you any better now. I think the knowledge that I'll be with you pretty soon is the only thing that keeps me sane.

I love you.
Sydney

P. S. There's a rumor that we'll be in the States by August 13th.

༄

Florence, July 23

Dear Mary,

I don't know whether it's worth writing many more days. I don't know how long the letters will keep getting there before I do. Most of the others don't bother to write anymore. It's going to be a short letter now as I went to town to the movies with DeWick and I have to get up at 4:30 tomorrow morning to go on K. P. It was a British movie and not too bad, with subtitles in Italian. I kept finding myself trying to make out what the Italian meant instead of listening to the English and so missed large parts of it. Afterwards we found some watermelon for sale, which was the first I've tasted for an awfully long time.

In this hot weather I just sit in a stupor all day. I can't even make my mind work, and then when night comes I wake up—a beautiful moonlit night tonight, the kind that makes you feel restless. I don't feel quite so irritated with the world now as when I last wrote. I got two letters from you tonight of the 14th, 15th, and the 16th and one from Father and one with a birthday check from Uncle Frank. Yours were wonderful long letters, and I've been writing such measly short ones.

I'm sorry Anna Mary has trouble with Mary, but I can see how it might be, perhaps, a little like having a governess. Do you remember?

I don't think the Browns have any Arabian horses now, but the stable DeWick was at had some of them. I'm glad Mother wants another one. When I heard "Cricket" was dead I thought of Mother, not Jane; I'd forgotten how Jane always rode her and thought of her as hers. It seems like such an awfully long time ago now. I hope you do get Mary Fyffe on a horse again. I guess she's just about forgotten how to ride. Once upon a time she used to care for nothing else, but Mother, in her blunt way, used to tell her that her legs were too short and that she couldn't ride very well anyway, and I wonder if that discouraged her. Mother used to think Jane had possibilities of learning to be a good rider.

I wish I could have been in Peterborough when all the children were there. It seems funny, at one time Mary F. used to talk about nothing but horses and ancient Greek sculpture and I was thoroughly bored, and now I, and not her, am the one interested in both.

It's just midnight and the temperature is getting to be quite comfortable and my mind is beginning to function normally, but I should go to bed. I have to hold a candle in one hand and balance the paper on my knee and write with the other. It's officers K. P. I'll be on tomorrow. Maybe I'll be waiting on Ombo. I'm going to tell DeWick that Mother is looking for a horse. Mother will be 70 in November. I think it's pretty good to be looking for a horse at that age. I'm very proud of her. Poor Father, there was always a horse for Mother and any old thing for Father to ride, though he did have "Rex," who had once been good.

I wonder what you did on your birthday. I hope it was something really special. The house sounds beautifully painted. I love you an awful lot. You'll have to be thinking of moving from that cot on the porch. We had one of those physical exams today where you run past the doctors and they write things down on paper without even looking at you—everybody passed. I wonder if any of Dick's old friends are still around Dublin. I'm awfully glad you've finally got "George." I hope you'll be alone, or with just the children, when I first see you.

I love you,
Sydney.

July 25

Dear Mary,

I was on K. P. all day yesterday and so felt sleepy in the evening and decided that maybe I'd be home as soon as any letter I wrote. But I decided today there was still time for one or two more. Anyway I hope it will work out so that if you go a few days without a letter you'll know that I'll be there any moment. I think I'll probably be sent straight from the boat to Fort Devens and will call you up from there. But I don't know anything definitely. It looks as if I'll just miss seeing Jane and Nat and Dick. If Arnold is coming east, and they could stay a bit longer, the whole family would be together at once. I don't know how many years it is since that happened.

I got a big package last night that said from "Mrs. Hotchkiss," one of your mother's labels on the outside with fruitcake and nuts and maple sugar. I wasn't sure whether it was really from your mother or you. The cake is all gone now, but I'm going to save the nuts and maple sugar for the boat as they starved me coming over. Today was hotter than ever and I lay on my bunk all day, as did everybody, comatose, irritable, and stupid.

I shaved off my mustache, which caused considerable comment and wisecracks. There seem to be two schools of thought; those who say I should have worn it home and that I was scared to, and those that sigh with relief and wish I'd cut if off long ago. Everybody wants to know what happened to the fauna and flora whose retreat was so rudely destroyed.

I came to town on purpose by myself this evening but I took a chance by coming here to the Red Cross, and of course I met several from C Company and now DeWick and Arthur are patiently waiting for me to stop writing and go to a movie with them. Just as I wrote that, Arthur came over to see if I'd finished yet. To me it seems terrible to come all the way to Florence and then just go to a movie.

Well I went and now I'm back in camp. I didn't get any letters tonight. Last night I got your letter postmarked the seventeenth, telling about riding with little Mary all the way round by Cashin's; that's a long ride. I think she's remarkable.

The others talk all the time about how wonderful to be in the United States, not just to be home but in the U. S. With me it's entirely a matter of going home. I don't care particularly about merely just being in the States. I like Florence better than Austin, Texas.

The rumor is now that we'll go to Camp Carson in Colorado after our furlough. I guess there's no hope of a camp anywhere near home, as I don't know of any. I keep wondering whether you know already that I'm coming, you may have seen it in the paper. I love you an awful lot. There's a full moon now and it'll be full again so we can watch it rise together the next time. I've been reading *Madame Bovary* which came in a package from your mother. I've also read *The American* by James and a book of Verlaine[160] that I borrowed from Stanton. They are all good books that I enjoyed.

I love you.
Sydney

Florence, morning, July 27

Dear Mary,

The last letters we can send have to be in in a few minutes. I should be home a few days after you get this. Last night was the last mail that came in and I didn't get any. Your last letter was written the seventeenth. We are going tomorrow from here to the port. Naples, I think, but I don't know when we'll sail. I went to town yesterday with Simpson, and, though we got some drinks and enjoyed ourselves, I was looking all the time for an opportunity to get away from him and finally did. Then I walked around and really enjoyed myself. It's extraordinary what a relief I find it to be when I'm alone, as if I'd broken my chains. I still haven't been able to see the Medici Tomb, and I've tried every day to get permission to leave in the morning when it's open.

I love you an awful lot,
Sydney

July 27

Dear Sydney,

I got your letter dated the 14th today. I did notice it was censored, and I also noticed the one of the day before was written on with pencil "bare censor." I assume that means a move is in the offing. But I already knew that from the newspapers of that same date, as I wrote you. All I don't know is whether the November sailing has been advanced due to this or if that stands. If so, I wonder where you are to be in the meantime, if the 34th moves in where you are now.

---

160. Paul Verlaine (1844–1896), French poet.

You spoke about the wood and maybe getting back this summer. I don't know if you meant to imply that was probable or possible. If there's any hope of your getting back here, or rather I should say chance, because, though my heart tells me I can't go on much longer this way, my head tells me the longer you stay where you are the better for your safety and the chances of your not having to go to the Pacific. But, as I was saying, if it's likely, I will stay up here longer until you get here!

This letter must be brief. Your mother, etc., came over and stayed 'til 6, and we were late all around. Then the Wilsons appeared and only just left. [It was] 8:30 when I settled down to write. Now the telephone rang and some friends of Anna Mary's mother are coming over. I'm awfully disappointed because I wanted to write you a long letter and go to bed early, too. But I'll do my best and hope tomorrow will be free of interruptions.

Mary remembers you out working in the studio, on the lady.[161] After all, it was about two years ago that you worked on that last. I think it was quite a while before Frank was born that you last worked on it. She and Sydney both remember us in the studio. She remembers everything else I've asked her about, at least. Frank is very vague. In fact, I think he still thinks this is the Wilsons' house. And their horse, too.

Speaking of the horses. They look just the same! (Here come these people, but now I don't think they are going to come in after all.) The horses are just the same. (They did come in and it's now 9:30! Anna Mary went out and I heard her say they couldn't come in, so my good manners got the best of me and I went out and invited them in personally and they came. Two old-maid nurses from Portchester, but very nice and friendly.) Well, as I was saying, the horses look just the same. "Jill" does seem a little stiff, but not as much as sometimes and "Nona" looks exactly the same! Not a day older, even your mother agreed on that! I've written you more about them all at various times before too. Especially "Wenny," who looks awfully well, though Mr. Wilson says she is lame some days. "Nona's" coat looks poorly, the way it has the last few years—bald patches on her neck, but they are filling in now. It seems to come when she sheds her winter coat. She is the same old "Nona" and up to the same old tricks, but she still has a nice trot and a wonderful canter and seems to be getting tougher.

This morning Mary and I rode around by Cashin's, through by Voorhees and back by Sargent Camp and home by Voorhees again, and, really,

---

161. The "lady" was known to us as the "Lady Rock." It depicts a Madonna, beautifully carved from granite and placed on a granite boulder, about six feet long. The Madonna stands about three feet high, and now sits outside my brother Willard's bookstore in Peterborough, The Toadstool.

I wish you could see Mary and "Mitzi." Now Mary carries a switch and to see her plying it while "Mitzi" is at a canter anyhow! She is usually way out ahead of me. And now she is getting so she can keep her off the grass and all—it's a riot! Mary, with her pigtails bobbing! So, really, all but "Cricket," the horses are fine, and we are certainly making the most of them this summer. I've been riding almost every day, I find, and good long rides, too.

Arthur isn't alright, but Miss Perry can't get rid of him or replace him. He wants a job that keeps him deferred! I don't know about the chickens. I haven't asked, but I guess not on a big scale. Pat's store isn't going yet, I don't believe, though she spoke as though she's done a house or two around. I bought the milking stand that Alec made, copying yours and using parts of yours. The seat and the stanchion lock, so that's what I use. If you should get home this summer don't worry about wood. We have that shed full! There'd even be enough to start us on the winter—"If." But I can think of other things for you to do rather than work!

This afternoon, while your family were here, "Becky" came prancing into the room! Your father got a great kick out of that! I must say it did look picturesque! I know people think the inmates of this house must be crazy "furriners." When a car goes by and three goats leap from the roadside and up the drive, and up on the grass are three, sometimes four, naked children, usually filthy dirty, too. Well, no one has complained yet or asked for my autograph.

Dick looks awfully well, much better than in Wellesley. He is awfully nice and so handsome. But not nearly as handsome as you are. Arnold is pale and thin, but otherwise seems fine. He's a little harder for me to talk to than Dick. He seems quite shy. But he's awfully nice, if a trifle on the serious side.

I must go up and go to bed myself. I scan the papers avidly for word of you. Today's papers mentioned strikes in Trieste. I wonder if you might end up thereabouts, even now for a little longer.

Many happy returns of August 5th. Perhaps this letter will get there on your birthday and may the next one, and every succeeding one, find us where we belong—in each other's arms! I love you an awful lot. Don't let that bar take too much of your time!

I love you,
Mary

EPILOGUE

"At last, the wheel comes full circle."

Cassandra Clare (Judith Lewis) (1973–) Clockwork Princess, 2013

Neither of my parents returned to Italy. In early July 1945, my mother left her parents' home in East River and returned to our house in Peterborough, which she had left just over a year earlier. She went by way of Wellesley, where, since 1889, my father's family have celebrated the Fourth of July with a softball game on the lawn of his great-grandfather's home.

The next month, on August 15, Japan surrendered unconditionally. That same day, my father arrived in Nashua, New Hampshire, on a troop train from Boston. In doing so, he fulfilled the prophecy of a dream I had had: "He dreamt of a trainload of soldiers, and it stopped, and you got off," my mother had written my father five months earlier. To this day, I can picture him walking toward the car, with me, my brother, sister, and my mother carrying Betsy, running toward him. On the way home, we stopped for a picnic in a field, across an iron bridge over the Souhegan River, just east of Wilton. His leave lasted perhaps a month, and then he had to travel to Camp Carson, Colorado, where he was officially discharged on October 23. While at Camp Carson, with the war receding in memory, he had little to do but reflect on what he had gone through. On October 19, he wrote my mother: "I become more surprised that I ever lived through it all. There would have been very few of us left if it had lasted any longer. Somehow, now, I feel as if you had been helping me all the time."

The home they returned to was a four-bedroom farmhouse on 160 acres, contiguous with about 400 acres belonging to my paternal grandparents. The house had no electricity, was not insulated, and was at the end of a dirt road, as a small bridge a half-mile north had been washed out in the '38 hurricane. Electricity was connected our first year back, the bridge was repaired, and insulation installed in the early 1950s. Five more children were born over the next ten years.

My parents opted for a simple life, centered around children, sculpture, animals, and skiing. Why this life? Even in his post-Harvard years before the war, my father had shown no interest in material things. But a combination of the Depression and then the war had to have had an impact.

My parents' adult life was different from the ones they'd had growing up. Both were artists and both loved animals. Horses were my mother's passion, skiing was my father's. My parents imparted values they saw as important—devotion to family, a sense of morality, personal responsibility, loyalty, honesty, and respect for others—rather than tangibles that fate might take away.

~

My father had little in his nature that was practical, apart from being able to fix barn siding, mend fences, and cut firewood. He was a "dreamer," as my mother noted, which was also his charm. While visiting Venice, he had written to my mother on June 9, saying, ". . . but I would like to wander around in a foggy sort of way, taking infinitely longer to see things and very likely not being able to tell anybody, even myself, what I had seen. But I would enjoy myself immensely and have been thinking the most exciting thoughts, which would also evaporate upon completion. I like to think, just the same, that the images and thoughts that seem to vanish so completely from my brain are perhaps distilled, rather than evaporated, and from great volumes produce just a precious little bit that become part of me."

My mother was more practical. Realizing that my father's dividend income would not support a family as large as the one they created, they started Red Shed Rubber Animals in 1947, combining their talents as sculptors with the concept of a home-based business. By 1949, more than 4,000 pieces had been sold to the Educational Equipment Company, a business run in conjunction with New York's Bank Street Nursery School. Within a few years, rubber animals were in schools in every state, and in countries from Japan to Saudi Arabia. But my parents wanted to keep the business small. They were not interested in building wealth, only in generating enough income to get by. They wanted to control the business, not have it control them.

Unlike many veterans, my father did occasionally speak of his experiences during the war, although never of the carnage or of his own heroics. He was proud of his service, but in a quiet way. He never went to reunions or sought out old comrades, but when he would see the 10th Mountain Division insignia on the hat or parka of a skier he would always speak to him. For him, the war was an interlude, not to be dwelled upon.

~

My father had been a longtime cigarette smoker and, while he gave up cigarettes in the early 1960s, he continued to smoke a pipe. But damage had been done. In February of 1968, he dropped a glass. Concerned, he went to a doctor. He was diagnosed with a brain tumor, which had metastasized from lung cancer. He spent months in Boston, undergoing lung and brain surgeries, but to no avail. He died that same year on December 2, predeceasing his mother by nine months. His youngest child was thirteen; his oldest twenty-nine. He had six grandchildren, the oldest four.

My mother gave up Red Shed Rubber Animals and started giving riding lessons, which she continued to do the rest of her life. In fact, she gave a lesson on the day she died. Her married life had been far different from the world in which she had grown up. (I have a photo of her at about age twelve (1923), dressed in a white pinafore, seated in her grandfather's carriage, on Hillhouse Avenue in New Haven. She is on her way to dancing class at Hampden Hall, two miles away. Hitched to the carriage are two horses, driven by Taylor, her grandfather's coachman.) In a recording she made about a year before she died, she remarked that her remembrances of her childhood seemed as though they were those of another person. Nevertheless, her humor never left her, and she was content with her children and growing brood of grandchildren. On the night of December 2, exactly twenty-two years after her husband died, and after writing to her youngest son George and phoning her lifelong friend Jean Kaiser, she went to sleep and never awoke.

ACKNOWLEDGMENTS

First, let me take responsibility for all errors. While others did a magnificent job in cleaning up after me, they could never have uncovered all the mistakes made.

As with my past two books, the folks at Bauhan Publishing have again produced a gem, at least in terms of design and print. Thanks to Sarah Bauhan, who runs the business; Mary Ann Faughnan, who had the task of making sense of what I had written and who placed the letters in a comprehensible order; Henry James, who designed the book, the cover, and who placed the photographs in appropriate places; and Jocelyn Lovering, who arranged places for me to speak before the book was published.

Thanks to all who fought with the 10th Mountain Division, those to whom this book is dedicated. But a special shout-out to two members who kindly spent time with me: Bob DeWick, who sadly has died, was a member of my father's squad. He is mentioned often in these letters. My family and I spent time with him at his home in Woolwich, Maine. He allowed us to learn more about the man we loved and who died too young in 1968. Tony Sileo of Bristol, Connecticut, is a man I only met recently, but whose decency was symptomatic of the 10th. He served in I Company of the 85th Regiment. His memoir, *My Life in the 10th Mountain Division*, was sobering yet inspirational. Like my father, he arrived home on V-J Day.

This book could never have been completed without the help and support of my family. My niece, Mary Gregg, inherited my mother's letters when her mother (my sister Mary, who plays a prominent role in this book) died twenty-one and a half years ago. My other sisters, Betsy, Charlotte, and Jenny, provided insight and assistance, as did my brothers Frank, Willard, and George. The spirit of Stuart, my brother who died seven years ago, has been a constant companion.

And last, but far from least, has been the love and devotion of my immediate family: First is my wife Caroline, without whom none of this would have happened. When I was discouraged, she encouraged me. When I was frustrated, she was patient. When I lost my temper (which was not infrequently), she provided balm. When I should have been remonstrated, she gave love. Our children Sydney, Linie, and Edward, and their spouses Beatriz, Bill, and Melissa, were always there for me and never lost faith in this project. And our grandchildren, Caroline, Alex, Emma, Jack, Anna, Margaret, Henry, George, Sarah, and Edith, provided timely (and needed) hugs, reminding me of what is most important in life. They are Caroline's and my gift to the world.

PHOTO CREDITS

Photos from cover: foreground – Walt Prager, (Hq. Co. 3rd Bn.) writing a letter home by Richard A. Rocker in his book, *This Was Italy,* 1946. From the 10th Mountain Division Archives at the Denver Public Library. Used with permission. **background** – A machine gunner and two riflemen of Co K, 87th Mountain Infantry, 10th Mountain Division, cover an assault squad routing Germans out of a building in the background. Sassomolare Area, Italy. Porretta Moderna Highway, 4 March 1945, Army Signal Corps Photo #: SC202949. U.S. Army Heritage and Education Center, Carlisle, PA. In the public domain.

Photos on pages 2, 8, 10, 12, 14, and 16, courtesy of the Williams family and used by permission.

Top photo on page 20: Map of The Gothic Line, August 1944. US Army Center of Military History. In the public domain.

Bottom photo on page 20: USS West Point (AP-23) on 22 April 1944, US National Archives photo No. 19-N-77620. In the public domain.

Photo on page 51: gravestone of Juan Barientos in American Cemetery in Florence, Italy. From 10th Mountain Division Descendants website, 10thmountaindivisiondescendants.org. Used with permission.

Photos on 66 and 156 are by Richard Rocker in his book *This Was Italy*, Denver, Colorado, 1946. From the 10th Mountain Division Archives at the Denver Public Library. Used with permission.

Top photo on page 142: Map of US IV and II Corps breakthrough into the Po valley, April 1945. US Army Center of Military History. In the public domain.

Bottom photo on page 142: Men in Company F, 86th Mountain Regiment, 10th Mountain Division, advance after air and artillery preparation in big "push" on Bologna, Italy. 14 April 1945. Army Signal Corps Photo No SC293381. U.S. Army Heritage and Education Center, Carlisle, PA. In the public domain.